DISCARDED

# ENGLISH DRAMA FROM EARLY TIMES TO THE ELIZABETHANS

GOTHIC DRAMA

Christ and the Tormentors by Grünewald

# ENGLISH DRAMA

## FROM EARLY TIMES TO THE ELIZABETHANS

### ITS BACKGROUND, ORIGINS AND DEVELOPMENTS

A. P. ROSSITER

*Late fellow of Jesus College, Cambridge*

BARNES & NOBLE, Inc., New York

Publishers · Booksellers · Since 1874

HUTCHINSON & CO. (*Publishers*) LTD
*178-202 Great Portland Street, London, W.1*

London Melbourne Sydney
Auckland Bombay Toronto
Johannesburg New York

★

*First Published January 1950*
*Second Impression September 1950*
*Third Impression October 1958*
*Fourth Impression April 1959*

*Printed in Great Britain by*
*William Brendon and Son, Ltd.*
*The Mayflower Press (late of Plymouth)*
*at Bushey Mill Lane*
*Watford, Herts.*

CONTENTS

Prologue: Of Dramatic History 7

PART I

I Pagan Rituals 15
II Rome and Christendom 29
III Christian Ritual Drama 42
IIIA Ritual Comic Relief 55
IV Gothic Drama 62

PART II

V The Castle and the Pin 79
VI The Morality Genus 95
VII Interludes 102
VIII Interlude of Church and State 113
IX The Stage of Academic Imports 129
X Mungrell Tragy-Comedie 137
Epilogue: from the Elizabethan Stage 148
Notes 164
Index 171

The publishers acknowledge the kind permission
of the Bayerischen Staatsgemäldesammlungen
to reproduce the frontispiece
from the painting in the Alte Pinakothek.

# PROLOGUE

THIS small book is intended to give directions rather than to "cover" its subject. It depends upon a certain limitation of the possible fields of interest in approaching "the drama", and particularly drama "from early times to the Elizabethans". It is partly the business of this introduction to define this limitation, and to make a rational statement of what is elsewhere implicit. It may be regarded as the author's embarrassed appearance before the curtain, burdened with the function which Prologues anciently had, of outlining enough of the Plot to assist the play without killing it; to which there may perhaps be superadded the function of some of Ben Jonson's inductions, viz. to minimize misunderstanding by giving some idea of what the author *does not mean*.

To different critics one main limitation will appear in opposite lights. One will say that the book treats of Medieval Drama in isolation, while another will say that it does not deal with that drama in itself. Both these partial views are correct. Early drama might be treated in a book which dealt with medieval literature in general, relating drama to the other writings and singings of its times, with the culture backgrounding them all, and with the lives and ways of the people concerned. This would be too much for a work of this size. W. P. Ker's work on *English Literature—Mediaeval* in the Home University Library (1912) is approximately of the same dimensions, and it excludes the drama completely. But even supposing that by severe compression both dramatic and non-dramatic writing could be "covered", the resulting generalizations would be so thin and abstract as to make the work in all probability quite useless to the kind of reader who hopes to learn from it; and—whether that was so or not—the effect of the whole would be to imply a dividing-line between "the medieval" and "the Elizabethan" and thereby to frustrate one of the author's purposes in discussing the drama at all. With this the second hypothetical critic can be met. The book does not deal with "medieval" drama in itself, because it is concerned with the cultural continuities which exist within and behind the stage for which Shakespeare, Jonson, Chapman, and Middleton wrote. Its purpose is to give direction in looking for these continuities, and this it attempts by following the metamorphoses of certain themes in different kinds of drama from what will doubtless seem preposterously distant "early times" to the verge of the Elizabethan outburst of major dramatic writing.

Rightly or wrongly, we assume that readers with a main interest in medieval literature (and specifically drama) are few: that those interested in the Elizabethan, and capable of being more deeply and subtly interested, are many; and that—setting aside all the requirements of a 'semi-popular' series of books such as the publishers intend with Hutchinson's University Library—what the general world of readers most requires from the academic or semi-professional reader and writer is much less the increase of specialized knowledge than the wider distribution of accessible understanding. To put it another way, we assume the existence of a public already interested in seeing more in Shakespeare (and possibly other Elizabethans), and capable of extending that interest backwards in time towards a rather hazy "medieval stage" in which it is not very easy to take a similar interest. Nor is this position indefensible. It has to be admitted that if earlier drama is approached from an Elizabethan beginning, the literary merits of it are far to seek and few, while the linguistic difficulties are sometimes considerable, even alarming, so that the whole enterprise seems to mean much labour for a poor reward. The born or luckily generated medievalist feels none of this, and therefore requires no light encouragement. He will find this book superficial; and from his point of view it is so. For it is primarily intended for the reader who wants to realize drama as a growing and altering thing in the English or European mind, as a result of which there are certain deep-rooted themes which, while an understanding of them adds depth and significance to our reading of Shakespeare, can also be taken up in far earlier work, and found to have a power and import which is only felt by us when we see them as items in a long-continued tradition—that is, as indications of something strong and persistent in the European mind. And, it might be added, perhaps strong and enduring enough to have determined other things which can be recognized later, in literature written long after Elizabethan times: possibly in our own century.

The conception of drama as a growing and altering thing can be handled solely in terms of literary form, or from the very different standpoint of one who observes that changes occur in (shall we say) plays with history-book names in them, and who then asks: "Under what forces and towards what end—if any—did these alterations come about?" It is in terms of this second approach that this book is conceived. We assume an as-if continuity in the mind of the Tudor audience, by which plays about Princes have hereditary linkages which make it unscientific to assume that because the Elizabethan blank-verse rhetorical drama is very different from anything known on the popular stage before Marlowe, there is a break in this kind of play-writing at what is called The Renaissance. So, too, with plays about Virtues and Vices, which, though standard histories of literature generally speak of them as obsolescent or extinct by Shakespeare's time, we assume from the start to have left some kind of mark on the popular mind. If it is asked: "What kind of a mark?" the reply need not be in terms of the Collective Unconscious or of archetypal patterns. It suffices to point to the mere habitual expectations of the audience: its accepted forms of illusion, of sentiment, or of humour—all of which, while a very considerable writer can modify, enlarge, or canalize them, have a strong tendency towards extreme conservatism. Those who think first of writers as originals consider such prepossessions in an audience as a limitation on an author: as an excuse which he can offer or the critics make for him, that he *had* (poor fellow) to please his fellow-men. Now audiences, to quote Mr. Podsnap, "do—I am sorry to be obliged to say it—*as* they do." But the stock of stuff in the heads of an audience is equally part of the live writer's stock-in-trade. It may provide him with nothing better than the chance of working off the same old joke that the oldest among the 'gods' or the 'penny stinkards' learnt to laugh at fifty years back: it may quite as well give him that sure touch which derives from an absolute confidence of where their minds start from and just how far he can go in giving a new turn to the application of a notion so old and traditional that a judicious and critical hearer might declare that it never was truly witty till now. Shakespeare frequently shows habitual humour —or the ground of conditioned-reflex laughter—turned to the springboard of wit.

Two light examples will show this playing on the known expectations of the audience far better than more abstract discussion. In *Midsummer Night's Dream*, Bottom the Weaver butts into the bower of the Fairy Queen with his ass's head. The line she speaks on awakening is delightfully absurd if we dwell on the text, sedulously imaging the object she addresses with:

> What angel wakes me from my flowery bed?

In the theatre it could not be relied on for a laugh: it is come and gone too soon. But when Shakespeare wrote it, he knew, even in the act of thinking of it, what its effect must be on an audience heavily pre-conditioned by *The Spanish Tragedy*: in which Old

Hieronymo made a highly melodramatic entry to the discovery of the body of his murdered son with the line:

What outcries pluck me from my naked bed. . . .?

It had passed into the language of the theatre-minded, become a regular catchword. Inevitably there mingled, in the roar of amusement which Titania's precise parody set loose, the laughter of 'the judicious' who had come to find *The Spanish Tragedy* comically melodramatic and the more astonished merriment of those who, since they still took Hieronymo quite seriously, were the less prepared to hear him echoed in this masterpiece of bathos.

The second example takes us further back. In *Twelfth Night*, Sir Toby Belch comes to Olivia to announce that there is a young man waiting to see her. The young man is Viola, disguised as Caesario. Sir Toby is drunk—manifestly so: Olivia sees it by his gait, before he lives down to his surname (with a confidential aside which complains of the ill-behaviour of 'these pickle-herring'). This dialogue follows: *Olivia:* "Cousin, cousin, how have you come so early by this lethargy?" *Sir Toby:* "Lechery? I defy lechery. There's one at the gate." Superficially, this is about as old a joke as belching. Sir Toby's wine-thickened tongue slips off the appallingly difficult word 'lethargy' on to the easier. But the point of applying the result of the skid to Caesario is as obscure as the later reference to the devil if we do not see that what Shakespeare sees in Sir Toby's mind is an image of lechery as a vice, lechery among the deadly sins, stage-presented as a smart young gallant of the age when there is nothing but 'getting wenches with child, wronging the ancientry, stealing, fighting'—as the Old Shepherd puts it in *The Winter's Tale*. The same body of expected awareness is as deftly touched on when one quibbling, equivocating servant says to another: "Your old vice still, mistake the word" (*Two Gentlemen*, III, i, 283). Give Vice its capital V, and the allusion changes: from our modern vagueness ('You're at your old games again, pretending to mistake all I say') to the Elizabethan complexity, in which the world of the morality play is as close behind this light quip as it is behind the much more serious jest of Richard III on his resemblance to 'the formal vice, iniquity' who can 'moralize two meanings in one word.'

These examples say nothing about the Elizabethan instances where a morality-play prepossession has been made thematic in later drama. The approach to such considerations lies through the later chapters of this book, and that approach supplies such 'plot' as it may possess. To discuss it here would be to burke the argument.

But the junction of what has been alluded to as 'thematic' and the light instances discussed above may be seen, if example is needed, in Prince Henry's description of Falstaff as 'that reverend Vice, that grey Iniquity': upon the interpretation of which depends, in some degree, our reading of Falstaff—upon which, beyond any reasonable doubt, hangs our whole understanding of *Henry IV*. And with it, one might add, our whole conception of Shakespeare's development as a dramatist of the historical-political between *Richard II* and *Macbeth* or *Coriolanus*.

Reliance on such 'continuities' in tracing historical developments necessarily implies some theory of 'tradition' or 'evolution', however conveniently vague we may contrive to be about it. This is not the place to discuss so difficult a question at length, since it necessarily leads towards the very complex problems of the transmission of culture and the interaction of an artist's conscious thought with all the subliminal influences of what can be roughly indicated by Samuel Butler's phrase, 'Unconscious Memory'. It must suffice to say here that an evolutionary principle is accepted as at least the analogy of what is to be observed in the changes of drama; and that this is not assumed dogmatically, but merely accepted as working-hypothesis and a convenient metaphor to elucidate description. The hypothesis seems particularly useful in providing an approach to those instances of what R. G. Collingwood labelled 'the law of primitive survivals': a generalization calling attention to that peculiarity of evolutionary developments in which some bit of the remote past is found, as it were, embedded in the present—useless, meaningless, perhaps even a trifle absurd, unless and until we read it in the light of a past equivalent to which it points back. Within the scope of the law of primitive survivals the human 'tail' (*os coccyx*) and 'appendix' represent a principle to which analogues may be found in the comparative anatomy of drama. The stupid conservatism which they seem to demonstrate is as much a part of evolutionary history as any apparently designed and directed or restlessly hither-and-thithering progressiveness.

A further justification for an evolutionary hypothesis rests on the assumption that the audience, as a representative of the mind-of-the-times, provides the *continuum* between past and present. This is not a denial of the usually emphasized literary influence, in terms of which the books an author reads are held to be important determinants of his own writing. It merely insists that, unlike the court poet or the élite novelist, the playwright does not truly exist as such until he has a public in the playhouse or the street—that is except under very unusual circumstances. As Johnson wrote for Garrick, at the opening of Drury Lane:

We who live to please must please to live.

It does not follow from this that 'the drama's laws' are 'given' solely by 'the drama's patrons'. But it does follow that the requirements, witting or unwitting, shallow or profound, of the mind-of-the-times provide a close analogy for environment in the biological theory of evolution. Adaptation is the law of existence: with this only mitigation in the sphere of artistic activity, that the mental environment itself can be worked upon by the originalities of a writer who is 'in advance of his times'—but not too much, too uncompromisingly, or antagonistically 'in advance'. This need not imply the compromises of dilution or cowardice. Only that the true dramatist does not write merely on paper, but on the sensibilities of his people. Their minds are his instruments, moved this way and that by his words, even as those other tools, the actors, are. His knowledge and apt expectation of the 'traditions' of the craft—whether these be stock tricks or unformulated formulae for emotional effectiveness, based on age-old experience and human wisdom—are another part of that environmental force by which his effective writing is determined. To feel such forces beneath the surface of the sequence of facts given in orthodox histories of drama is to enter into a more vital understanding of drama itself.

In Shelley's *Defence of Poetry* I read how 'epitomes have been called the moths of just history; they eat out the poetry of it.' That is to say they end as 'a catalogue of detached facts', the dead opposite of what Shelley called 'a poem', viz. 'the very image of life expressed in its eternal truth.' Sceptical as our century may be about all claims to approaching 'eternal truth', his comment is one which all writers of small books on big subjects must end by taking seriously. Those who find themselves in tune with the 'image of life' which this book suggests will understand it without the lame assistance of these lines before the curtain. They will see that these notes of mine attempt to catch at subtle ghostly refrains which continue as ground-bass to the trumpets of Marlowe and the huge resolutions of discords in Shakespeare. For the rest, there is, I hope, an adequate 'catalogue of detached facts' with which the poetry of the goblin-element does not materially interfere.

A. P. Rossiter

# PART I

## CHAPTER I

# PAGAN RITUALS

I doubt me, that you do not thoroughly beleeve the truth of this strange nativity; though you beleeve it not, I care not much: but an honest man . . . beleeveth still what is told him, and that which he finds written.

Is this beyond our Law? . . . For my part, I finde nothing in the sacred Bible that is against it. (RABELAIS, Chapter VI.)

BEYOND the beginnings of recognizable dramatic art lies a world of rituals. The simplest and most primitive is the dance: always at its beginnings a religious act, a wordless rite of temporary physical and emotive dedication to the unseen powers by whose virtue nature is as man takes it to be. In this primitive religious act the dancer becomes one with the spirit to which he gives himself, and the god becomes a real presence in the rite. Thus in the drunken orgy of the bacchanal or the sexual orgy of the primitive fertility-cult, the gods not only show their power but *are*, as their true selves, in the frenzies of intoxication or of animal lust. In other rites the 'heartless witless' cruelty of nature is conjured to a human presentness, and the urges to strike, to kill, and to horrify with blood are equally the god in being. In the possession by the gods, the dancer must retain some vestige of his normal disgust at mouthing raw flesh and drinking warm blood; but the horror is an aspect of the divine power and as truly the god as the ravishment of sex or the hunter's flush of triumph when the spear strikes home. Moreover, fear enters into rites which might seem to us only convivial: for wine is a spirit twice over, first because it 'inspires', so making a man not himself, and secondly because it is a red juice and 'naturally conceived as the blood of the vine'. (Frazer: *The Golden Bough*, 1900, i. 359, etc.)

The simplest device for releasing the spirit-driven marionette from the ordinary man is, however, the mask. The funny noses of the Christmas party which shield modern self-consciousness, and require no prepared 'part' to live *down* to them, are but primitive survivals. Palaeolithic man assumed the hide and 'mask' of the animal he hunted, and achieved a comparable transition to a world of wish. Often his dance was a ritual of hope, in which, as among the Red Indians, any exhausted dancer *became* the bison itself, to be shot down with a dummy arrow: thereby constraining the real bison to an analogous fate. Here what we call 'acting' is one with sympathetic magic: in which a constraint is put upon nature by an imitative or 'mimetic' ritual, as in the old-style sailor's whistling for a wind.

Other masked pantomimes of great antiquity do not constrain the future but re-evoke past triumphs. Here the ritual is of memory, though the human urge to self-assertion is still present. If the rite concerns a beast-god with established myths, the service is at once commemoration, re-creation, and constraint: the divinity is recalled to mind—that is, to present being—and is urged to commit nature to yield his customary blessings. Whether of hope or memory, all such rites bear mankind towards the consummation of their wishes, and beyond the constraints of time. The modern cinema audience, still, but masked in darkness, is not in so very different a case when the pale or painted shadows of the screen bear it towards the transient adumbrations of its conceptions of heroism or love, high adventure or golden fecundity. To the primitive, what we call 'tension' or 'thrill' was a presence, and 'surprise' the jab of other worlds on this; but so long as lusts or longings dance, a kind of rite, a kind of veneration is there—however little defensible once the shadow-show is over.

Whether we seek beyond the beginnings of a recognizable drama among the Chinese of 2000 B.C., the Greeks of 500 B.C., the Romans, or our own more immediate cultural ancestors, we find that the ritual of the dance, more often masked than not, is a point of departure for the dramatic. As much is true for the shadow-theatres of ancient India and of Java: for the development of the Japanese *Nō* from the danced pantomime called *Kagura* (thirteenth century); and for the types of drama preserved in the geographical isolation of such island-cultures as those of Java, Bali, and other parts of Indonesia where Mohammedan influence has preserved ancient forms by prohibiting all that a European would call 'acting'. The same principle applies to a theatre such as the Japanese *kabuki* or 'popular stage', which developed from seventeenth-century marionette-shows; for the marionette is, as it were, the mask in isolation—a performer who is all 'part', and therefore 'seraphically free from taint of (the human actor's) personality.' In this connection it may be remarked that some such ideal of de-personalization as this suggests is to be seen in the fact that, with only rare exceptions, the dramas of ancient China, Greece, and Rome, like the Japanese, the Javanese, and our own Elizabethan, were played exclusively by men, or men and boys. In turning our attention from our modern plays and films and towards other and earlier forms of the dramatic, it must be borne in mind that a marked lack of our wonted 'realism' may be a measure not of the crudeness of the drama but of the more subtle mutual adjustment of actor and audience. In a ritual dance where the myth, its persons, and its importance are known or felt by everybody, this subtlety of adjustment is at its height: the mask and the stylized gesture (a kind of mask-of-an-action) provide the completest illusion; and the state of mind of the normally critical modern theatre-goer is, to say the least, an improbable aberration.

Yet if the historical facts of the derivations of the Greek and medieval stages are admitted, and both recognized as religious, we can still make an imaginative effort to overcome the feeling that they must of necessity be *contrasted* to all that we can feel as drama. Any art which is in the smallest degree 'representative' or 'imitative' offers two distinguishable aspects. One is what might be called an EVENT: something which exists or existed in time, or was supposed to exist—such as Van Gogh's sunflowers, or the France of Shaw's *St. Joan* or of Shakespeare's *Henry VI*; Renoir's servant Gabrielle or the Jerusalem of a miracle-play or the background of Bruegel's *March to Calvary*. These might be called REFERENCES, and can be as close to some actual state-of-affairs as the material of a 'documentary' film, or as remote from factuality as the stuff of Tennyson's *Idylls* or Strindberg's *Dream Play* or Kafka's *The Castle*. Much in artistic 'treatment' depends on the degree of imaginative distance between the items presented and the EVENTS to which they seem to point. In Velasquez' *Rokeby Venus* the REFERENCE seems to belong to the world of statement: the imaginative distance is small. In the dome at Florence which Brunelleschi modelled on the contour of Cléo de Mérode's breast, the REFERENCE belongs to a world of allusion, and the imaginative distance is great.

With this aspect of an 'imitative' work of art there may be contrasted another which can be called RITUAL. By this I mean nothing specifically religious in any narrow sense. Armies, regiments, ships, societies, academies, freemasonries, professions, and even government departments all have their rituals: often (as with the Royal Air Force and the Inland Revenue) accompanied by an esoteric and largely unintelligible language. In a work of art, the RITUAL is the offering, or the hinting of an offering, of a gesture of regard or respect for something which goes beyond the state-of-affairs or the EVENT. Seen from this aspect, every work of art is the presentation or adumbration of a ritual of veneration. The essence of this RITUAL aspect is that it appeals from time to timelessness, though both the artist and his appreciators may be quite unconscious of this, both feeling only a 'satisfaction' with the performance which does not require analysis, or which entirely defies it.

The realization of a ritual aspect may effect great changes in one's reaction to a work of art. The apparently abject flattery of Spenser's references to Queen Elizabeth becomes something very different if they are recognized as part of a ritual of kingship, which is in turn part of a great ritual of order. Verrocchio's statue of Bartolommeo Colleoni at Venice assumes a deeper significance if it is once seen as a magnificent and terrifying ritual of human pride (an aspect caught by the detail of the man's figure in Burckhardt's *Civilization of the Renaissance*). In approaching earlier dramatic material it is particularly important to be able to accept the advice given by Seami, the original genius of the Japanese Nō plays (*c.* 1423):

> Forget the theatre and look at the Nō. Forget the Nō and look at the actor. Forget the actor and look at the 'idea' (*kokoro*). Forget the 'idea' and you will understand the Nō.

A point to bear in mind here is that 'a gesture of regard' may be given to things which do not seem in the least 'venerable' to us, though we may be forced by the evidence to admit that they have been heeded widely enough from 'venerable antiquity' till today. For this reason the phrase 'a gesture of regard or respect' was used above. It will often be necessary for the reader of early drama to reflect on how certain quite unrespectworthy things go on being done, and that their persistence is a measure of their value as rituals. Bawdry and derisive denigration, buffoonery, and basely cynical rascality may all represent some appeal to, some influence with, something *lasting* in human nature, if not permanent. Ritual commonly survives the overt beliefs which once were attached to it; and in the survival of these and other unvenerables, we must look beyond the actor and the 'idea' and seek for the rituals of negation (of order, decency, etc.) which these persistencies imply. This approach is particularly necessary in considering the connections between primitive folk-rituals and the religious dramas which followed.

## II

The importance of the primitive underlay of Greek drama does not depend on any direct derivation of the English from the Greek. Few Elizabethans reached any nearer to Greek tragedy than what is found in Seneca—a Roman and bastard descendant of Euripides—and no medieval writer reached as far. The pagan underlay of Greece concerns us (1) because it has been carefully examined by the anthropologists; (2) because their examination reveals *European* types of ritual which dance their way down the ages in the background of more reputable arts, lasting on from remote pre-history to medieval and even modern times; and (3) because it shows some connections between the primitive dance and those developed conflicts and surprises which are the essence of the dramatic. To this we might add (4) that in the nominally Christian Europe of the Middle Ages the pagan underlay of dance, rite and revel had some effect at least on the nature of drama and the dramatic, because the older gods had been subsumed by the legions of the Christian devils.

The details of all the processes by which Greek drama developed need not concern us here. Aristotle said that both Comedy and Tragedy began as improvisations, but that while the nobler singers went the way of the dithyramb and became tragedians, the singers of the base produced Comedy, which originated from the phallic songs. He remarks in the same place that it was some time before the dignified manner of tragedy replaced the grotesqueries of the earlier satyric form; but that this change involved the dropping of the trochaic tetrameter which had suited the satyrs (or the satiric) and was better for dancing.

These are the remarks of a lecturer who knows that he is understood at a hint: just as when he mentions the phallic songs as 'still in use in many of our cities.' What sort of extempore-cum-dance precurred tragedy has been a battleground for scholars, many of whom might have had more profitable (if less exciting) lives if Aristotle had only said that 'tragedy' did mean 'goat-song' and added a hint on why so odd a name was attached to something so serious and philosophical. But it is now widely accepted that the Satyr Play, which came at the end of the tragic trilogy, closing it on a note of burlesque or of earthy humour, was the surviving link with some ritual dance of beast-men, the primitive object of which was the service of fertility. If a vase-painting of about 400 B.C. at Naples is to be credited, the appearance of the satyr-chorus left this connection in no reasonable doubt. It shows ten young men getting ready for the play, among whom one has put on his shaggy-bearded, prick-eared, Silenus-like mask and is rehearsing his capers. The rest lounge about, most with mask in hand. Except for one in a kind of fancy bathing-slip, all wear no clothes but a hairy loincloth with a tail behind; and sprouting from these limited non-coverings, each has a realistic representation of the male organs —and in the state which the decencies of classical scholarship describe as 'ithyphallic'.[1] This is common in early figures of man-beast hybrids. It belongs to a mental climate where the phallus appears as universal symbol of fertility, to be borne in processions like a banner, manufactured in all sizes and materials, and identified with as many objects as the most single-minded Freudian could wish. Whether the satyrs began as horse- or as goat-hybrids, they bore into the antimasque which followed 'Thebes' or Pelops' line' the relics of ages when fertility could be magically controlled by appropriate rituals. With them, too, was borne some echo of the innocence of the Age of Saturn, the shamelessness of the Golden Age, which was shared by the phallic processions with Phales naked above them. An innocence perhaps already touched by the spirit of the *enfant-terrible* and the clown: the 'natural' who is so natural as to make free with all the decencies.

Whatever the satyrs stood for, they were connected with Dionysus, at whose festival and before whose altar Greek tragedy became the austerely beautiful thing we—if but partly—know. His was the most familiar of nature-myths. His parents were the sky-god and the earth-mother, and his name is simply 'Dios the younger'. Left to his own devices, he mounted the sky-throne and grasped the thunderbolt; whereupon the Titans plotted to destroy him, and succeeded. Stalking upon him with whited faces while he played with a mirror (when the grip of the endistanced soul is weakest), they fought him in all the shapes he assumed, till he was caught in a bull-metamorphosis and died as a bull dies. They cut him up and cooked him; they ate him; and Dios Papas returned and blasted them to pieces. The bits of the body were, in one account, buried at Delphi; but the heart given to the earth-mother to drink in a potion; whereupon she conceived and bore a son, a divine being, Dionysus. The torn god dies only to live again, and in his magical resurrection his virtue is made manifest.

At the roots of this lie beliefs which are anterior to anything that we can think of as 'believing': primal intuitions which have no existence as 'myth' or 'gospel' apart from the rituals which convey and implant them. With Osiris, the Egyptian god, the same. To us these are allegories of the indestructible vitality of nature, of the course of the dying and new-born year: of the seed which goes down alive into the grave, and dies to rise once more: of the whole rhythmic course of vegetation, sex, and all fecundity. Or, looking another way, they are the wild hypotheses of a primordial science, which we call magic; stories drawn upon the weft and woof of rituals mean to constrain the fertile powers to pour their riches forth and be to man as man would have them be: unfailing, inexhaustible, prodigiously vital.

All these are but aspects and abstractions. They do, however, enable us to recognize a similar RITUAL significance in other ancient forms and myths. At Eleuthera there was a combat between a 'fair man', Xanthos, and a 'black man', Melanthos, in which Xanthos was killed with the help of a Dionysus 'of the black goatskin'—presumably a god of the nether-world. The sequence of the seasons can be dramatized either way: as the victory of Spring or (as Shakespeare's folk-lore had it) as the funeral of old John Barleycorn:

> all girded up in sheaves,
> Borne on the bier with white and bristly beard.

The fight may be between the old king and the young, a Jack and a Giant or Monster, or Father and Son: may be a ritual battle between groups, or a mere altercation or slanging-match. It may assume a different aspect, in which Evil is driven away, as a scapegoat (the *Pharmakos* of the Greeks was human, an echo of human sacrifice), or in which a Death-and-Dearth symbol is maltreated and then buried. Here the symbols are what psychologists style 'over-determined': the maltreatment of the negative is affirmation of the positive, and the two opposites are present at once. The connection between 'phallic songs' and 'iambizing' (lampooning?) may be no other: the turgid symbol asserts good cheer, and the abuse castigates all niggard and skinflint spirits. (Hence the lasting use of sexual epithets in 'bad language'!) Finally, among the deeper mysteries, the Greeks had a ritual orgy in which a beast dedicated to Dionysus was torn asunder by his worshippers and the flesh eaten and the blood drunk in a sacrament of life-renewal and rebirth. There survives the ritual of the primitive, who achieves *Mana* (inclusively, Force, Vitality, Prestige, Sanctity, and Power-of-magic) by ingurgitating the vital spirit of his dying god, the taboo animal.

The more the anthropological background is considered, the firmer grows one's conviction that one and the same nexus of never-quite-realizable notions is in control throughout. (I use the term 'notions' only *faute de mieux*.) The *Dromenon* or ritual embodying the death and resurrection of Dionysus may have reached 'playing' only through the educative terrors of mock death and rebirth in a ceremony of initiation into manhood. The satyrs may have become the band of dancing revellers which accompanied

Dionysus (the *thiasos*) because they 'stood for' the young men who were initiated into the fertility-rite. The essential nexus is one and the same. The rites of the satyrs centred in the Thraco-Phrygian Semele, the earth-mother, and the mystic child whom the dancers tend is the same Dionysus—subsuming in one person the reborn initiate, the satyr of satyrs, seed of seeds, the wine of life, the vital principle itself. However primeval and compulsive-magical the 'notion', it was still living in St. Paul's time and he can use it allusively: "Thou fool, that which thou sowest is not quickened except it die. . . ." (I Corinthians xv, 36.)

Far more than this. Pass over the intervening centuries and consider the old Mummers' Play of St. George and the Turkish Knight (or the Dragon, as the case may be). To some this is perhaps no more than a bit of 'local colour' in Hardy's *Return of the Native;* but for those who can say, with the present writer, *et ego in Arcadia vixi*, it is a different matter. I can remember how they came to my Gloucestershire home when I was a child—'before the First War', as we say nowadays. They wore furry hats like busbies, one at least had a furry costume, and they had swords—perhaps wooden, I don't know. The champion announced himself, the other denied: they fought and St. 'Jarge' was killed. It was plainly a serious quarrel and as they were grown men, I took it seriously. Accordingly the next astonishing lines have stuck:

'Ere come I, ole Dr. Grub,
Under me'arm I carry a club,
In me pock't I carry a bo'le (*bottle*).
An' a gr't big volum' o' Harris To'le . . .

The club was poked into the corpse in a way that struck me as improbable even in doctors, but St. Jarge came to life. I forget how many times he or the Turk succumbed; but at the end the latter was certainly dead, and Father Christmas took a collection—which struck me as a profane thing to do, not being in church (though this may depend on the receptacle, which I only remember as something odd)—and they all had drinks, invoked doggerel blessings for Christmas, and went their way.

About the same time a more elaborate performance was being noted by anthropologists in various parts of Thrace and Northern Greece. A group of masqueraders went from house to house demanding presents of food or cash, chief among whom were two in masks, goatskin caps, and bells, of whom one had sometimes a blackened face. One carried a phallic club with which he knocked at the doors. There was an old woman with a puppet-baby in a basket, and though this was not general, in some places it was a seven-months-by-blow which grew up so fast that it was soon crying "A boire!" like the young Gargantua himself, and even demanding a wife. There were two boys dressed as girls (one of whom became the 'wife') and a chorus of gipsies and gendarmes with swords. The show began with an obscene pantomime of copulation between a man and 'woman' on the straw-heaps before the houses. A hand-in-hand dance followed, in which two gendarmes brandished their swords. Next came the mimed forging of a ploughshare by the gipsy 'smith' and his wife, a ritual repeated at the end, and then (in the places where it was kept up) the turn of the old woman and the precocious baby. Then the hero with the phallic club took over, the baby becoming a bridegroom. But the second goatskin principal intervened, they fought, and he was killed; whereupon the victor skinned him, and the bride, the chorus and all joined in loud lamentation. But after a mock-funeral he came to life again: sometimes assisted by a doctor; and to complete the show the ploughshare was forged again, the two 'girls' were yoked to a real plough, which they dragged round the village square, followed by a man scattering seed, while players and people cried out a prayer for wheat, rye, and barley at the prices they hoped to see, ending with: "Amen, O God, that the poor may eat! Yea, O God, that poor folk be filled!"[2]

Taken with the Dionysus-myth these two twentieth-century survivals speak for themselves. In all we find a proud champion, an enemy, a fight, a death, and a resurrection. The Thracian mumming keeps the obscene phallus which in modest England is only a life-giving club. The modern versions have a burlesque note which goes with the capering satyrs. But if we seek the RITUAL aspects, all are one. The fertility-symbol is at once the god, the hero, and the saint; and the swords are one with the club and the ploughshare, whether they do or don't also stand for those of the ancient sword-dance, in which armed men danced to scare away ill spirits while the seed was sown. An ancient vase depicts a row of naked men carrying a huge phallic plough with eyes; but without it we can understand how Shakespeare is making Agrippa use the same tongue when, in a half-bawdy-toned passage in *Antony and Cleopatra* we read:

Royal wench!
She made great Caesar lay his sword to bed:
He ploughed her, and she cropped.

No one in Racine ever says anything like that. It belongs to a conception of tragedy in which the satyrs were not relegated to an irrelevant appendix. The opposite conception, which we can call 'classical', makes a complete severance between the 'serious' and the 'comic': thereby breaking any continuity with the death-and-resurrection rituals of the old gods, the wellnigh deathless persistence of which is the main point in dealing with Greek drama here at all. But if we consider the amazing survival of these queer primeval death-and-resurrection rites, we must realize that the death and lamentation is only part of the whole story; and that what we may broadly call 'the comic' (including the 'broadest') is part and parcel of the other side. That is to say, the joy, the triumph, and defiance of the resurgent spirit, which finds its active symbol in the prancing horned indecent hybrid, in the shameless roaring gusto of the rites of Phales—of all the 'monkey-song' (*Sarugaku*) as the Japanese called it, which lures the Sun-god from his cave, as the goddess Uzumé did when she 'bared her breasts, let down her skirt, and danced; and the gods laughed till the high plains of heaven shook.'

Greek tragedy, at any rate from the time of Aeschylus, took a different way, and yet one where the essential movements of the ritual drama of the fertility-god can be discerned. As Professor Gilbert Murray showed, the tragic pattern usually contains the following sequence:

(1) A contest (*agon*), as of Life and Death, or summer plenty and winter dearth.

(2) A death or scene-of-suffering (*pathos*), perhaps even with the hero torn to pieces (Hippolytus and Pentheus), narrated (3) by a messenger.

(4) A lamentation (*threnos*), followed by (5) a recognition (*anagnorisis*), and (6) an apotheosis or 'in some sense his Epiphany in glory'. The recognition may be that of the justice of Fate, so that the primitive resurrection pattern is obscured. The invention of the tragic mask by the half-legendary Thespis (*c.* 536 B.C.) in which the *human* took the centre of the stage, barring out all those monstrous faces which savages have made to themselves to shadow forth the features of divinity—the rapidly developed sense of a *moral* strife in man and about him: these by themselves bore the tragedy far into a new world. How near the old remained can be seen in the *Bacchae* of Euripides, where the fertility-pattern determines the whole play: the torn and slaughtered Pentheus is one and the same as his rival Dionysus against whom he has blasphemed. And finally,

the moral conflict itself, much as it may owe to the jar of wills and purposes in Homer, is foreshadowed in the drama of the year. The notion of *law* is present in compulsive magic: for to act as if a rite can compel nature is tantamount to an assumption that there are determined regularities in natural phenomena—relations of cause and effect which can be exploited by the man who knows them, and which the captiousness of the gods themselves cannot alter. Beyond this, the notion of inexorable *Fate* is present in the very conception of the year as an anthropized being. The glories of the grape and grain are born from winter death only to die: 'the grass withereth, the flower fadeth': *sic vita.* The merciless determination of the sun's course binds the sequence of the seasons, and gives pattern for the predestination of the accursed houses of Tantalus and Laius. From this point of view the *Hubris* of the Greek heroes—the tragic pride and self-sufficiency which calls down on itself the retribution of the universe—is little more than man's pathetic rationalization of the pitiless course of life. The gods *must* be just (how else can they be *super*-natural and better than the supermen of power with whom Xenophanes compared them?) Therefore the tragic fall *must* have been deserved. Therefore the heroic greatness, the sublime self-assertion must be a sin; and *Hubris* is its name. But human restlessness and 'zest-for-life' (as Sir Charles Sherrington calls it) protests against this theologic chain. It answers Sophocles' lines from *Oedipus at Colonus:*

> Who longs for more allotted days,
> Who scorns the ordinary span
> Of human life, I judge that man
> A bloody fool who walks in folly's ways

and whether the answer is the death-wish of the same chorus or Shakespeare's 'As flies to wanton boys are we to the gods,' the protest is the same. Therein lies the essential conflict which makes Tragedy. The religious purpose of serious Greek drama was to explicate this clash of man with man, man with law, and man with Fate. Their tragedies were mystery-plays, aimed to explain at once some rite of a particular place, some ancient taboo or traditional institution (such as a torch-race or a lamentation-rite), *and* the deep-down rightness of divine law, the absolute necessity of submission. But even this is found nascent in the fertility-rite. 'For the life of the year-dæmon, as it seems to be reflected in tragedy, is generally a story of Pride and Punishment. Each year arrives, waxes great, commits the sin of Hubris, and then is slain. The death is deserved; but the slaying is a sin: hence comes the next year as Avenger, or as the Wronged One re-risen.'[3]

It is hard for us to share this theologic background. Professor Murray and Dr. Bowra (in his *Sophoclean Tragedy*) may cajole and persuade, but a modern reader tends still to be left with an intense conviction of the boundless injustice of the tragic gods, a downright refusal to accept the comfortable voices of Sophocles and Milton with their 'All is best, though we oft doubt' and the explanation that all 'zest-for-life' is 'sin'. Those who share this view will find in Greek tragedy a profound pessimism; and yet one which, on reflection, is consequent on the fullest acceptance of Life—whether of the Year, the Plant, or Man himself, with his foredoomed cycle of birth, maturity, the yellow leaf, and dusty death. Greek drama flourished and perished because it was so perfectly adapted to the social and religious environment which shaped it. Hence the failure of every attempt to revive or imitate it. The results, however excellent as words to read, belong to no theatre: however accurate, they inevitably tend to resemble the reconstructions of the Age of Reptiles in a geological museum—where one gapes in wonderment, but never quite believes. Even *Samson Agonistes* is like Lenin in his glass case at the Kremlin.

To return to our goat-songs. If the basic pattern of Greek tragedy descended, as Aristotle said, from the satyr-play *via* the Dithyramb (the overtly Dionysiac element), then Aeschylus effected one of the immensest simplifications of the literary art in thrusting all the jocularity and rankness of the human mind out of the trilogy, to leave it (if he did) only in a traditional appendix. The intensely pure and splendid drama which resulted has little to do with later European sequences, apart from its contribution to the lasting belief that Comedy and Tragedy were opposites and no man could engage the favours of both Muses—a belief which Socrates seems once to have tried to upset, though Plato leaves one guessing as to whether he meant it seriously. (*Symposium*, at the end.) But the fertility-rituals from which the ideas of conflict (*agon*), change of fortune (*peripeteia*), calamity (*pathos*), and recognition (*anagnorisis*) grew persisted in the underworld of the European mind, undivorced from the jocularities and the ranknesses, the crude rejoicings of the inexpugnable pagan.

Professor Cornford has very ingeniously traced the 'Old Comedy' of Aristophanes to a similar point of departure in ritual. Its *agon*, a wordy warfare not always without blows or missiles, goes back to the phallic rites in which the contestants stood for the opposed forces of spring and winter, and others in which abuse was employed as word-magic against ill spirits. Its *Parabasis* of conflicting semi-choruses (each as big as the chorus of tragedy) which egg on the rivals echoes the widely distributed sham-fight rituals which have the same significance: one of the most engaging of which is the tug-of-war. The whole leads up to the *Komos*, a procession celebrating (with more gusto than dignity) the ritual 'marriage' of a pair who represent the gods, and who are—to put it bluntly—the sexual representatives of the entire community in a magical coition which has replaced the more ancient common promiscuities of the savage. If this is so, then once again Aristotle is justified by modern scholarship, and the basic pattern of comedy was the phallic procession, some shadows of which survive in the Thracian mummers' play discussed above. The same basis of ritual underlies the traditional King and Queen of May in later times, with all the perils ascribed by the godly to 'gathering nuts in May', and all the long war of the Puritan with the Maypole. (The last is gone, save as a pious fake like the Dickensian Christmas; but I believe the superstition still exists that it is 'unlucky to bring white may indoors'.)

Whether Cornford's theory finds acceptance or not, the fact remains that the dramatic heights of Greek civilization left but a very transient mark. Before we generalize too freely on the fineness and restraint of their taste and make their culture a reproach to all others, we must accommodate the truth that the satyr-play was for these same Greeks; and for them too the comedy of Aristophanes—which no scholar has ever dared to render fully and frankly into the English tongue. It is tempting to assume that the satyr-play made a considered descent to the inglorious, the rude and earthly, and so rounded off an artistic whole. Easy, too, since there is but one complete specimen surviving (by Euripides), one sizeable part (by Sophocles), and some fragments. Could we see the whole, we might find the same disconcerting incoherence that we suspect in the Elizabethan jig (an impromptu of which no proper account survives).

The important fact to bear in mind is that though Greek drama was a literary cult at Rome, it never enjoyed a real life in the theatre. Rome had its own 'primitive underlay', and of the same types as those we have considered. With the closing down of the Greek civilization the staged results of these and other 'primitivisms' (including some specifically Roman) became 'the theatre'. With the fall of Rome, the way back to the heights of Greek drama was closed; and what persisted, to be condemned as *ludi* (plays), was in many ways nearer in spirit to the state of things before Aeschylus confined the satyrs. Thus the introduction of tragedy (and comedy) to the Romans by Livius Andronicus (*c.* 240 B.C.) and the Euripidean derivatives, Ennius, Pacuvius, and Accius, are no more to the present purpose than is Seneca (d. A.D. 65). It would be excessive to say that the finer drama of Greece died of democracy; but though Julius Caesar wrote closet-drama, he could no more impose it on the Roman audience than he could on the Ancient Britons. Between the fall of Rome and the tenth century, the wavering and uncertain fate of a tradition of plays and playing rested almost entirely on the laps of the old gods. Dance, Mask, and Pantomime, from which drama had grown through ritual to a human art of noble simplicity and majestic calm (*edle Einfalt und stille Grösse*), went on and lived, with all the restless force of man behind them. The triumphs of Aeschylus, Sophocles, and Euripides lay still in 'brown Greek manuscripts', silent, unacted, little read, unknown.

## CHAPTER II

# ROME AND CHRISTENDOM

MR. ALDOUS HUXLEY once committed himself to the dictum "we needs must love the lowest when we see it." Without pondering the implication with regard to the by no means unpopular author himself, we might apply his comment as an explanatory theory of the Roman theatre. Roman plays and players concern our story only in two ways, viz. (1) because they determined the attitude of the Christian Church towards 'theatrical spectacles'; and (2) because whatever tradition of professional entertainment survived the disintegration of the Empire goes back immediately, if not finally, to Rome. We should add, however, (3) that some Roman rituals also play an important part as 'primitive survivals' in a later age.

The normal attitude of the noble Roman towards players was one of contempt. Though the ritual games of the circus had been established by Romulus, permanent theatres were not allowed before the declining days of the Republic, and the gradual infiltration of actors into influential positions was regarded by the Roman satirists as a disgraceful mark of decadence. But by imperial times the giving of *Spectacula* had become an irremovable part of public life, as everyone knows from the formula *panem et circenses*. (From Juvenal, A.D. 60-130, *Satire X*.)

The earliest entertainments came from Etruria, and the 'fescennine' songs which survived in the dirty doggerel verses sung by soldiers at a triumph may have a phallic extraction, though Fescennium (a town) is usually held responsible for them. Greek tragedy and (new) comedy came in through Sicily and Southern Italy, but could not compete with their rivals in a field where 'giving the public what it wants' rapidly became the sole criterion. Thus the *Comedia palliata* (Greek-cloaked) and the *Comedia togata* (of Roman manners) came and went: Terence (*c.* 184-159) followed Plautus (254-184) in an exit to the library; and the theatre was left to the tastes of the mob, the soldier on leave and the tired business-man. *Spectacula* included shows of all kinds from chariot-racing to gladiators and menageries to farce. They were given not only as part of a national celebration (like the Olympiad) but as part of an official's public duties, and also for private celebrations, etc. Even an emperor who detested or despised them (as Marcus Aurelius did) could no more venture to suppress them than a twentieth-century 'austerity' government dare close the cinemas.

The amphitheatre apart, what made the strongest appeal to the *magnanimi Remi nepotes* was the farcical and the suggestive. An ancient rustic farce, the Atellane, which had come to Rome in the third century B.C. from the vicinity of Naples was a long-lasting favourite. It had stock personages named from their masks: Pappus (called Casnar in the original Oscan dialect), an old fool like Pantaloon, possibly descended from Father Silenus (*Silenopappos*) in the satyr-plays: Maccus, a lean ironical clown, a prototype of Harlequin: Bucco, a fat and blockheaded clown: Dossennus, a hunchbacked pedant or 'doctor'; and possibly a boastful 'fighting-cock' (Cicirrus), an ogress (Lamia), and some ghosts (Manies) for special occasions. Surviving titles show that the resemblance to the *Commedia dell'arte* is fairly close, the 'plots' being arranged to show Maccus (say) in some sort of absurd situation (e.g. as soldier or as a virgin), and the dialogue largely extemporized. The appeal of it depended on cross-talk comedians, and though they burlesqued other plays, and went in for topical side-cracks, their wit and antics were often of the lowest. Through them the humours of wind pass over from Aristophanes to a long tradition of buffoonery, which can be traced through the explosions of scandalized medieval churchmen to *Othello* and *The Alchemist*. Worse still, they made much of that age-old staple of broad farce, the humours of cuckoldry, an easy theme for indecent clowning.

Suggestiveness was taken further still in the Mime, which came from Magna Græcia. It was a kind of revue or Variety, centring about cross-talk between an Archimimus and *stupidi* (like Maccus) and *parasiti*—our 'stooges', presumably. Here the *mimus* had his *mimae*, and played bare-faced—in all senses. The performance included much obscenity, with dancing, horseplay, bawdry, topical (including political) allusiveness, satire, and the kind of neatly put sententiousness which survives in books of quotations under the name of Publius Syrus (*c.* 42 B.C.). While the strip-tease turn was left for the New World to invent, the Romans could make the actress (*mima*) either strip or play naked at the Floralia; and though this was a piece of folk-ritual for the Roman Queen of the May, that consideration would not improve it in Christian eyes.

Under the Empire a variety of mime called the *Pyrricha*, a choric ballet imported from Greece and given a mythological plot, became a spectacular show somewhat like a Stuart court-masque gone mad. That the Christians' antipathy to *spectacula* was not mere 'puritanism' or 'other-worldliness' is self-evident from Suetonius' story of the *Pasiphae* done for Nero and from the account of Heliogabalus as his own stage-manager: *in mimicis adulteriis, ea quae solent simulato fieri effici ad verum iussit.* Domitian, with a different taste in realism, had a mime devised to include a genuine crucifixion. Too much should not be made of such details from the more obviously superhuman among the Cæsars; but with the tale of blood from the amphitheatre and the quaintly horrible entertainments of Tiberius at Capri, they mark the way from mere coarsening towards wild enormities of obscenity and sadism. Hard and narrow as Christianity became in its attempts to destroy all the arts but those of the diathetics (and even logistics) of theological controversy, the intolerance is an instance of Newton's third law. A charitable view of Christian uncharitableness will allow that only a company of saints could have had Roman paganism as their enemy for over three centuries and survived without a cock-eyed persecuting attitude towards all 'zest-for-life' that comes from sex and the senses.

There were other grounds of condemnation, evidenced by the pantomime; which began as an upper-class entertainment derived from breakdown-products of dramatic art, and became a kind of one-man ballet to the accompaniment of a choir, which had replaced both the flute and the spoken dialogue to which the earlier Pantomimus danced. Though some of the themes were satirical, most appear to have been erotic and derived from mythology (such as the Amphitryon story or other amours of Jupiter), and the performer, who mimed all the *dramatis personae* unaided, was expert at libidinous gesture and lascivious movement. At best an art of degenerate refinement, it was condemned by the satirists as by the Christians: who used against it and the stage at large the argument that the pagans dishonoured their own gods in the theatre. The name *histrio* commonly applied to the *Pantomimus* (though not always distinct from meaning the *Mimus* or *planipes:* i.e. devoid of 'buskin' or 'learned sock') passed into Christian history as a term of infamy. Whether the Christians saw the possibility of mime or pantomime getting loose on their own mythologies we do not know; but the later use of 'propagandist' mimes in the long dialectical warfare of the Christian creeds, in which 'the most sacred symbols and mysteries of the Church' were ridiculed by controversialists, suggests that the danger may have been realized.[4]

In the bloodshed of the arena (quite apart from Christian martyrdoms), the broad bawdry of the mime, the lubricity of the pantomime, and the plain revelation of the old gods in the most innocent fertility-ritual there was more than any thinking Christian could accept. It was only natural that Christians were forbidden to be *histriones* or to marry them, and that on conversion the *scaenicus* (or *scaenica*) abjured his (or her) profession. Yet such was the lasting rage for *spectacula* that even when the Empire became Christian under Constantine (307-37) they were insuppressible. It is notable that though Christians were forbidden to spectate on Sundays and festivals, they could not be further restrained. The abiding complaint that the cinemas are full and the churches empty goes back at least to St. Chrysostom and A.D. 399: to be duly echoed some thousand years later by John Bromyard who objected to the miracle-plays on the ground that those who have plenty of time to witness them insist that business prevents them from listening to sermons. The idea of having a Christian theatre, *alleged* to have been thought of by Arius—an idea which might have altered the cultural history of Europe, was of course damned with Arius. He was certainly accused of 'beguiling the ignorant by the sweetness of his music into the impiety of his doctrines.'[5]

From the *De Spectaculis* of Tertullian (*c.* 200) through St. Jerome to Paul Orosius (*c.* 417) and the later Salvian the voice of Christian condemnation thunders down the centuries. Tertullian (and Salvian after him) maintains that renouncing the devil at baptism means inclusively the theatre and all its works; yet even that fierce African ascetic seems to make some allowance for the invincible lust for dramatic spectacles when, in a famous passage, he offers the patient Christian the rewards of the Last Day: telling him that *then* will be the time to hear the tragedians, made truly poignant by their unfeigned agonies, and *then* the hour to admire the antics of the quick comedians, made nimbler than ever by the sting of unquenchable fire! Two centuries pass, and the pleas of Augustine for the higher forms of the literary art are unavailing. In the fifth century his pupil Orosius is anticipating the Elizabethan Puritans: the evils of the time are due mainly to the theatres. A little later Salvian almost looks to the barbarian Goths for a resolution of the general decadence, in which *fecit romana iniquitas iam non esse Romam*, Rome is destroyed by romance. To him the Roman people have eaten of the insane root, so that, dying, they still laugh. *Moritur et ridet.* So, among the ruins, he wrote Rome's epitaph, adding thereto the words of Christ: "Woe unto you that laugh now! for ye shall mourn and weep."

The barbarians did, in fact, solve the impossible dilemma in which the Christian emperors were placed by the conflict of rituals. On the one hand, the line of Tertullian might promise them hell eternal as the price of not deferring all dramatic spectacles till Judgement Day; but on the other, the turbulent Roman people threatened them with an immediate foretaste if their damnable amusements were stopped. But though the solution was provided, the Ostrogoths continued to give the conquered their wonted bait, if with the contempt the situation invited; and the end came only with the Lombards (568) whose simple barbarianism was untainted with the Roman. At last it was over:

> Thou hast conquered, O pale Galilean; the world is grown grey from thy breath. . . .

And of the Attic Gods and Heroes it might be added:

> In the darkness of time, in the deeps of the years, in the changes of things
> Ye shall sleep as a slain man sleeps, and the world shall forget ye for kings.

* * * * *

The old gods, however, were of tougher stuff. Condemn as we must the amusements of the Romans, we can still see them in a RITUAL aspect: as survivals of essential paganism, in so far as that identifies divinity in nature with nature's frivolous cruelty and bloodshed, nature's full and unregardful fecundity and indecency; and with human attitudes of high-spirited (if low-minded) rejoicing in sexuality. We must allow *some* connection with the all-too-human gods of Homer.

There could be no peace between Christianity and the fertility-cults with their sacrificed gods, their spring festivals of resurrection, their unnatural births from magical mother-goddesses, their communion of the regenerate in sacraments of flesh and blood, their tau crosses and sacred trees, their pantheon of godlets only too readily confused with saints in charge of special interests. Ritual must fight ritual if only because the symbolic 'accidents' were so alike, however different the spiritual 'substance'. And there was so much for common human nature in paganism—so much that a hardening Christian asceticism denied—that it was only natural for mere men to cling stupidly to the old magical rituals and to be of the devils' party in the (mainly beneficent) interests of good cheer, good fellowship, and good harvests.

Thus while considering Roman rituals with an evolutionary bearing on the dramatic future, we must briefly look at two other devices of the heathen—the Saturnalia and the Kalends.

The first was a festival of winter, on 17th-24th December, in which the jollity and liberty-equality-fraternity of the Golden Age was restored: when a reign of topsy-turveydom obtained, restraints were abandoned, and masters and men diced and drank together. The mighty put themselves down from their seat, the lower classes were given the utmost licence; and in the revels directed by the Rex Saturnalitius it was expected that the most absurd orders (or disorders?) would be issued and carried out. The RITUAL aspect of such revels enshrines the primitive 'belief' that order is restored and renewed by a temporary plunge into chaos; and with it there goes the deeper conviction that the freedom and innocence of primordial or prelapsarian times is only to be achieved by an *inversion of civilization*. (A belief which, in a very different form, is central to modern psycho-analysis.)

At the Kalends, a New Year festival, the same sort of disorder prevailed, but now for three days. The houses were lit up, their occupants no less: they were decked with greenery; and revellers carnivalled in animal-skins or dressed in women's clothes. Special presents were exchanged, called *strenae*: a word meaning 'twigs' and connected with the Golden Bough itself.

The resemblance to 'Christmasing' is obvious; but the damnability of the pagan merrymaking is only seen when one realizes that the Christian festival of Christ's birth was not fixed for 25th December much before A.D. 336. Previously that day was sacred to Sol Invictus (the undefeated sun). It was not accepted in Jerusalem till the sixth century.

These two social-religious rituals of revelling and levelling, of disguise, mask, dance, and merriment against a background of evergreens and presents survived all specifically Roman religion. As rituals they remained part of the perpetually resisted, persistently recurrent pagan underlay of subsequent Christendom.

The results can be pursued in the long series of extracts printed by Sir Edmund Chambers as an appendix headed *Winter Prohibitions* (*Med. Stage II*): an astonishing record of the detritus of Roman religion and rustic superstition which the Church had to contend with. Anthropology was unknown and comparative religion unthinkable, and by consequence the priests were not well armed against their protean adversaries—in whom (if only as devils, demons, imps, or evil spirits) they often devoutly believed. The Bible does not provide much to damn acting with, and consequently a passage in *Deuteronomy* tends to appear with comical persistence in the literature of histriomastics (player-thrashing). There (xxii, 5) between an injunction not to look the other way when your neighbour's ox or ass falls and one on the proprieties of birds' nests it is written: 'The woman shall not wear that which pertaineth to a man, neither shall a man put on a woman's garment; for all that do so are abomination, etc.' Where there is a Christian will and a biblical text, there is usually a . . . way; and thus these words become a whip as well for the misarrayed revellers of the Kalends as the starveling *histrio*, thrust out from the ruined theatre and left, another Touchstone, 'like honest Ovid among the Goths'. (And, as I am sure Shakespeare meant, 'not so "honest" neither'.)

It was, in fact, the least 'honest' elements of Roman entertainment which were best fitted to survive in a theatreless world. Whereas a tragedian requires a tragedy and some at least of the refined resources of illusion, a tumbler needs no more than a mat to fall back on, a juggler can carry his whole apparatus at his shoulder, and the back-chat comedian need be no more than a lazy scamp clever enough to make a living by begging from those whom ordinary wags are generous enough to entertain gratis or for the mere hope of another round of drinks. Given a female companion the last could make a fair shift at a mime, if not on some local scandal then at any rate on the perennial scandal of the ways of men with maids—or with honest men's wives. If both could dance and sing, the normal human weakness for entertainment might assure them a living, even in a nominally Christian world; and for the life to come they might, with Autolycus, 'sleep out the thought of it'.

By such poor itinerant vessels the vestiges of a tradition of acting a part survived, to be somehow combined with the very different tradition of the Scop or Gleeman of the Teutonic peoples: a singer of heroic legend who—at least until corrupted—did not act his poems. Of such was the famous Taillefer who sang of Roland as the Norman conquerors rode into action at the Battle of Hastings (alias Senlac, for dignity). But though the Scop was historian and poet rather than mere entertainer, a lofty being venerated for his mysterious talent—and therefore most different from the dancing, grimacing, rough-and-tumbling bastard spawn of Roman mimetics—there is still a certain relationship to 'playing a part' in the formal style and histrionic bearing of the inspired reciter. The bard, if the term is used in its loose modern sense, is part of the ritual of a tribal cult of heroism; and though he never acted the part of any of the people in his epical tales, the assuming of the bardic role is a kind of acting. The kings who on occasion took the harp themselves, like the Norseman singing his own death-song, turning life to epic in a final Nordic frenzy as he fought his way to a heroic end: both drew about themselves that 'frame' which marks off the dramatic from mere narrative; and either, with a very slight extension of terms, might be said to have acted a part. The very principle of chivalry, with its implied contrast between the man as he is and the ideal which is his by virtue of his position (as Knight, Lord, Gentleman, or Lover), was enough to keep one kind of histrionic tradition alive. The whole psychological apparatus of the 'idol ceremony' requires something analogous to the actor's talent if it is to sway 'the tide of pomp which beats upon the high shore of this world' or give one man the power 'to monarchize, be feared, and kill with looks'. Hence Christendom set itself in vain against all survivals of the theatrical. Its vanities persisted in cathedrals no less than courts; for human nature is such that only a very great man can be prince, prelate, or even Prime Minister without taking some thought for the dramatic occasion of the morrow: without some concession to *populus vult decipi*. . . .

There were other reasons why the 'fall of the theatres' by the end of the fifth century marked no firm line across the cultural page. In Western Europe, to which England or Britain was a remote and barbarous appendix rather than an erratum, the Roman Church made the same kind of concessions as were practised by sixteenth-century missionaries in China, but which have (one gathers) become unusual since then. Finding an established culture based on pagan faith, they set out rather to christianize than to extirpate it, relying on the doctrine of Augustine (d. 430) that Christians should not reject a good thing merely because it was pagan, for God is author of all good things; so that to continue good pagan customs and even to preserve their buildings (as churches) is not borrowing from heathendom but returning his own to God. This shrewd policy of spoiling the Egyptians appears in a letter of Gregory the Great to the missionary Mellitus (A.D. 601) advising him against destroying heathen temples. As quoted by Bede (d. 735) it trenchantly observes that it is 'impossible to efface everything at once from obdurate minds'; and therefore the temples should be de-idolized, purified with holy water, and converted from the worship of devils to the service of the true God. In Rome this policy enabled Boniface (Gregory's successor) to boast that everything which had been pagan was now Christian: Apollo's temple had become the church of the Apostles, and the Pantheon of all the idols the church of the Virgin and All Saints.

This sounds admirable; but if one imagines the position of 'obdurate minds'—i.e. ordinary unreflective Saxons, not infrequently 'converted' by their king's command, quite unsupported by any theological conviction of their own—it is evident that a queer doctrinal hotch-potch must result. There is a profound truth in Shaw's epigram: 'The conversion of a savage to Christianity is the conversion of Christianity to savagery.' The results of these antithetical conversions are to be seen in the positions of Christian festivals and numerous saints' days in the (pagan) solar year (e.g. Christmas, Easter, St. John's Day); in the quasi-identification of reputable saints with much older divinities; in the wealth of apocryphal saints of more-than-usual legendariness who turn out, on investigation, to be reputed 'kings' with quite disreputable godlets behind them (a phenomenon immediately remarked in Cornwall); and in innumerable infiltrations into Christian ritual of such devices of the heathen as fire-festivals, duckings in or with water, holy stones, wishing-wells, Easter-eggs, and the like. What Sir Edmund Chambers called 'the religion of the Folk' did not so much start outside the walls of the Church as *within*. Thus the widespread ceremony of lighting a new sacred fire on Easter Saturday has no Christian sanction, being but one European survival of the kind of solar-fire ritual found among the Incas, the Mexicans, and the Eskimos. Yet at medieval Durham and Norwich immense Easter Candles towered in pagan triumph, while in the churches of Athens and at the Holy Sepulchre crushing multitudes awaited the hour of midnight when all would fight to light their little candles from the magic fire. The link between such practices and the more overtly dramatic fertility-rituals is shown by their being sometimes accompanied by the hanging and burning of a Judas-guy: the scapegoat of evil cast out as the living fire is reborn from winter darkness. The Sacred Fire tended by the Roman Vestal Virgins was renewed on 1st March; and though the Easter Lights were suppressed by Edward VI (1547) and again by Elizabeth (1569), presumably as 'fond things vainly invented, grounded upon no warranty of Scripture' (as the Thirty-nine Articles puts it), the association of chastity with unlikely combustions survived in the Elizabethan superstition that a girl's virginity was proved if she could blow up a glowing taper to flame again.

In short, Rome was christianized, Rome fell, the *circenses* passed away, *mimus* and *mima* tramped the rough roads in obscurity towards promised damnation: pagan ritual survived. Reversing what happens in Milton, the old gods became the new devils—

when the priest was preaching. When not, they lurked still in the Gothic shadows, venerated by ancient practice if by no stated creed. All that was cruel, apprehensive, lustful, and jolly in normal unascetic unspiritual humanity clung to them; and in the rich confusion of the Middle Ages a kind of Manicheeism tended to supplant Christianity, at least for practical purposes. At their lowest, they begot Black Magic; and even on consecrated ground, where the bells should have disposed of them, they often seem to have placed the devout in the compromising position of the old Irish-woman who always curtsied when the Devil was mentioned in church, 'because there's no knowing, and 'tis as well to be on the safe side.' Betwixt and between, but nearer White Magic than Black, they persisted in village feasts and seasonal revels, many (if not most) of which involved something like 'playing a part', while some included masks or other forms of disguise. It matters little whether we call these seasonal customs 'folk-plays' or merely 'play': whether we imagine behind them a strongly persistent fertility-veneration which can be called 'religious', or assume with the ironical Dr. Sisson[6] that folk-customs go on by mere habit in a state of cheerful ignorance and spring-fever appropriate to May-queens in Tennysonian Lincolnshire. Their constant condemnation by the Church, which set its face as firmly against them as against the so-called *ludi* of the minstrels, serves to show that their connection with the old religion was recognized at the time. A narrowly ascetic church came by slow degrees to admit the arts to its service; but though architecture, sculpture, music, painting, pageantry, and even a kind of acting were redeemed by the tenth century, the ecclesiastical aversion to dancing was inexpugnable, at any rate in principle. There is no need to wonder how 'prehistoric solemnities' can have 'degenerated into mirth' (Sisson, p. 157). *The veneration* in the pre-Christian fertility-rituals *was in the mirth* (or mockery); and it was that impish or farcical spirit which was opposed to strict Christianity and condemned by the official Church as what it was—pagan, diabolic. Thus when Sir Edmund Chambers observes that, besides bearing witness to 'the deep-lying dramatic instincts of the folk', the village revels made a 'contribution to medieval and Renaissance drama and dramatic *spectacle* . . . greater than has been fully recognized', we might add that this contribution rests particularly on the fact that to a formally ascetic and Christian world-picture they opposed a *kind* of devil-worship: an odd mingle of magic, tricks-for-luck, dancing and fooling, farce and blasphemy, from which springs the strong element of the grotesque in all medieval art. It represented, as it were, 'the Other Side', the antinomy of the numinous; but behind it there yet remained the shadow of a numen—some vague adumbration of the spirit of unredeemed nature as men find it who most make contact with it: life-giving but capricious, generous and cruel by turns, joyous but tricksy, full of kindliness and the cussedness of things, suddenly terrifying, wantonly malicious or crudely undignified, inspiriting as wine and coarse as dung: 'the very devil to deal with', no matter whether you farm or sail or mine or only venture alone in the woods, or on a steep crag when the weather is changing. For all those things the old gods stood. A new creed made them devils, just as older snake-gods had provided the Serpent of *Genesis;* but while some established themselves in an 'underground movement' among the saints, others lived on just outside the temples from which they had been expelled with aspersions and fumigations, and, as occasion offered, they slipped back within the Gothic arches. There Tinia Tin or Tan, subsumed in the slippery St. Anne and still patron of a Tan Hill Fair held within a week of Lugnasad (1st August), might exchange an unsanctified wink with his quondam fellows as they appeared on corbels and misericords, on the gargoyles without and the Judge's left hand in the mural of the Last Day; and on All Souls' Night (Samhain, in the octave of which fire-rituals yet survive, on 5th November) we can fancy the whole troop running loose, like the souls of the dead at the Greek Anthesteria. In such a world of spirit our medieval forerunners lived, and their dramatic preoccupation with devils must be reckoned an intrinsic part of their essential religion. It is expecting far too much of human nature to be surprised that it soon came to play a part in the ecclesiastic drama which can be traced from about the tenth century, in which —though proof is impossible—we may occasionally suspect the intention to pillage paganism of its delights in the interests of a creed too remote for common clay.

The hazy line of derivation which connects the disintegrating Roman world with the medieval through a kind of tradition of acting preserved in minstrelsy shows reason for an ambiguity of Christian attitude towards all entertainments which could be called *ludi.* The *ioculator* (a vague term covering jugglers or rope-walkers quite as much as what we think of when 'minstrels' are mentioned) inherited all the ill-repute of the *histrio* or *mimus;* and as such all entertainers or minstrels were condemned by Canon Law as codified by Gratian in the twelfth century, and again by the Decretals of Gregory IX (1227-41). In 1244, when a religious drama had come into being, Bishop Grossteste of Lincoln wanted it suppressed, for he put it in the same category as drinking-festivals (*scotales*) and the spring and autumn revels of the folk. But as Thomas de Cabham, later Archbishop of Canterbury, remarked some time before 1300, it was really true that the indecent dancers, the wearers of horrid masks, the mockers and railers were different from those other minstrels who sang of saints and princes. Some of these sang dirty songs, which was of course damnable, but the difference existed, and is part of the evidence for the descent of minstrelsy from the Teutonic gleeman or official poet, as we might call him. In this distinction we can see a reason for the failure to choke minstrelsy. But to this it must be added that as *ioculatores* were established as courtly diversions, it need surprise only the high-principled to suggest that the interests of governing classes have usually made churchmen ready to compromise, at any rate in practice. Atop of this there is ample evidence that Christians, even when in orders, are often distinctly human. Indeed no small number of monastic Christians were of the minds of Chaucer's Monk, while some went so far beyond his latitudinarianism as to welcome the visits of the wicked *ioculatores* in open defiance of Tertullian, Canon Law, the Decretals, and all the rest.

We should, in short, be careful not to oppose too cleanly 'the Church' and 'the World' (with its minstrels). Similarly, scholars have perhaps tended to mark too clear a line between the heritages of the base *mimus* and the noble *Scop*. Since 'those who live to please must please to live', we can without undue rashness suppose that even specialists in the 'noble' (or the saintly) might be capable of a 'low turn': that as the evening drew on and the cups were emptied, the equivalent of *Idylls of the King* gave place to *The Northern Farmer* —or rather some equivalent suited to those tastes in amusement of which *Piers Plowman* gives one broad hint:

> Ich can nat tabre ne trompe . ne tellen fair gestes,
> Farten ne fithelen . at festes, ne harpen,
> Iapen ne iogelen . ne genteliche pipe. . . .

The importance of minstrelsy lies in its having preserved among the high and noble as well as the poor and lowly some vestige of comic acting. Most of the motley rout of which Chaucer gives us glimpses matter as little as Colle tregetour or the 'tombesteres fetys and smale' noticed by the Pardoner, or the talented person who seems to have invented the art of the Abseil at Basle in 1276 and achieved a first descent of the cathedral undamaged. But when we read how '*L'uns fet l'ivre, l'autre le sot*', it is plain that *acting* is going on; and even if it suggests the worst ribaldries complained of by John of Salisbury and Adam of Bremen, it is one with the Roman mime on the one hand, and, on the other, with the buffooneries of the profane interludes which found their way into the developing religious drama: which had, in its original development, no discernible connection with any drama of the Roman world.

With the exception of Terence who (in one of A. W. Ward's rare neatnesses of phrase) bore 'a charmed life in the darkest ages of learning', the drama of the past was almost entirely a closed book. Only rare scholars such as John of Salisbury even glimpsed the possibility of an acted play: as may be seen from a passage in Lydgate's *Troy Book* (ii) where the 'ancient poet' recites in a pulpit in the theatre, while visored players accompany him in dumb-show. Nor can we now attach any dramatic importance to that over-noticed tenth-century aberration, the Benedictine nun Hroswitha or Hrotsvitha of Gandersheim who wrote piously intended but improper Terentian prose comedies. Conceivably her convent acted them, for all that (in Chambers' phrase) 'they abound in delicate situations' (a nice meiosis). Though Ward attempted to fit her into the development of drama, her soul, though not quite 'like a star', certainly 'dwelt apart'. Earnest, naughty, well-meaning, inefficiently frivolous and unconvincingly pious, would-be Latin and yet somehow incurably German, indecently chaste and modestly indecent, she appears on a stage no larger than a convent refectory could hold, perhaps teaches her nuns to play, perhaps only to recite; and then the puppet goes back into the box. Others may have been born to blush even more unseen 'And waste sham Terence on monastic air'. The dialogue *Terentius et Delusor* (printed in *Mediaeval Stage II*, Appendix U) may have been written for a couple of minstrels, possibly as a prologue to some such unlikely attempt. Whatever may be lost to us among the fossils of the past, it is improbable that its effect on the new ritual drama was great.

CHAPTER III

# CHRISTIAN RITUAL DRAMA

. . . *usum quorundam religiosorum imitabilem ad fidem indocti vulgi ac neofitorum corroborandam . . . hoc modo decrevimus.*[7] (St. Ethelwold.)

A KIND of drama in ecclesiastical Latin and closely connected with the Church liturgy of the great Christian feasts is generally regarded as the restarting-point of dramatic history after the barbarian interregnum of the Dark Ages. Between the ninth and twelfth centuries the liturgic developments of the Carolingian Renaissance—as a literary movement finding expression in elaborate services—led to semi-dramatic additions to the established rituals, in some of which direct impersonation of biblical personages found a place. For this one point of departure was antiphonal singing: a practice said to have originated at Antioch, which was brought to Italy by St. Ambrose before 400 and standardized in the Gregorian *Antiphonarium* at the end of the sixth century. But though Antiphones, or the singing of semi-choir against semi-choir or choir and precentor in turns, can be dramatic—as in oratorio—the mimetic actions of true drama are lacking. Here the example came from the general use of symbolic gestures and devices, the appeal of which—and, indeed, the utility—is evident with rituals not conducted in the common tongue. (Chaucer's Summoner, who shouted '*Questio quid juris?*' in his cups, was not untypical: he heard more Latin than most, but it remained hocus-pocus to him.)

Such devices as the hanging candle-star (*Stella*) for Epiphany, the Whitsun dove or descending censer (which one Elizabethan remembered from his boyhood), the crucifix laid down on Good Friday, restored to its place at Easter, and raised aloft at Ascension all served the same purpose. So, too, the hieratic gestures of the celebrant in the very dramatic ritual of the Mass, of which Amalarius of Metz wrote in the ninth century: '*Sic est immolatio sacerdotis in altari quodammodo Christi immolatio in cruce.*'[8] And again, all the pictures in mosaic or enamel, paint or needlework, which met unlettered eyes on walls and floors, on vestments and on banners. Many rituals touched the edge of mimetic action: among them the Palm Sunday procession with palms or olive-branches, which came from fourth-century Jerusalem: the washing of the feet of the poor on Maunday Thursday: the offering of gold, frankincense, and myrrh at the Chapel Royal: the Lenten veil which hid the sanctuary at Wells and Sarum, to be split at the appropriate words in the gospel; and an elaborately dismal rite at Durham, known as Creeping to the Cross.

Still nearer drama is the ninth-century dedication-ritual in which the bishop's procession approached the new church to the 24th Psalm (*Tollite portas principes vestras . . . et introibit Rex Gloriae*), when, after he had knocked thrice, a clerk hidden within answered with: 'Who is that King of Glory?' (*Quis est iste Rex Gloriae?*) Thereat the choir answered that the Lord of Hosts was King of Glory, the doors flew open with impetuous recoil, if not with jarring sound, and the ejected black spirit of unconsecration ran out as if in flight to join the tail of the forces of triumphant and glittering sanctity as they entered. Here the flying devil-deacon is plainly not from the Psalm: rather from the near-manichean world of belief that all is richly bedevilled wherever unblessed. But though 'dramatic' the ritual falls short of acting: for the 'parts' have only a generalized or allegoric significance. As much can be said of the celebrant's cross-spread arms, when he is certainly not acting the part of Christ.

Ritual drama is therefore traced from the germ of the famous *Quem Quaeritis*, as a trope or sung interpolation, in the *Introit:* the chant sung while the celebrant approached the altar. 'Troping' as a process of interpolation resulted from the elaborate extension of the chants till they came to 'torture one poor word ten thousand ways': especially in procrustean rackings of the tails of Alleluias. Words fitted to these winding bouts of linked sweetness—called *Neumae*—were known as *Prosa ad sequentias* or 'words to the sequences' and a developed addition to liturgy may be called a 'prose' (*prosa*) or 'sequence' (*sequentia*) or a 'trope': though properly speaking the last is not derived from the Alleluia (Young). Some of their authors are known: among them Notker Balbulus and Tutilo (of St. Gall) and Adam of St. Victor. They took their words from scripture, but only some half-dozen tropes are in dialogue form; and chance or divine inspiration may be called in to 'explain' why Easter had one of these, which Tutilo may have compounded, from Matthew xxvii and Mark xvi; which fell into a ritual context already fecund with mimetic device. The removal of the crucifix to show that, as modern Italians have been known to say on Good Friday, 'God is dead'—its 'deposition' in a tomb (*sepulchrum*) originally perhaps no more than the receptacle of the Host consecrated from Easter Thursday and 'reserved'—the rites of the 'elevation' on Easter Day: all these led logically to a 'visitation' ritual, in which 'the women went to seek their Love and found an Angel in the Tomb'.

The dramatic combination seems to have been made by bringing together this *Visitatio* ritual (from Matins on Easter Monday) and the sung Introit trope in which one set of voices sang: 'Whom seek ye in the sepulchre, ye followers of Christ?', the other replied: 'Jesus of Nazareth, the crucified, O heavenly ones', and the angelic voices concluded with: 'He is not here; He is risen as He foretold; go and tell how He is risen from the tomb'.

Thus the *Quem Quaeritis* (whom seek ye) trope appears in a ninth-century manuscript of St. Gall. In the reign of Edgar (959–79) St. Ethelwold, Bishop of Winchester, gives a developed little scenario in his *Concordia Regularis* (an appendix to the *Rule* of St. Benedict), and there is no longer any doubt that 'ritual drama' is the right word. One of the brethren, with an alb and a palm, is to go and sit in the Sepulchrum unnoticed. Three in copes, with censers, are to approach, walking tentatively like seekers (*pedetemptim ad similitudinem quaerentium*). After the *Quem Quaeritis* dialogue, the three turn and sing: '*Alleluia, resurrexit Dominus*'. The angel recalls them with: '*Venite et videte locum*' ('Come see the place, etc.') and to the accompaniment of the anthem they lift the linen cloths in which the crucifix was wrapped. These borne to the altar to the anthem *Surrexit Dominus*, the prior opens the *Te Deum*, and all the bells chime out in Easter jubilation.

The instructive aspect is pointed to by Ethelwold's own words given at the head of this chapter: its success *ad fidem corroborandam* is measured by the fairly rapid growth by a process of accretion, evident by the eleventh century or early in the twelfth. As the trope was interpolated into the service, stretching it (as it were), so further incidents extend the *Quem Quaeritis*: the visit of Peter and John, the *Planctus* (lament) of the Maries, Christ's appearance to Mary Magdalene (where her mistaking him for the gardener is quaintly shown by his being *praeparatus in similitudinem hortolani*—i.e. disguised as such), the journey to Emmaus, and even the non-scriptural episode of the purchase of spices from a merchant (*unguentarius*). This *unguentarius* illustrates in little the whole process of evolution by accretion and elaboration. He is merely *deduced* from scripture to play mute in a dumb-show: later he speaks: last, in the German vernacular, he has become a comedian.

This accretive process altered the Easter trope, changing it to developed playlets like those of Orléans (Adams, p. 15) or the 'Dublin Q.Q.' (Chambers ii, Appendix R, and Adams, p. 11).

Meantime trope-forms had been developed for both Christmas and the Ascension; but though one for the latter is strikingly dramatic, Easter and Christmas were to be the true growth-points. A Christmas *Quem Quaeritis* of Rouen, probably eleventh century, has the crib (*praesepe*) as material point of complication (analogous to the crucifix and the later *Stella* of Epiphany). Five canons, arrayed as shepherds (*pastores*), approach from the West door the images of Virgin and Child to the music of the *Gloria*, literally *in excelsis* (for a boy sang in the heights of the cathedral to represent the Angel), and are met by two priests, 'like the midwives' (*quasi obstetrices*), who turn the old formula to: '*Quem quaeritis in praesepe, pastores, dicite?*' ('Whom seek ye in the manger, shepherds, say?') To this beginning was added the *Stella* or *Tres Reges* (three kings) or *Magi:* to that the visit to Herod, his rage, the Angel's warning not to return, and—in a twelfth-century text from St.-Benoit-sur-Loire—a first hint of 'heroding Herod', where the vanished star reappears and the monarch and his son '*minentur cum gladiis*' (i.e. flourish their swords in threatening manner). Finally a complete Nativity-drama is made by the further accretions of the Massacre of the Innocents, the Planctus of Rachel 'weeping for her children', and the Flight into Egypt. (A long Fleury play gives as sequel the return, with the deposition of Herod.)

Here there is more than what St. Ethelwold and Pooh-Bah, from their different standpoints, would call 'corroborative detail'. The sequence has got so long as to interfere with the liturgy—supposing that anyone attempted to include even most of it—and while the original *Pastores* belongs to Christmas Day (having grown from the Introit at the 'great' third Mass, and then been transferred to Matins), the Innocents belongs three days later, and the *Magi* or *Herodes* to Twelfth Day. The natural tendency was to evolve a single Christmastide play, still ritual, still sung, but no longer tied to the placenta which had nourished it. Already we can see a little *Divina Comedia* with a real plot (a child is born, is threatened, and escapes): an earnest naïf infant-drama almost crying out for delivery from the womb of Mother Church. And Christmastide is the natural time for entertainment in its own right (or nearly so); for it might savour of heresy to underdo the merrymaking. Priscillianists and others fasted then, holding with the Gnostics and Manichees the body only evil; so that to honour the Nativity *secundem carnem* was decent and orthodox. The latitudes of the Christmas season were extensive: witness the Feast of Fools —marks of some connection with which appear in both the

Rouen *Pastores* and *Magi*. It seems possible that the first of the rumbustious Herods was none other than the *Rex Stultorum* (king of fools) himself. (See later, p. 58.)

A similar process of accretion is shown in the procession of the Prophets (*Prophetae*, or *Ordo Prophetarum*), but with a different sort of diversion towards a potential future development. It is based not on a trope, but on a 'dramatically' rhetorical passage from a sermon against Jews, Infidels, and Arians (heretics), then ascribed to St. Augustine. This passage was originally read in Advent, for in it various worthies are quoted for their prognostications of the Messiah: among them Isaiah, Jeremiah, Moses, Daniel, Habakkuk, Simeon, and John the Baptist, with his parents. (Presumably a Jew was not supposed to find that this use of such prophecies begs the question.) Worthy pagans were represented by Virgil (for the 'prophecy' of *Bucolics* iv, 7), Nebuchadnezzar (who saw a fourth person with Shadrach and the other 'children' in the furnace), and the Erythræan Sybil (for the verses on the signs of Judgement given in Eusebius). By the eleventh century, when it was some 500 years old, the *Sermo* was cast into verse, and Israel (i.e. Jacob) included at the expense of Zacharias. Finally the thing became a procession in which each worthy said his piece in turn; and in this stage of being a kind of pageant, some germs of dramatic growth can be seen. At the same time some striking accretions slip in, themselves dramatic.

In a long prose version from Rouen, Nebuchadnezzar has a furnace and an idol, and these probably indicate some *action*, beyond merely saying his piece: Simeon takes a boy in his arms; and Balaam is given a dramatic episode in which some unlikely 'properties' are required. These we can illustrate from a Laon text much shorter than the other and cast into neat rhymed verses. (Text in Adams, pp. 41-8, with the Rouen *Balaam*, p. 48 n.) The pageant is carefully costumed, and the prophecies are separated by two theme-songs which two Summoners and a chorus repeat with a totalitarian persistence in iteration:

| | | |
|---|---|---|
| Iste cetus | 2 *SS:* | All united |
| Psallat letus | | Choir delighted |
| Error vetus | | Error nighted |
| Condempnetur. | | Execrating. |
| Quod Iudea | *Chorus:* | Guilty Jewry |
| Perit rea | | Perished surely, |
| Hec chorea | | Choir we duly |
| Gratulatur. | | Jubilating. |

Nominally, that undistinguished prophet Balaam appears for his 'There shall come forth a Star out of Jacob, etc.' (Numbers xxiv, 17); but this is inadequate to explain his donkey and the comical little episode when it shies at the Angel whom he cannot see. The prophet is directed to beat the animal and to speak in anger thus:

| | |
|---|---|
| Quid moraris asina | Neddy, why do you shy and back, |
| Obstinata bestia? | Stubborn brute you, obstinate, slack? |
| Iam scindent calcaria | Now my spurs shall rip and rack |
| Costas et precordia. | Your ribs to the diaphragm cardiac! |

After the 'stage-direction' *Puer sub asina respondet* we have the lines for the boy hidden under the trappings: the Ass's speech[9]

| | |
|---|---|
| Angelus cum gladio | An angel with a sword I see |
| Quem adstare video | Standing there in front of me |
| Prohibet ne transeam; | Forbidding me to pass him by; |
| Timeo ne peream. | I'm afraid I'm like to die! |

Now Balaam has no place in the pseudo-Augustinian *Sermo*. Possibly he slipped into fame rather on his ass than his merits. If so, this episode may be a sign of one attempt to christianize some ancient entertainment, perhaps ritual, involving a donkey. Real donkeys were sometimes brought into the *Flight into Egypt*, which was not always seriously treated: as is shown by complaints about pretty girls riding round churches and by one assertion at least that the chosen fair one was the priest's concubine. The wooden Palmesel (Palm Sunday donkey) which long survived in Germany as a wheeled figure with an image on it may have some connection with this. (Picture in Young *i*.) So too may the fact that the (mainly dead-serious) *Prophetae* of Rouen was called *Processio Asinorum*, which is a term synonymous with Feast of Fools, in which 'assing' went to remarkable extremes.

If we wish to see what evolved from Balaam among the prophets, we need but turn to the Chester pageant played by the cappers. (Adams, pp. 132 ff.) The main intent is serious. It begins with Moses and the commandments, but the Balaam episode is treated at length. Only now it is a real playlet, since it ends with Balaack's conversion: he standing for all the pagans. But the ass Burnell—a most reasonable and moderate creature—is still there, and the turn is a comic one. Since the stage-directions and the prophecies are still in Latin, it is a reasonable inference that the *Ordo Prophetarum*, deriving from the church-procession and not the trope, is the germ of all later dramatization from the Old Testament. The process of accretion and elaboration, already glanced at, would lead from mere lines in a processional pageant towards episodes with action, and so to separate plays. Whether Balaam's ass first appears to meet the desire for Christmas jollity (i.e. as 'comic relief') or as an attempt to sanctify an indecent animal:

> the Devil's walking parody
> Of all four-footed things[10]

all that must remain obscure. The comic already touches the ritual drama of the Church; and we can only speculate on what environmental forces lurked behind it, like the shadowy figures of the Ox and Ass in old pictures of the Nativity or the Magi: in which again we may sometimes read more significance than that of mere incidental detail (e.g. in Bruegel's *Magi* in the National Gallery and Baldung's *Nativity* at Munich).

Many reasons are given why drama 'left the Church' to become 'secularized' in streets and markets. Increase in length, interruption of ritual, the growing demand for spectacle, the detachment of episodes from their proper seasons, the intrusion of the common tongue and common humour, and the objections of the strict have all been suggested. But it must be remembered that it was only the evolutional growth-points of drama which came 'out of God's blessing into the warm sun': within the Church liturgical histrionics continued, even as troping did. But by the end of the twelfth century, all that was closely connected with the liturgy was static; future development lay with what came nearest to being plays in their own right.

A noteworthy example of one approach to this is the *Play of the Image of St. Nicholas* (*Ludus super Iconia Sancti Nicolai*) perhaps written *c.* 1125 by Hilarius, a pupil of Abelard and wandering scholar. It belongs to the saint's day (6th December), but is quite separable from ritual and might indeed have been given merely as entertainment. Though in Latin, it has recurrent French refrains, one of rather comical rejoicing. (Text in Adams, p. 55 and also in Pollard: *English Miracle Plays*—otherwise rather a collection of snippets.) In it one Barbarus (Chambers perplexingly calls him a Jew!) entrusts his treasure to St. Nicholas' image, only to have thieves steal it (done in dumb-show). Barbarus returns and laments, and then goes so far past barbarian patience as to flog the image with a whip. The saint suffers in silence, but then appears to the thieves and blackmails them, with a touch of humour and a pun. They return the treasure; and when Barbarus comes back, he rejoices in a comical mixture of French and Latin to the tune of

'*Jo en ai*' (roughly, 'It's all me'own again' or 'She's come back'); and then apologizes to 'Nicholax', who politely and properly passes the credit—and the barbarian—to God. Barbarus takes the hint, and is converted in two neat stanzas, with as much impulsiveness as he has shown throughout.

In the play of the Bridegroom (*Sponsus*) and the Wise and Foolish Virgins from early twelfth-century Angoulême, there is an extensive use of a local dialect, and also the first incursion of devils. The bridegroom's coming connects it with Advent, and Chambers suggests a connection with the Anglo-Norman Adam-play which is commonly regarded as the first clear example of the drama outside the Church and which he dates *c.* 1150. This included a Creation, an Adam and Eve, a Cain and Abel, and a Prophets; and as another play on the Resurrection mentions the 'Harrowing of Hell' (i.e. the descent of Christ to liberate the souls of the patriarchs, including Adam), it is possible that before 1200 the essential parts of the great Christian 'cycles' were already being assembled. A development by accretion would extend the end of the *Sponsus* (where devils rush in and seize on the Foolish Virgins) to a Last Judgement (*Juditium*): before which the release of Adam and the Prophets would logically come. Since Christ 'harrowed Hell' in the days when He lay in the tomb, this sequence would connect with the derivatives of the liturgical Easter plays; which are thus drawn towards fusion into one single plot with the episodes grown from the *Prophetae*, and also with the material of the plays for Advent, Christmas, and Epiphany, etc.

This certainly happened, though whether just within the Church or just without we do not really know. Size alone does not seem enough to have caused the removal: an extensive Christian drama might have remained one with the home of architecture and painting. Here Chambers and others seem to have made too much of the Tegernsee *Antichristus* (on which see p. 81–2). It is admittedly a big contrivance, but there is little to show that other plays made such demands on space and numbers. Nor can the objections of Gerhoh of Reichersberg (d. 1169) be taken to stand for those of a majority opposed to dramatics. True he wrote that the Augsburg monks were only at home for a Herod show. But when he argued that the *Antichristus* was itself a limb of Antichrist, he wrote as a galled jade—the political moral of the play being directed against his clerical party. Similarly, when Aelred of Rievaulx regrets that histrionic gestures more suitable for the theatre than the oratory have entered the liturgy, an objection to the frettings of some thwarted Alleyn or Olivier is not the same as an objection to all drama. Histrionic clergymen have not become extinct or unobjectionable with the coming of a theatre of which Aelred knew nothing. There is ample evidence of *some* opposition; and Gerhoh's raising of the standards of Tertullian was plainly dangerous, with his justifiable insistence that the Church and divinity should abhor *spectacula theatralia*, and pay no regard to such false insanities—or rather, true ones—where men shamed themselves with women's disguise, clerks turned soldiers, and humanity transformed itself into deviltry.[11] Others more compromising lamented with the abbess Herrad von Landsberg that Epiphany playings should have become a riot of drinking, unseemly jokes, shameless wenches, and clanging weapons, not all of which ended without being used.

The simplest explanation of the 'exit' from the church is that the secular world gave more room for developments which were already pressing on inventive 'literary' minds. The secular world gave freedom, and an impulse we may properly call artistic took the line of least resistance. Pressure from within doubtless helped; but it is hard to be sure how objectionable a twelfth-century divine found Provençal or Norman in church, though Samuel Johnsons no doubt existed, adamant against disgracing consecrated walls with anything beneath the dignity of Latin. It is hard to see how the Passion-plays, which began *c.* 1200, could have rubbed shoulders with the Mass—which Catholic authority has called 'truly mimetic' and 'a liturgical drama'. (Dom Lefebvre, 1925.) The earliest surviving text among these, from the *Carmina Burana* of the Wandering Scholars, gives a longish sequence to Mary Magdalene at her most mundane, living in sin and singing very charmingly:

> Mundi delectacio dulcis est et grata
> Cuius conversatio suavis et ornata[12]

—lines out of keeping with any liturgic pattern. Outside the Church, however, these signs of an impulse towards presenting 'men doing and suffering' are what we should expect to find in a young and sprouting art with all the world before it.

Passion-plays may have been among the more important growth-points. If one from Vienna represents an early stage (despite the manuscript being of the fourteenth century), they made important suggestions towards cycle-formation, for the Passion-play proper is preluded by a *Fall* and followed by a *Judgement*—in the form of a kind of debate in Hell, where a monk, a robber, and a sorcerer are tried, and the monk fails even the infernal matriculation. A *Creation* and *Fall* existed at Regensburg as early as 1195, and if we ask *WHY?* and take up together the evidence from the Anglo-Norman *Adam*, the admitted liturgic dramas and the rest, the secret of expansion and cycle-evolution is in our hands. The Christmas, Easter, and other ritual dramas omitted the Passion. The *Prophets* foretold a Messiah—a Redeemer; but the ritual drama left the Passion alone (so far as we know) and was not explicit on the *necessity* of the Redemption. Hence Adam is put among the prophets: to show the Fall, followed by Cain ('who did the first murder', as Hamlet remembered)—and, in due time, by Noah's flood. Among the prophets, while in theory any might hatch a plot, few did. A principle of selection is at work, which takes Abraham and Isaac (because the Father's sacrifice 'prefigures' the Crucifixion), takes Moses (for the Commandments), but quite rejects all the wealth of histrionic fable centring in Elijah.[13] The vast plot had no more use for Samuel or David than for those very dramatic persons Jezebel and Joab. It was controlled by a logic which was theologic; and it is this consideration which makes nonsense of the opinions of Professor Allardyce Nicoll and others who make the medieval plays 'distinctively the creation of the common people'. (*British Drama*, p. 23.) Such a view derives from the formula '*Das Volk dichtet*' (the people turned poet) as applied to the Old Ballads. But though there is much alike in 'miracle-plays' and ballads, though both show marks of a genuine People's Art, yet in the structure of the cycles there is what the people as such could never have arrived at.

Thus we trace the chain of episodes from Adam through the Old Testament to the Nativity group: notice how sketchily Christ's ministry is passed over; and so reach the Easter group. To this are added the Harrowing of Hell (from the *Gospel of Nicodemus*), with the release of the pent-up prophets; and the Last Judgement is a logical conclusion. Like Samuel Richardson, when correspondents begged him not to kill his Clarissa, the medieval planner might say: "I should not think of leaving my heroine short of death." Add the end of the world to the one end, and start with the creation at the other, and the whole magnificent conception is complete: a vast cosmic drama 'of man's first disobedience *and* the fruit', beside which *War and Peace* almost seems small and Milton himself parochial.

We may smile at the *simplesse* which stages the Creation (as all four of our English cycles do): laugh outright at the account-book's dry 'Paid for the making of three worlds, 3*d.*'; but the magnificence of design of this Christian cosmic drama coterminous with Time's full extent is beyond denial. With all due reservations, it deserves Goethe's exclamation at Marlowe's *Dr. Faustus*: "How greatly it is all planned."

The whole is indeed a remarkable contrast to its parts, and to the liturgical cells from which those grew, with their tinkling rhymed Latin, their small, remote, illuminated-missal-like effect as they appear to the imagination, deep in the candle-light far down the tunnel of a great church, wrapped in the fumes of incense and the murmur of the chant. The huge theologic pattern which scaffolds the cycles has no counterpart in the design of the episodes or 'pageants' which it orders. Within them another spirit reigns, not seldom of 'most admired disorder'. Yet it is an error to make this only the result of 'secularization', and to talk as if the 'mystery miracle plays' stood for a clean escape from clerical influence. Of the popularity of the new diversion, its appeal to Europe at large, there can be no doubt. In 1204 a *Prophetae* was given at Riga: it had an *Interpres*, who may have been an interpreter (not merely an expositor), and is described as 'what they call "a comedy" in Latin'. Three bits of players' parts from Shrewsbury give sung Latin and spoken English together: leaving scholars to guess whether each speech or the whole show was done twice *seriatim*. About 1220 a *Resurrection* was done in the graveyard of Beverley Minster, beyond doubt outdoors, for it was accidentally recorded by what the twentieth century would call 'an accident': a boy fell from a window to which he had climbed, like Zacchaeus, because he was small and couldn't see, hurt himself, and was restored by a miracle. (Here, as with the 'devices and gestures' discussed above, it must be remembered that all these 'rituals' belong in a context of sacred images and relics, which are not merely *evocative* but also capable of an abrupt passage to the realms of supernatural power.) From Finland to Sicily, from the Czechs and Magyars to the Cornish with their pagan kelly-rounds, in Siena and Padua as in Sarum and Beverley, Christendom threw up its queer little rituals of the undying God. At Rome, Christian spectacle appeared in the blood-beghosted Colosseum itself. *Vicisti, Galiliae!* The 'pale Galilean' had indeed conquered; no grey world either.

From that conquest came the items which flowed together in the vernacular drama. It was 'assembled' by 1304 at Cividale in Friuli, and in England probably not much later. But neither in shaping nor in 'literary' execution is it divorced from the influence of clerics. (Our notion of which should carefully include Chaucer's 'jolly Absalon' as well as him of Oxenford!) It was a *secularized religious drama:* in the vernacular: latterly in the hands of Craft Guilds: filled with much comedy and farce, especially in England; but the forces of RITUAL still direct it. In the words of Miss Evelyn Underhill, 'it is the art-work of the folk-soul in the religious sphere'; and therefore 'full of the elemental passions and instincts of a thinly disguised folk-lore.' If it could speak for itself it might anticipate Faust's '*Zwei Seelen wohnen, ach, in meiner Brust*' (Alas, two spirits dwell within my breast). Sometimes, like Balaam's Ass, this fact does 'speak for itself'. The drama of the Church set out to christianize humanity: the miracle-plays humanized Christianity. Sometimes they bedevilled it. It is that other spirit which largely accounts for the contrast—even clash—between the grand logic of the plot of Man's fall, Man's hope, and Man's redemption by the Second Adam, the more-than-history of the more-than-world, and the detailed episodes which hang on that huge frame. It is hard to hold the parts and the main lines in proportionate view, for the parts clash between themselves; and modern readers have the disadvantage that while the comic and profane can amuse them, the pious, devotional, and didactic appear flat and insipid. Yet the opposition is not so different from what must be coped in Chaucer, in passing from the Knight's tale to the Miller's, and from the Prioress' to the Nun's Priest's, and the Merchant's. To lift a title from Sir Charles Sherrington, we have in both 'Two Ways of One Mind'. A strangely comprehensive two-ways-facingness brings together in medieval art the remote, the transcendental, the noble, and the vulgar, the gross and the base: often switching abruptly from the one to the other, from pathos to brutality, or from reverence to blasphemy. The piquant clash of biblical persons and their entirely medieval, often English-village, settings is but one most obvious example. The contrast between the 'divine comedy' of the real design (which is also the world's tragedy) and the homely, vulgar, absurd, or human-trivial detail is but another aspect of the recurrent tonal clash between the rituals of devotion (which are of God) and those of the grotesque.

That this clash of tones is large in Gothic art is there for anyone with eyes to see, if he can once remove the film of acceptance and quasi-habituation which inhibits surprise at grinning corbels, gaping fiend-faced gargoyles, and 'all the crank variety of hell', as contrasts to the spirit of the familiar architectural and sculptural features. Those large unresting energies of arch, vault, and buttress writhe in distortion in the grotesque details, and with another and an alien restlessness. Even if it is only some cusp-framed space filled with a carving from the everyday life of the people, it is like an aberration—and often carved as such. If you look at Notre-Dame de Chartres as it appears from the distance, you are assailed at once by the imaginative, the soaring magnificence of the original design, and by the brooding, approachable-yet-unapproachable spiritual intensity of those elongated superhuman figures in living stone, in which every curve and ripple still moves and speaks in imperceptible stillness and a motion not of this world. Near to, or following more than unaided eyes can reach save in photographs, you are absorbed in the quaint, phantasmagoric more-than-world of the carvings which are only *seen* when too near to master the design of the architecture. Grotesque and homely, weird and distorted, telling of forgotten religious legends or proverbs, old-wives' tales or craftsmen's tricks and ways of life: now human and still near at hand, now demonic and remote, they echo in speaking stone, even when it gibbers, the apparently irreconcilable clash between the grand sweeping cosmic-minded conception of the medieval drama and the often distasteful oddity and absurdity of so many of its component episodes. But there is one great difference. Whereas the craftsmen of the Middle Ages had mastered stone for their own particular purposes—words proved for them too hard a medium. The very fact that the drama found its most expansive environment near the ground and without more than the casual benefit of clergy kept it apart from the linguistic and semantic developments of the English fourteenth century. Its language, its world, are close to Langland's 'field full of folk'; and so much the further from the subtle dexterities of word and movement of Chaucer. So much the further still from any possibility of developing its strange juxtapositions, its twists of tone and mood, its harsh and nerve-jarring contrasts, to the edge and poignancy of comparable clashes in the Elizabethan dramatists.

## CHAPTER IIIA*

# RITUAL COMIC RELIEF

Truth, 'tis supposed, may bear all lights; and one of those principal lights or natural mediums . . . is ridicule itself. (SHAFTESBURY: *Essay on the Freedom of Wit and Humour.*)

OUR uncertainties about the 'removal' of the evolving drama from the Church give a certain value to glimmering sidelights, even if they are literally *ignes fatuorum* or will-o'-the-wisps. Hence this brief divagation to the strange phantasmagoria of the Feast of Fools.

In 1207 Innocent III issued a decree against some kind of *ludi* in church; but a gloss of *c.* 1263 makes it clear that devotional Christmas and Easter plays are not intended. None the less, William of Waddington distinguishes between 'representations made modestly in the office of Holy Church' and 'miracles' done by 'foolish clerks', and in the *Handlyng Synne* of Robert of Brunne (1303) the decree is applied to all outdoor playing 'in weyys or greuys', all 'miracles' being 'a gaderyng, a syght of synne'. These and other data make it difficult to accept Dr. G. R. Owst's contention: "It was *popular preaching*, we believe"—an activity entirely overlooked by Chambers—"that brought about the 'secularization' of the drama." (*Literature and Pulpit in Medieval England*, 1933, p. 478.) Dr. Owst seems entirely justified in claiming that sermon-literature is over and over again identical in source-material with the vernacular drama, to which the preachers' handling of English tongue no doubt contributed; but direct derivation from the sermon (however true of the morality-play) cannot well explain the strange profanities of the popular drama, nor its choice of comic turns. For instance: By what sermonic authority could the preachers' common abuse of women, or of marriage, have 'picked on' the harmless necessary wife of the biblically intemperate but certainly not henpecked Noah? Moreover, the *Sermo*-derivative, the procession, is already budding out into Balaams before there is time for Dr. Owst's scenario of the sacred pageants following the friars to the churchyard 'with a sermon retained as the prologue'.

The transition, in short, remains obscure. As Chambers points

*The reader may skip this and follow the dramatic thread to Chapter IV.

out, the documents of the first 'secular' plays would naturally tend to vanish in the world's fires and ruinations, since they were not in the safe keeping of long-lasting organizations such as the abbeys and the guilds. The 'performances' resulting from something very like the *Joculator* spirit got loose in church and cloister have therefore an interest as giving a possible light on the comic side of the new drama. It is conceivable that, like Saul, some spirits of Christmas revelry went out for asses and found a kingdom. If the bolder farce of the vernacular found any precedent in the spirit of the Feast of Fools, a fairly rapid mutation-process would be natural; and this would explain the condemnations of the preachers as something more Christian than the envious vilification of one sort of popular entertainer by another.

The Feast of Fools, as the gay day of the subdeacons, is mentioned by Joannes Belethus, not later than 1190, as one of a series of *tripudia* (revels) in the days following Christmas. By his time it seems firmly established as the *festum hypodiaconorum quod vocamus stultorum* (the subdeacons', the fools' feast as we call it), held at the Circumcision, at the Epiphany, or its octave. It enjoyed a long and—in every sense—parti-coloured existence, and though chiefly known in France, we have records of it from Lincoln (where it took strong measures to suppress it), Beverley, Salisbury, and St. Paul's. In Germany it was little known; but Innocent's decretal against *ludi* and masks (*larvae*) was originally directed against Gnesen, in Poland, which seems to argue a wider geographical distribution than the detailed records bear out; and it may have been its special type of fooling which made Herrad von Landsberg lament the decline of the *Magi* (see p. 50 *ante*).

The *festa follorum, ubi baculus accipitur* forbidden in France in 1212 (before Gregory IX set canon law against it in 1234), by its reference to the taking-over of a staff or wand (*baculus*), shows some relationship to the *tripudium* of the choir-boys on Holy Innocents' Day. In this a boy bishop was appointed, and commonly officiated at a serious service in which all the senior positions were taken by children, the men becoming their inferiors in the ecclesiastical hierarchy for that one day. This happened in England in the thirteenth century at Salisbury, St. Albans, Lincoln, and York. Later, the two 'christmassings' tended to get both combined and confused, the boys were corrupted by the evil communications and ill-manners of the subdeacons; and a complaint from Wells in 1331 tells of tumult and foolery (*ludibrium*) in divine service from the Nativity to the octave of the Innocents, with *ludi theatrales* in the cathedral. A similar complaint about Exeter and churches near it says that about 1360 *ludi inhonesti* (naughty plays), which not only mocked the service at Vespers, Matins, and even Mass, but also did material damage to vestments and ornaments, were performed at Christmas and the three days after it.

In the earlier stage the choristers seem to have taken the inversion of normal order with a touching—if slightly comical—gravity: as is shown by the story of King Conrad I visiting St. Gall in 911 and telling his courtiers to roll apples along the pavement to tempt the boys, who, however, neither stirred nor heeded them. The subdeacons, a despised species, were quite otherwise. The implications of would-be-reformatory fiats are betraying enough. They give an imprecise but no less striking impression of 'wild enormities' of pagan scurrility and a profane freedom with sacred things which is at once very comical, rather shocking even to the undevout and culturally puzzling.

"The ruling idea of the feast," as Chambers says, "is the inversion of status, and the performance, inevitably burlesque, by the inferior clergy of functions properly belonging to their betters." One main item in it was the supplanting of the normal holder of a *baculus* (wand of office) by an elected Lord of Misrule. From this *festum baculi* came to be synonymous with *f. stultorum*, *follorum*, or *fatuorum*, as those names did with *asinaria festa* or Feast of Asses. The delivery of the staff took place at Vespers, in the *Magnificat* and at the words '*deposuit potentes de sede, et exultavit humiles*' (He hath put down the Mighty from their seat, etc.); and the earliest reformatory note, of 1199, betrayingly ordains that the word '*deposuit*' is to be sung five times at most. One infers that the despised '*humiles*', who were scarcely 'meek', howled their *deposuits* in saint-corrupting iteration, so that five times was austerity.

That they howled is certain. In the full asinarian ritual they also brayed. If documents from Beauvais represent the unreformed rites as they existed before 1222, an ass ridden by a pretty girl with a baby was taken into church—representing the Flight into Egypt, nominally—and a Mass sung with the trio at the altar, each ritual portion ending with a bray. At the end, instead of saying '*Ite, missa est*', the celebrant '*ter hinhannabit*' (shall bray thrice), to which the congregation of self-appointed asses replied in kind.

Nor was this all. Even in the modified ritual there persisted the 'Prose of the Ass', no small amount of which is detailed travesty of

Christian hymns in dog-Latin rhyme. From the full text the following verses suffice as illustration:[14]

| | |
|---|---|
| Orientis partibus | From the countries oriental |
| Adventavit asinus | Comes an Ass in state advental |
| Pulcher et fortissimus | Fairest, strongest of his nation |
| Sarcinis aptissimus | Expertest at back-portation. |
| *Hez Ser Asne, Hez!* | *Haw, Sir Ass, hee-haw!* |
| | |
| Hic in collibus Sichen | He, from birth on Sichem's hill, |
| Enutritus sub Ruben | Nourished under Ruben till |
| Transiit per Jordanem | Crossing over Jordan's stream |
| Saliit in Bethleem. . . . | He bounded into Bethlehem. . . . |
| *Hez Ser Asne, Hez!* | *Haw, Sir Ass, hee-haw!* |
| | |
| Aurum de Arabia | Gold from blest Arabia |
| Thus et myrram de Sabba | Saba's frankincense and myrrh |
| Tulit in ecclesia | To the Church he bears with his |
| Virtus asinaria. . . . | Asinine capacities. . . . |
| | |
| Cum aristis ordeum | While he chews at barley-bristles |
| Comedit et carduum | Eating up the prickly thistles, |
| Triticum a palea | Grain he sorts from chaff and straw |
| Segregat in area. . . . | On the judgement threshing-floor. . . . |

Beside such wanton parody of sacred phrase it is not much to remark that in various places orders were issued against the straying revellers crowning themselves with flowers, wearing women's clothes, bringing *theatrales ludi* into church, or opening the proceedings with a drinking-bout in which the elected monarch of misrule was borne shoulder-high. Sometimes he was 'baptized'; and much can be reasonably read between the lines when a Sens 'reformation' of 1444 moderately ordains that the maximum quantity of water to be poured over the *Precentor Stultorum* at Vespers must not exceed three buckets (*nec proiiciatur aqua . . . ultra quantitatem trium sitularum ad plus*), and that naked persons (*nudi*)—presumably 'debagged' (*sine brachis tegentibus*)—are not to be brought into the church but dealt with 'without injury' but 'with buckets of water' at the well. Here the term *precentor* shows the connection with the ceremony of handing over the *baculus;* and possibly with the directions at the end of the Rouen *Pastores* and *Magi* mentioned earlier (p. 46) that in the Mass which follows, the Shepherds (or the Three Kings) are to 'rule the choir', thus taking the Precentor's office. The unfortunates whom the order tries to safeguard from a ducking were probably opponents of the reign of folly, who were submitted to a pagan custom belonging to St. John's Eve. Elsewhere they were taken round the town in deplorable carriages (*vehiculis sordidis*), again without the coverings of decency. In a few places (Sens and Dijon) the ritual of shaving—which survives in Neptune's Barber in the ceremonies of 'Crossing the Line' and in other and less amicable 'raggings' of the English gentleman—was practised. But almost everywhere the reformers and repressors cry out against masks (*larvae* and *personae*) and 'monstrous' or 'hideous' disguises.

Too much should not be made of the famous letter issued by the Dean of the Faculty of Theology at Paris in 1445, for it is an *ex parte* statement aimed at getting the whole game suppressed. But as a collection of the evidences of an utter inversion of Christian order and decency, and of deliberate parody and profanation, it has its value:

> Who, I ask you, with any Christian feelings, will not condemn when priests and clerks are seen wearing masks and monstrous visages at the hours of Office: dancing in the Choir, dressed as women, panders, or minstrels (*histrionum*), singing lewd songs (*cantilenas inhonestas*)? They eat black-pudding at the horn of the altar next the celebrant, play at dice there, censing with foul smoke from the soles of old shoes, and running and leaping about the whole church in unblushing shameless iniquity; and then, finally, they are seen driving about the town and its theatres in carts and deplorable carriages (*vehiculis sordidis*) to make an infamous spectacle for the laughter of bystanders and participants, with indecent gestures of the body and language most unchaste and scurrilous.

One most interesting thing about all this is that our 'modern' explanations in terms of a day's release from ascetic repression, and even the anthropological framework itself, were anticipated by contemporary churchmen. Before 1223 William of Auxerre explains that the Roman *Parentalia* had to be removed by the Church, and since its customs could not be extirpated, a substitute was provided. He meant the *Kalendae*, which *was* a time when a day of good fortune meant a year of happiness; and as he names this superstition, his slip over the name means nothing. In 1445 the Faculty of Theology state in plain terms that the origin of the *Festum* is in the rites of the pagans, of which only this Janus-worship has been permitted to survive. They also state—only to dismiss it—the argument for relaxing the bent bow awhile, recognizing it as a piece of the wisdom of the ancients, but not foreseeing what it might become in another 600 years.

The importance of the *Festum Stultorum* or *Asinaria Festa* in dramatic evolution is uncertain. But one can at least see in it, and within the Church itself, the inversion of normal order and the hierarchy of Christian values. We can even speak with licence of 'the influence of the devil'; for the Paris theologians, who knew both parties well, ascribed it to that versatile source of employment for idle hands and wits. There is a certain comic irony in some of Time's revenges. Tacitus caught it well: '*Mihi quanto plura recentium seu veterum revolvo, tanto magis ludibria rerum mortalium cunctis in negotiis observantur.*' (For myself, the more I reflect on events whether recent or remote, the more I am haunted by the sense of a mockery in human affairs.) Once Christian Fathers had derided the pagans who defamed their own gods in the theatre. They could not heed Horace's '*Naturam expellas furca, tamen usque recurret*'; though they did not so much drive out Nature with a fork as give it Neptune's trident and the satyr's horns and mask, and set it up as an anti-god —to be worshipped in superstitious awe and pagan outbreak.

As Horace said: "*Tamen usque recurret*" (it comes back again). The Fathers and the preachers after them, and even the erudite Wakefield shepherd Gyb, saw a prophecy in Virgil's famous lines:

> Iam nova progenies caelo dimittitur alto,
> Iam rediet Virgo, redeunt Saturnia regna.[15]

But they made inadequate allowance for the well-known fact that Virgil was a sorcerer. The words of sorcery, like those of other magical books, are equivocal. Indeed we have it on patristic authority that the words of Holy Writ must necessarily be so: for how should the Infinite confine itself in single statement of one poor only meaning? Virgil was used for *Sortes*, or fortune-telling from a fortuitous text, as late as the time of Charles I: just as Pierre used the Bible in *War and Peace*. The famous lines could be read in quite another way. In the Feast of Fools *Saturnia Regna* returned indeed.

Beside this, it is only another of Time's light jests that the so-called *Missel des Fous* from Sens, now in the Bibliotheque Nationale, with a ritual for the Circumcision which includes the Prose of the Ass, should be 'enshrined in a Byzantine ivory diptych' of the sixth century, the leaves of which display a Triumph of Bacchus and one of either Artemis or Aphrodite.

In the Gothic drama we can see marked analogies to the profaning spirit of the fools. In France a type of fool-play (*sottie*) descends directly from these blaspheming riots, which are better regarded as pagan rituals to unknown gods. Their spirit endures even beyond the time when Francis Bacon took a hand in Christmas revels with a Lord of Misrule among the law-students, or when New College and King's had their boy-bishops, and Merton the appropriately named *Rex Fabarum*, or King of Beans.[16] *Twelfth Night* was synonymous with 'What You Will' many centuries before Shakespeare associated it with cakes and ale and ginger hot i' the mouth, not to stress St. Anne. One of its essential spirits descended to him in the clown: the appointed or natural ass, sometimes simply the 'natural', who is the professional inverter of order, seriousness, decency, and even virtue.

CHAPTER IV

# GOTHIC DRAMA

My husband Timothy Tattle, God rest his poor soul! was wont to say there was no play without a fool and a devil in't; he was for the devil still, God bless him! The devil for his money, would he say, I would fain see the devil. (JONSON: *The Staple of News.*)

HENCEFORWARD our scene is England. At the time of the evolution of cycles a difference of presentation generally distinguishes the English plays from the Continental: the latter using fixed stages, often of huge size, the former mainly favouring the processional method in which each play or 'pageant' had a wheeled dray (also 'a pageant') to itself, the episodes literally 'following each other' about the town as through the day. Detached from their several seasons, the assembled plays tended to arrive at some time of year when outdoor amusement is pleasant; and commonly this was Whitsun or the Corpus Christi festival finally established in 1311, though first devised in 1264. The pageants began by following the procession of the Host, stopping at the same 'stations': so that the audience could either stand still while the 'theatre' ran about, or, if so minded, see the same play several times by pursuing it. The appeal oi some plays makes it easy to see why the procession and the pageants drifted apart. Texts show marks of the necessity to silence a rowdy holiday-spirited crowd in addresses to it or attacks on it by some rumbustious character crying aloud for silence, as Chaucer's Miller did, 'in Pilate's vois'. This dodge and the analogous one of direct self-presentation is common to both minstrelsy on the one hand, and the Elizabethan stage on the other. It is noticeable in the Wakefield (or 'Towneley') plays, where Cain's Garcio or plough-boy (a clown), Herod, Caesar Augustus, and Pilate (in three several plays) all use it, generally with threats.

The management of playing is known in some detail from Chester and York, whose cycles survive; and from Beverley, Coventry, Lincoln, Norwich, and Newcastle, from which we have only fragments. It is assumed that similar arrangements obtained at other places which are known to have had plays: *inter alia*, Canterbury, Bungay, Louth (Lincs.), Hereford, Worcester, Leicester, Preston, Lancaster, Kendal, Dublin, and Aberdeen. Two important cycles, however, are outside these generalizations: the group belonging to Cornwall and played in Cornish in such 'rounds' as those of Penrhyn and St. Just; and the so-called 'Ludus Coventriæ' or 'N-town Cycle' (the more modern term) which is possibly an East Anglian travelling-company's repertory, and which seems intended for a fixed stage at 'our pleyn place'.[17]

How dramatics got into the hands of the craft guilds is unknown. It may have originated in their practice of supplying watchers at the Sepulchrum from Good Friday to Easter, armed like soldiers for the occasion. If we combine details from the York records and the account of playing at Chester given by Archdeacon Rogers near the end of the sixteenth century, we get (with some confusions and contradictions smoothed over!) the usual text-book account. At both places separate guilds took single episodes on their own if they were large enough, but combined—usually with cognate trades—if not. Professional players were excluded (York), and the Chester banns boast of 'craftes men and meane men', not 'playeres of price'. It would seem that acting was popular, for York imposed a fine of 40*s*. for taking more than two parts (exactly how this was possible in a processional 'continuous performance' is beyond me to explain)—whereas being late cost a mere 6*s*. 8*d*. The York plays occupied one day 'from dawn to dewy eve', for they began at 4.30 a.m.; and in 1432, when there was a rumpus about the buffoonery of one Fergus and the *Burial of the Virgin* was suppressed, they were not over by dark (8 p.m. G.M.T.). It is improbable that all their forty-eight plays were ever given together; for at Chester, with only twenty-five, the full show took three days. These were at Whitsun, but were still called Corpus Christi plays. Those of York, though dislodged to the day after the procession as a precaution against either the York beer or the natural exuberance of Yorkshiremen a-waking, dislodged the Corpus Christi procession itself about 1426. The organization was in the hands of the Corporation and Chapter jointly, and financed by a levy of 'pageant-silver' on the guilds, who were fined for not playing or for a bad performance. Individuals could even be fined for not knowing their parts: obviously a somewhat serious matter when acting on 'a high scafolde with 2 rowmes, a higer and a lower', for 'back-stage' was underfoot when (as Rogers tells us) 'in the lower they apparreled themselves, and in the higher rowme they played'. How big the 'pageants' were is unknown. Rogers gives them four wheels in one place and six in another. Possibly they varied. The Noah plays needed room for shipbuilding operations, and the 'Towneley' *Secunda Pastorum* is but one example requiring two distinct 'scenes' in the one 'set'. Probably most 'effects' were nearer children's improvisations than 'production', but fifteenth-century records of Liturgical Drama include payments '*pro faciendo novas nubes*' (to making new clouds, i.e. for an Ascension), '*pro pingendo vulnera*' (to painting wounds), etc. Hell-mouth was a regular property, the damned presumably exiting down the hole in a hideous face—echoes of which survive in the pictures of Hieronymus Bosch and Bruegel's *Dulle Griet*. On one occasion an ingenious soul salvaged the head of a stranded whale for this purpose, and had the jaws worked by two men, so that boys could run in and out. Devils probably made a practice of descending to scare the crowd, and Herod is certainly directed to rage in the street as well as in the pageant (Coventry). Here the Evil One and the bully Tyrant belong together to the comedy of the terrifying-grotesque, and hilarity touches hysteria. In ages of faith it is all very well to *know* that the horned and black-faced monster is only Black Will showing 'his lightnesse and maistrye'; but there is no being absolutely *certain* that he has not become possessed. It rests on good authority, as miracles go, that the devil appeared on the stage in Elizabethan times at a performance of *Dr. Faustus* at Exeter; indeed contemporary writers were convinced that this was what made Alleyn found Dulwich College.

In general, no attempt was made to get round things difficult or impossible to stage. Thus the non-universe before the Creation, the fall of Lucifer, the flames of the Last Day: all were staged. 'A link (torch) to set the world alight' goes down with the material for Eve, 'a Rybbe colleryd red'. Adam appears naked and unashamed at both Chester and N-town, and though Chambers rebukes those who have followed Warton (revised by W. C. Hazlitt in 1871) in jumping too far from the (much later) direction 'aparlet in whytt lether', the accounts of shows of naked girls given in Huizinga's *Waning of the Middle Ages* leave one wondering. The 1611 translation of the Perranzabulo *Ordinalia* calls for 'ffig leaves redy to cover ther members', and though the frank paganism of the *Floralia* was no doubt too much, it seems plain that 'the exigencies of medieval realism' were less modest than Sir Edmund, and quite as sceptical.

The serio-comical tale of the account-books shows that many before William Withers of Chelmsford (1562-3) took great 'paynnes' over properties and costumes. The unscholarly but customary procedure of bundling a mass of references together does at least give an impressionistic glimpse of the 'lean unwashed artificers' buzzing with preparation, the 'busy hammers' mending pageants or making ironwork 'that Burle occupied for the hell', and the patient clerk who entered all the expenses and checked the stores: '2½ yds. of buckram for the Holy Ghost's coat, 2*s.* 1*d.*': 'Paid for a pound of hemp to mend the angels' heads, 4*d.*': '50 fathom of line for the clouds': '5 prophets cappes, one wanting': 'iij flappes for devils'. Sometimes there is a mysterious care for esoteric particulars: 'Item paide to Robt. Mathews for a pair of Wombes' (presumably for Elizabeth and the Virgin, with or without the addition of the *Trial of Joseph and Mary*): 'ij wormes of conscience, 16*d.*': 'a chawbone' (Cain's no doubt), 'a new balk line to the star and ryving the same star' (from Yarmouth, presumably nautical in terminology); and so on. Nor are the players omitted. The Coventry Drapers paid 3*s.* 4*d.* 'for pleayng God': at Hull in 1483 it was only 6*d.* against a shilling for Noah. At Coventry, while a versatile person named Fawston earns 4*d.* for cock-crowing and as much for hanging Judas, a fine impartiality gives 5*s.* to three white souls and the same to three black. This happened in 1573, when Shakespeare was nine years old.

Touching this question of the connection with the Elizabethan stage we may remark in passing that miracle-plays should mainly have been stopped in Elizabeth's reign as 'popish impostures'. The York plays on the Virgin were suppressed in 1548 (Edward VI), but the cycle was played in 1569, and probably later, though it was then taking turns with morality-plays. In 1579 the books were handed in to the archbishop and dean to be accommodated to 'a reformed mouth' as Zeal-of-the-Land Busy called it; and those careless or erastian dignitaries either lost them, as they said, or tactfully pigeon-holed them for good as beyond reformation. The Chester cycle went on till near 1600. In 1572 and 1575 mayors were arraigned by the Council for allowing plays, though the text had been revised; but in 1600 there came as mayor 'a godly zealous man' appropriately named Henry Hardware, with something of Justice Overdo's nose for 'enormity', and he 'would not suffer any Playes'. He also stopped the Midsummer Show with its giants and other beasts, 'the divell in his fethers' and another called 'god in stringes', the dragon and the naked boys, and the representatives of the craft-plays who rode in the procession, among them 'the Doctors and little God' for the Smiths, and Balaam and his Ass for the bricklayers. But though Hardware fell (*sic semper tyrannis!*) and the show went on next year, the date 1600 on the manuscript of the cycle seems to mark only the intended revival which he prevented and which was never attempted again. By so late a date the old 'pageants' were of course quite outmoded in London and the less old-fashioned towns. But it is plain that there was a true contact between the medieval 'miracle-play' and the Elizabethan world, and that the allusions of Shakespeare and others touch on living memory and not mere legend or antiquarian myth.

One important item, however, could not exist without the close relationship with the guilds: the principle by which a well-acted play was not only *ad maiorem Dei gloriam* but also a display of craftsmanship—a discreet form of advertising, often of special workmanship which the episode was chosen for requiring. Thus the goldsmiths, orfevers, or goldbeaters did the *Magi* at York, Newcastle, and Beverley: the armourers, cutlers, and other guilds making weapons (e.g. at York the blade-smiths, shethers, bowyers, and fletchers) did scenes with armed men, such as the taking of Christ and the scourging. The Wakefield litsters (dyers) did Pharaoh, for they could show their skill in incarnadining the Red Sea, which is directed to overwhelm the Egyptians. The skinners in *Adam and Eve* is what we might expect, but the plasterers in *The Creation* seems far-fetched; *The Deluge* by the Chester waterleaders and drawers in Dee is nearly as comical to our minds as the cooks and innkeepers in the *Harrowing of Hell*. But Jonson gave the same association of ideas to the puritan Wholesome in *The Alchemist* (iii, 1), still with 'Satan our common enemy' attached, not to mention glass-blowers (who shared this play at York). The bakers of Beverley, Chester, and York either did alone or shared *The Last Supper;* and a similar near-punning (like the heraldic rebus) gave the York parchmenters and bookbinders *Abraham and Isaac*, since parchment is sheepskin and ram is sheep. Though these ingenuities amuse us, we must remember that to Donne punning was no more undevout than it was necessarily low to Shakespeare. These odd inappropriate appropriatenesses are one with a world where the nailmakers and ironmongers appear in the *Crucifixion* to display what beautifully horrible nails they can make: just as the York ropers share a pageant on the scourging of Christ.[18]

From the literary point of view the workmanship is never far from crude and, in the older strata, insipid to a degree beyond *Hymns Ancient and Modern* at its tritest. Criticism is confused by the discoveries of recent researchers that all four of the English cycles (Chester, York, Wakefield, and N-town) have been extensively revised, never completely; so that what one reads by nature's light is a kind of palimpsest with geologic 'intrusions' of varying date and intention. The earliest in origin is Chester, dating from *c.* 1327. Five of the twenty-five plays are from the Old Testament, and it is probable that the whole grew from a small group of episodes with an expositor (*Preco*, *Doctor*, or *Nuntius*), based on a few prophets (including Balaam and Burnell), the Nativity, Epiphany, etc.—i.e. in close contact with the liturgic stage. It is consistent that the cycle is the most low-toned and didactic, with the farcical little developed: though there is some 'rough-stuff' from the shepherds Trowle and Tudd, and Christ is vigorously reviled and maltreated.

Of the forty-eight surviving York plays, eleven are Old Testament, the rest including three on the Virgin. The basis, according to Greg, is 'a simple didactic cycle . . . in elaborate stanzas' dating from *c.* 1350; but the whole has been rehandled by several writers in a second stage, marked by the work of an accomplished metrist, and finally by 'the York realist', a rugged and tumultuous alliterator who concentrated on the Passion and made a masterly sketch of Pilate. His work is not earlier than 1400, and it is not very likely that he drew the engaging puzzled figure of old Joseph (which Chambers pushes with Agag-like delicateness towards 'the metrist'). The York plays show humour, though less robust and coarse than is found in the 'Towneley' or Wakefield which, however, somehow and somewhen 'conveyed' (as the wise call it) five plays from the older cycle. But as we know that the midwives were cut out of the *Nativity* for going too far, it is possible that York once had much more of the kind of thing which made the well-brought-up Byron describe miracle-plays in general as 'very profane productions'.

The Wakefield plays ('Towneley' only from quondam owners of the manuscript) have long been known to have been incompletely revised by 'a writer of genuine dramatic power, whose humour was unchecked by any respect for conventionality' (A. W. Pollard in EETS ed., 1897). Their earlier history, never clear, has become the obscurer since Pollard's neat sorting into three strata dating between 1360 and 1410 has been upset by the economic evidence that Wakefield did not flourish as a wool-town till round about his end-date; so that one is left guessing whether the two earlier stages belong to some other place, before the collection came to Wakefield and the reviser at all. But there is no doubt of the reviser nor his genius, save only in the erudite and valuable work of Dr. Owst, who displays an admirable persistency in setting that word 'genius' in those quotation marks which ought properly to be called 'marks of derogation', he being assured that all this writer's merits derive from the arts of popular preaching.

Of the thirty-two extant plays, eight are Old Testament, the original sequence having been: *Creation*, *Fall* (now missing), *Murder of Abel*, *Noah*; *Abraham*, *Isaac*, *Jacob*, *Pharaoh*, *The Prophets*. The Nativity-group includes eleven plays: *Caesar Augustus*, *The Annunciation*, *The Salutation*, two shepherds' plays (*Prima* and *Secunda Pastorum*), *Magi*, *The Flight into Egypt*, *Herod*, *The Purification*, *The Doctors*, and *John the Baptist*. Christ's ministry is represented only by the tail of this and by *Lazarus* (No. XXXI). In the Passion-group ten can be included: *The Conspiracy and Capture*, *The Buffeting*, *The Scourging*, *The Crucifying*, *The Play of the Dice* (*Processus Talentorum*), the *Hanging of Judas* (No. XXXII, out of place), the *Harrowing of Hell*, *The Resurrection*, *Pilgrims* (*Perigrini*), and *St. Thomas:* unless we call it six and separate a Resurrection-group of four. The two remaining are an *Ascension* and a *Juditium*. The distribution gives a fair idea of what happens in the other cycles, barring the Cornish, except that a *Pentecost* is probably lost. It is a cycle of length midway between York and Chester and comparable with Beverley (thirty-six, all lost), though Norwich and Newcastle had but twelve plays and Coventry ten or twelve (of which only two remain).

The mark of the Wakefield Master (*pace* Dr. Owst's 'genius') is a very unusual nine-line stanza, most noticeable in the *Juditium* perhaps; for there a play of the York type has been expanded by adding forty-two such stanzas in which a devil called Tutivillus deals with subordinates who bring in 'returns' of lost souls. A terrific energy speaks out in fierce social criticism directed against perjurers, extortioners and unjust, swindling tax-gatherers, bargainers and lovers of simony; against hazarders and dicers, 'kirk-chatterers', slanderers and backbiters; against women, with their moods and hypocrisies, their vanity and exaggerated dress with horns on their heads (shared, to speak Elizabethanly, by their husbands), against male dandies, servants who don't know their due place, toss-pots or 'ale-sitters', and lechers with their 'Janets of the stews'. The writer has a sarcastic vein in satire which is cruel as well as comic: Ten Brink's phrase, 'young infernal humorist' for Tutivillus needs emphasis on the middle term, for he is a sadistic comedian, giving a foretaste of the chuckling jocular fiends-incarnate of the Elizabethans, who go about their dragging of souls to hell with 'Pleasure and action make the hours seem short' or with the gloating amusement of Volpone.

Five other plays share this stanza and a kindred power or spirit; but the latter appears in others where the stanza does not, so that we can either extend the Wakefield Master's work to include the coarse, rough comedy of the *Mactacio Abel*, the harsh ten-line stanzas on death in the *Lazarus*, and some other passages of biting realism, or, alternatively, infer the existence of something like a school of northern 'realists' whose mark is on both this and the York *Crucifixion*, on the *Processus Talentorum*, and on the *Scourging*: which last the Master has half rewritten. But without conjecture the five plays recognizably from the one hand show a remarkable variety. The *Noah* makes the most of the usual comedy between well-meaning husband and shrewish wife, and Noah improves the occasion by advising married men 'if ye love your lives' to beat wives while they are fresh. (All the English plays but the N-town are agreed that the Noahs were funny and Mrs. Noah no good. It is improbable that such a libel originated with the preachers, however hard they strove to surpass St. Francis in exhibitionistic sensationalism. It is extremely likely that that age-old staple of farce—marital difficulties—slipped in from minstrelsy. Its survival can be seen in Heywood's *Johan, Johan*, *c.* 1530.) The humorist reappears in the two shepherds' plays, drawing Yorkshiremen from the life and, at the same time, commenting satirically on contemporary abuses (especially by the rich), on women and marriage, and—Bethlehem or no—the English weather. The rascal-comedy of Mak the sheep-lifter in the famous *Secunda Pastorum* is too well known to need description; the first shepherd's play, however, deserves to be better known, if only for the pure comedy of the row between Gyb and John Horne about the pasturage of an entirely imaginary flock of sheep.

In the *Buffeting* we meet at once that disturbing doubleness of tone and point-of-view which marks the two Crucifixions mentioned above, the *Scourging* and (to some extent) the Dicing-play. It seems to me one of the most noteworthy things about Gothic drama, and I believe that the easiest approach to it is through the two paintings by Bosch of Christ and his tormentors, one in the National Gallery, the other in the Prado. In both, two spirits are at variance: *one* focuses on the pathos, emphasized by the simplicity of the Christ: *the other* takes a cruelly humorous delight in the different epitomes of derision in the hard and mocking faces which imprison Him. Take this back to the *Crucifixion* and a similar ambivalent effect is seen. The executioners have made the auger-holes too far apart, and so they hitch a rope and stretch and rack out the body till the hand will reach the hole for the nail, shouting together as they heave. This is repeated with the feet. Then they raise the cross and agree to let it fall with a bang into the mortice, to jar the hanging body; and the fourth of them then opens the mockery with:

'So, sir, gape against the sun!'

A fiendish delight in the inflicting of savage pain appears throughout the scene; yet the fiends are heartless comedians at the same time. Only when they have done does Jesus speak: words heavy with pain, of a sad naïve dignity. Then the same movement is repeated: the torturers lift and drop the cross again, and the heart-wrung pathos of the Mother follows, before the torturers come back once more. A devilish gusto is juxtaposed to the human agony in an ambivalence which the more durable medium of painting has preserved for us in Bosch and his greater successor, Bruegel. Not merely the macabre, the torturingly horrifying, as it can be seen in Grünewald's Isenheim altar-piece: rather, the presence of two rituals at once, of which the one is the negation of the faith to which the piece is ostensibly devoted. The very values of martyrdom—of *any* suffering as significant—are implicitly denied by thus making game of it.[19]

The soldiers in the *Buffeting* are very near to Bosch's *Crowning with Thorns:* those jeering eyes in hard peasant faces. The sneering sham-jocularity is at once like the hateful zest of the crucifiers, the hand-rubbing delight of Tutivillus, and the playing-up of their own humour by Cain as the stingy farmer who cheats in his tithing, by Pilate as the unjust judge (in the *Scourging*), and by Cayphas as the bully on the ecclesiastical bench in this same play. It is distinct from the drawing of Herod or Pilate, here and elsewhere, as vain-glorious noisy tyrants; for these are frightening devils without the sly meanness and spiteful malice of what Middle English called 'the shrew'. (The enjoyer of *Schadenfreude*, to whom others' pain of mind or body is a jest. The type is caught by the face in the left foreground of Bosch's picture at London.) But sometimes these bullies have their own diabolism. In the *Processus Talentorum* Pilate not only silences the rowdy audience and is funny at the same time: his Latin half-lines are parodies in his mouth, and in 'old odd ends stolen out of holy writ' he profanely usurps the titles of God himself:

Stint, I say, give me place, quia sum dominus dominorum
He that against me says, rapietur lux oculorum
Therefore give ye me space, ne tendam vim brachiorum
And then ye get no grace, contestor jura polorum,
Caveatis

Rule I the Jury
Maxime pure,
Town quoque rure
Me paveatis.[20]

A like profanation of sacred phrase is given to the First Demon in the Chester *Antichristus:* he says he was born 'in clene horedom verament', and then later tells the wicked:

'With me thou shall, from me thou come,
Off me shall come thy laste Dome. . . .'

exactly echoing the Latin of our 'from whom all things, by whom all things, in whom all things shall be' (as in Abelard's hymn: '*Ex quo sunt, per quem sunt, in quo sunt omnia*'). Examples could be multiplied of this expression of the devilish as the inversion, reversal, or parody of the divine.

The Wakefield *Secunda Pastorum* can be taken as an extreme example of the *contemporaneity* which marks the medieval drama as, too, the Elizabethan. The shepherds who speak against the 'gentlery men' who treat poor men as they please, and who warn young men that 'had ah knawn' is worth 'nowt' once you're married, belong to the same world as the very Chaucerian Summoner in the N-town *Trial of Joseph and Mary* with his catalogue of mere-English names, Cock Crane and Davy Drydust, Miles the Miller and Robin Reed, all whom he warns to come with full purses, 'for else your cause may speed the worse'. But the placing of Joseph and the Virgin in this context of bribery and suspected fornication makes a different thing of it: especially as two comic backbiters spread the scandal, and the first slyly remarks on the advantages of a young man to a wench with an old husband. The play goes well beyond its source[21] and the Wakefield parallel, which is humorous rather than comic, a simple character-piece, in which Joseph doesn't really blame Mary, it is just 'woman maners' after all. In short, though a magical ordeal ends it happily, the N-town play is managed in the tone of the tragical farce of the servant-girl who has slipped up, and who is bullied and nagged with every shaming comment and indecent inquisition. For all this, the whole is *not* made coarse and absurd: the pathos of the girl's plight is felt, and indignation, with a kind of fear, is evoked by the busy slanderers with their leering eyes and prurient tongues. Yet they are funny.

The same 'two ways of one mind' appears over the parallelism between Mak's stolen sheep hidden in the cradle and discovered only because the remorseful shepherds return with christening-presents, and the scene which immediately follows. Either Mak's cottage was used again for the stable at Bethlehem, or there was a crib on the one side to balance the cradle on the other, emphasizing the offering of gifts, Mak's assertion that 'any Lord might have this child to His son', and Gill's vow to eat the child (the lamb) if she is cheating. A travesty is effected by nearly-exact parallelism, of lines in what Euclid called 'opposite senses'. Clowning and adoration are laid together, like the mystery and the boorishness in Bruegel's *Adoration of the Magi*, or mystery and surrounding nescience in others of his pictures. We are left to wrestle with the uncombinable antinomies of the medieval mind: for these immiscible juxtapositions constantly imply two contradictory schemes of values, two diverse spirits; one standing for reverence, awe, nobility, pathos, sympathy; the other for mockery, blasphemy, baseness, meanness or spite, *Schadenfreude*, and derision. Above all, it is the fact that the 'other spirit' is *comic* that compels reflection and analysis; for the evaluated effect of the ambivalence reaches out towards a searching irony.

It is a far cry from Wakefield about 1425 (*Henry VI*, Part I) to Lear on the heath in the London of 1606 and the Gunpowder Plot; but an equivocal 'prince of darkness' is about in both places, and though the ambivalence of Mak and the Shepherds is a very different thing, artistically, from the ambivalence of *Macbeth*, the strong native vein of the Gothic grotesque connects them. Gothic drama differs utterly from the classical in its laudable (if rarely artistic) desire to get everything in; and no 'Senecan' or other 'Renaissance' influence gives precedent for Elizabethan temerities with action, time, place, or tone. With 'historical' matter the earlier Elizabethans are often recklessly medieval in their following a prose source through thick and thin, stageable and seemingly unstageable. Their technique is often no more than a more concentrated form of unconcentration, of the sort seen everywhere in the Miracles: whose authors have mostly no idea of either compression or emphasis, beyond 'dwelling on it', 'piling on the agony', etc. Thus they have tragic strength only where *naïveté* will serve: in the pathetic submission of Isaac or the still and suffering dignity of Christ. Though some few characters have more than one facet to their minds—e.g. Joseph in conflict between kind-heartedness and cuckoldry, Pilate divided between justice and policy—nothing complex appears. Signs can be seen in all the cycles of a nascent interest in humanity as such stuff as plays are made on, and if space permitted, more might be said on such 'non-cycle' pieces as the sensational *Play of the Sacrament* from Croxton (Adams, p. 243 ff.) and the very interesting fragment called *Dux Moraud* (The Vagabond Lord) which I for one do not believe to be a 'miracle of the Virgin' at all, but a primitive tragedy on incest and expiation. (Text in Adams, p. 207 f.) The interest in mankind, as separable from Man's redemption, is plain enough in the Wakefield and Chester *Shepherds*, in the well-made *Dicing* of Wakefield (not the Master's), in more than one Joseph and Pilate; though there could never be scope for character-development so long as the technique of playing demanded just as many God-the-Fathers, Christs, Herods, Pilates, and Judases as there were separate plays including them.

In contemporaneity of conception, *and* of presentation, the Elizabethans followed medieval precedent, just as the painters did. (The Botticelli *Magi* records the riding of the Three Kings at Milan, as it happened in 1336, when Herod waited to roar at San Lorenzo.) Their Caesars and Cleopatras all appeared 'in modern dress'. Their stage hangings (*Horestes* and *Sir Thomas More*), decapitations (*Apius and Virginia*, *Atheist's Tragedy*, and *Byron's Tragedy*), and torture-scenes (*Cambyses*, *Bussy D'Ambois*, and *King Lear*) kept the popular tradition; and in similar fashion Noah's Ark and the Flood, all forty days of it, gives example for Elizabethan temerities with shipping *and* with time. The English disregard for all pseudo-Aristotelian 'rules' of place and time is typically Gothic. The stage is *where* you please and the time is *when* you please, and goes just as fast as you please, or, if you please to stop it, time stops. And similarly with tone. Contemporaneity of conception opened the way to the *intrusion* (a geological metaphor, as Dr. Chasuble would explain) or *infiltration* (a military one) of non-scriptural matters, often comic in themselves; and the establishment of such juxtapositions in profoundly serious episodes results in the evolution of that peculiar kind of 'comic relief' which descends from the Gothic drama as what this chapter has called The Grotesque. It derives from that opposite and antithetic world of the diabolical, in which the shadows of primitive paganism survived; where an *unholy zest*, like that of Cain beating up his Garcio or of the none-too-nicely-spoken mothers of the Chester Innocents who beat up the braggart knights, readily turns to a positive *zest-for-unholiness* in which the Spirit of Negation almost speaks out loud and bold. Cain's backchatting the Almighty with 'God is out of His wit' and bidding Him go to hell to look for Abel is one with the profanations of the Chester Joseph consoling himself with the thought that there have been (as Leontes remarks) 'cuckolds ere now' and with the N-town

Summoner and the backbiters. In all the legacy of Joculator and Jougleur has become one with the spirit of the comic rejoicings of the folk, as a kind of opposite to or negation of their nominal religion. A ritual of defamation, sometimes reaching an adumbration of the undermining negatives which threaten all human values and respects, regards and venerations, is the true basis in the English legacy of the clashing comic contrasts of Gothic drama; and this comes down to later times as the most important part of the medieval heritage. There is no need to speculate on whether young Will Shakespeare saw the Coventry players, who certainly toured when he was a boy and who at least intended to play their cycle in 1591. Those who mark off the old religious drama with 'the Old Religion' have not reckoned with the Devil's Advocate.

* * * * *

## POSTSCRIPT

Having said so much, I might as well add my own impressionistic sketch of the man who has a certain claim to be called the first comedy-writer 'in English tongue'—the Wakefield Master.

So far as one can tell, he was a later contemporary of Chaucer's; but though he has something of a Chaucerian sense of rude fun, his is a more harsh and sarcastic vein in satire. Of that wit-tickling, never-quite-graspable ironic subtlety he has nothing. He is caught by clash of wills and his Anas and Caiphas jar in a conflict which is dramatic enough; and in most of his plays the persons have in them that suggestion of more-implied which makes the stage-character. If he did the ten-line stanzas on death inserted in the *Lazarus*, he had a gift for the harshest mortification. If so, his zest-for-living—of all sorts—makes him the fuller man. His shepherds (in both plays) are as alive as his tormentors, and in the *Secunda Pastorum* we see but one side, for there his grimness and slash are wanting.

Dr. Owst wants him to have been a priest. A clerk he certainly was, and whether frocked or unfrocked does not much matter. The man is dead, and to attach a name to him, as the architectural experts are now doing to those who cut the sublime and grotesque figures in Gothic stone, would add but little: unless it led to the discovery of such small details as we know of old Bruegel with his taste for frightening people with 'all sorts of goblin noises'. But the jolly Friar Tuck that some would make of him will not do. There is an uncomfortable twist in his vision. He not only saw as far as the 'medieval' eye of Donne or Webster, but saw too in men's suffering and squabbling—even about the Son of Man—a grotesque nightmare comedy, beside the pathos. The visual soul of it is in Bosch's *Christ bearing the Cross* at Gand: a chaotic sea of human-devil surging against the islands of Christ and Veronica.

It is this that makes the Master's work remarkable: though it would be less *generally* important did a like spirit not appear, less sharply, in places where he can have had no influence.

But with all his strength and ingenuity, his words are rougher than a Yorkshire tongue, and the crudeness of his Middle English, untempered by Chaucer's French, is like a gag in his mouth. It hurts to think what the man might have done, given a more swift and flexible language: even what he might, given other opportunities, have done in his own age and country.

Master he is, none the less, in half a dozen crabbed old plays, maybe ten if we boldly identify his 'spirit' where his extremely difficult craft-master's stanza is not. Trying to label him, I think first of Langland—but this man lacked his vision, and Langland was too embittered for that broad humour—and then of a medieval Ben Jonson. Ben loved cheating as he loved broad farce: his toughness was similarly compounded of a huge zest-for-life and the moral strength to see through its glitter, its hypocrisies, its shame, and its rewards, and to face the hollowness beyond. He too was cruel in his humour, and his great stage of fools rides like a liner over the vanished wake of the *Narrenschiff*, capsizing the cock-boats of position, zeal, and pretension with the vast inconsiderateness of a sporting leviathan.[22]

Yet when all that is said, one has to generalize and end with the reflection on how much might be made of all this, given a better tongue. The vision of the shifting and ironical doubleness of all things is in the Gothic drama at large; but we *see* it best in the Flemish painters who inherited the uncourtly spirit of terrifying farce, and *feel* it to the full only when an Elizabethan writes as a man of both worlds.

# PART II

CHAPTER V

# THE CASTLE AND THE PIN

Simple folk . . . judge of divine things from the analogy of corporeal things (Walter Hilton, in defence of Images, quoted by Owst in *Literature and Pulpit*, etc., iii, from an unpublished MS.)

FROM about 1380 an apparently new kind of play begins to be noticed which becomes the standard type for the later half of the fifteenth century and lasts on into Elizabethan times. The records of court-performances under Elizabeth demonstrate that 'the Moralities' were dramatically alive till after 1600, and show that those who accept Mr. S. L. Bethell's implication in writing 'they had not quite disappeared in the boyhood of Shakespeare himself' (*Shakespeare and the Popular Dramatic Tradition*, N.D., ?1945, p. 14) are themselves the victims of popular tradition. Forty years ago Dr. C. E. Vaughan wrote:

> I cannot convince myself that either the Mystery plays, or their successors the Moralities, had any substantial bearing, anything more than a sporadic influence, upon the subsequent course of tragedy. (*Types of Tragic Drama*, 1908, p. 103.)

Since such statements affect the whole importance of the Morality, on which this and the following chapters will lay a very different emphasis, they had better be met at once. This can be done by placing them in their literary-historical context, which is that of the character-minded nineteenth century, still dominant in text-books. The assumption is that a form of didactic play, peopled with 'colourless abstractions' and pointing a moral much rather than adorning a tale, endured—or *was* endured—till about the 1580's, when Marlowe's discoveries of dramatic 'character' sent it for ever to the most inspissated regions of the Limbo reserved for historians of the drama. (As visiting Dantes, be it understood.) The beginnings of this transformation, so the books say, are seen in Bale's *Kynge Johan* (*c.* 1539?), where abstractions turn, for a time, into named historical personages. Marlowe's merit 'lies in his humanizing the puppets of the *Kynge Johan* type', as Gregory Smith wrote in *The Cambridge History of English Literature*, which may be consulted by those curious to see how 'the didactic or satirical' intent can be noted by a nineteenth-century historian, only to be immediately forgotten in the pursuit of more congenial—and more 'romantic'—prepossessions. (*C.H.E.L.*, V., pp. 151-2. cf. Saintsbury on history-plays, p. 184, same vol.)

The accepted premise beneath all such views is that with the Renaissance 'interest in character', an old order passed, and abruptly. In dealing with the morality-play, the interlude, and the subsequent history-play we assume nearly the opposite. In the Morality—a field of reading for the most part admittedly and unrelievedly dull—we assume that we are already dealing with the making of Elizabethan patterns, and that that lends interest to medieval matters which might otherwise appear remote and dramatically dead. For what might be called 'the Morality habit-of-mind' is a medieval heritage of the first importance to the understanding of the Elizabethan drama.

The first Morality was in existence by about 1378, and was perhaps a Wycliffite production, for a tract refers to teaching the Paternoster 'in English tongue, as men seyen in the pley of York'. It is described as setting forth the goodness of Our Lord's Prayer, 'in which play all manner of vices were held up to scorn, and the virtues held up to praise'; and although no text remains, this datum, with the additional fact that it included a *Play of Sloth* (*Ludus Accidie*), makes its classification reasonably certain. Sloth is one of the deadly sins—meaning not mere idleness only, but the slack and depressed failure of the will which makes a man indeed beyond redemption. There were seven deadly sins and seven petitions in the Lord's Prayer, each requiring the sevenfold operation of the Spirit; and from this Chambers argues that each part of the *Paternoster* play dealt with a several vice. We know there was a Guild of the Paternoster by 1389, so it was probably responsible for the play; which supplanted the York cycle at intervals till 1572, when the archbishop called in the book and no more is heard of it. But in 1469 a *Paternoster* play was acted at Beverley, and this had seven 'stations' but eight 'pageants': seven for the deadly sins and the eighth for one Vitiosa, whom we might call either 'Vicious' or 'Mr. Frail', and who was probably the unheroic hero of the piece. One presumes that the lay-out was something like that in *The Castle of Perseverance*, and that Vitiosa displayed his versatile frailties on the seven stations after an introductory scene of some kind (perhaps with good and evil angels attending).

So much for the earliest indications of a continuous tradition of acted Moralities. The line continues through *The Pride of Life* and the *Castle* (*c.* 1425), examined later on. But if Morality is roughly defined as allegoric drama presenting the conflict of opposed powers for the soul of man (or mankind)—*humanum genus*), then one much earlier piece must be given a passing note.

The twelfth-century Advent-play of *Antichristus* belongs to a stage when drama is still attached to Church-ritual. It is the earliest piece to use personified abstractions, and the first (since Roman times) to be written so as to have what the Elizabethans called 'application' to current political affairs. It is based ultimately on the mere hint of 2 Thessalonians ii, 3-12, which was developed into theological fiction in the *Libellus de Antichristo* of Adso of Toul. This in turn provides the material of a complicated pageant-play with a procession of the Emperor, the Pope, three European kings, and personifications of Gentilitas, Synagoga, and Ecclesia, attended by Misericordia and Justitia. These personifications are from the pseudo-Augustinian *Altercatio Ecclesiae et Synagogae* or Contention (or debate) of the Church and the Synagogue. In both cases something like sermon-material has been used. But while one can freely admit Dr. Owst's introductory remark to his study of the Moralities: 'Here, at the outset, we are *already on firmer ground* in making a similar claim for pulpit influence' (p. 526 op. cit., but my italics)—it is strange, if his thesis is sound, that the morality-generative sermon remained barren from the twelfth century to the fourteenth. The *débat* of the Four Daughters of God, where Mercy and Peace plead against Truth and Righteousness for man's salvation—the whole an invention on Psalm lxxxv, v. 10—though written in the twelfth century by Bernard of Clairvaux and Hugo of St. Victor, seems to show that this indubitably influential piece of the literature of the pupit was without *dramatic* effect till well after the period of 'secularization'.[23]

The conclusion must be that while such themes as this and 'the Beseiged Castle and the Vices personified' owe everything to the Sermon, the non-allegorical drama is not of the same stock. Dr. Owst does not consider the *Antichristus*, but it anticipates much of what he finds in the English moralities when their authors have their eye on particular contemporary evils while affecting to deal in generalities or universals. The Hypocrites who prepare by propaganda for the victory of Antichrist over the Kings of the Greeks, the French and the Teutons and persuade Synagoga that he is the Messiah, stand for the supporters of the Papacy against Barbarossa. The King of the Franks is squared with gifts and marked on the brow with A by Antichrist because Louis VII supported Pope Alexander III, and the German imperial party thought he 'followed but for gain'. Apart from this the play is only an elaborate military pageant demanding unusual resources in space and in performers. (Text in *Young*, ii.)

Besides the sermon-literature which deals with the conflicts of the inner life and the fortunes of the soul as it fares through the world towards death, the Morality draws on the semi-dramatic field of the *débat* or *éstrif:* a formal contest in words between two persons who are opposed like the two counsels in a law-case or the contestants who held open debate or logical disputation in ancient universities and schools. The forensic pattern of accusation and defence or argument and rejoinder has the elements of the dramatic in it; and it is possible that some surviving medieval pieces on this pattern may have been performed by minstrels, each taking a 'side'. An example is the *Interludium de Clerico et Puella*, of which only two 'sequences' survive, so that we are left uncertain (though hardly 'without a clue') as to whether the clerk conquered the maiden, or vice versa. Nor is it impossible that the deservedly famous *Nut-brown Maid*, with its gradual turning of the screw on the girl's heart and the sudden surprise of the 'discovery' (*anagnorisis*) at the end, was intended for some merryman and his maid to dance and sing. (Text in *Oxford Book*, No. 25.)

In clashing, yet not inappropriate contrast to anything so charming is the side of the Morality which draws on not only the theme of death in the sermon, but the Dance of Death itself as a pictorial allegory. To many, this will be familiar from the works of Holbein. Emperor, King, Cardinal, Bishop, the Pope himself, the knight, the lady, the merchant, and the beggar are approached by the skeleton, their power, their sanctity, their astuteness or misery notwithstanding; and often the scenes are composed in a way that suggests a 'dramatic denouement'. There is a clear relationship to those once-popular poems, earlier than the dance, which ask: 'Where are (they)?' or '*Ubi sunt*?', with a list of fallen fames, which we can trace down the centuries till we are moved by an *ubi sunt* for all past times.

In the thirteenth century the *Love Rune* of Thomas of Hales catches the note:

> Where is Paris and Eleyne
> That were so bright and fair to see,
> Amadas *and* Ideyne,
> Tristram, Yseude and alle they;
> Ector, sharp of might and main,

And Caesar, rich of worldes fee?
—They be y-gliden from domain
So the sheaf is of the clay.[24]

It is in Villon's famous *Ballade of Dead Ladies* early in the fifteenth; and before that the sting of his refrain is in Chaucer's *Troilus and Criseyde:*

Yea, farewell all the snowe of ferne year. . . .

The context is ironic, and there is no overt moral any more than there is in Villon: who answers a question by a question, and whose refrain—'burden' as the Elizabethans called it—tells you in the *Envoi* that if you ask '*Ubi sunt*', the echo will only answer '*Ubi sunt*'.

It can be picked up a century after Dunbar's *Lament for the Makers* in Nashe's song from *Summer's Last Will and Testament* (1593):

Adieu, farewell, earth's bliss,
This world uncertain is;
Fond are life's lustful joys,
Death proves them all but toys,
None from his darts can fly. . . .

In the third stanza Helen crosses the stage, in the fourth Hector, and, as the refrain tells, one brute-fact connecting all these is simply medical: the outbreaks of bubonic plague which, from the Black Death to Elizabethan times, set the sudden skeleton at any man's elbow. There is no need to go further, to the last ironical recrudescence of *ubi sunt* in:

Where is Napoleon the Grand? God knows:
Where little Castlereagh? The devil can tell:
Where Grattan, Curran, Sheridan, all those
Who bound the bar or senate in their spell?

* * * * *

Where's Brummel? Dished. Where's Long Pole Wellesley? Diddled.

No one who has noticed the paradoxical recurrence of the 'mutability' theme among the life-hungry Elizabethans can fail to recognize this particular heritage, and its closeness to a kind of ritual of death. The preaching tradition is but one side to it: how powerful is demonstrated by a tremendous passage from the Dominican John Bromyard, with the *ubi sunt* running all through it, which Owst translates. (*Literature and Pulpit*, p. 293.) Yet the conception of death as 'a skulking ghostly tyrant, who flits through all lands from place to place, sparing none, be he rich or poor, high or low, king or emperor, pope or prelate, religious or secular' (id., p. 531) owes much to that brute fact which Nashe wrote most in mind of, and not a little to the silent sermon of the Totentanz. The plague explains why the earlier tale and pictures of 'the Three Dead and the Three Living' (usually kings, nobles, or gallants) were supplanted by the dance, where all estates take part; and again why that beings as a dance of the *dead*—a visitation of corpses and not of allegorical skeletons. The continuity of this Morality-like personification of death-by-epidemic is obvious if one puts beside *The Pardoner's Tale*, where the old man (as Age) directs the drunken rioters to where death is to be found, the passage which Dekker printed in 1603, after 40,000 had died of plague:

> Imagine then that all this while Death (like a Spanish Leaguer, or rather like stalking *Tamberlaine*) hath pitched his tents (being nothing but a heap of winding-sheets tacked together) in the sinfully polluted Suburbs. The Plague is Muster-master and Marshal of the field: burning Fevers, Boils, Blains and Carbuncles, the Leaders, Lieutenants, Sergeants and Corporals: the main army consisting (like Dunkirk) of a mingle-mangle, viz. dumpish Mourners, merry Sextons, hungry Coffin-sellers, scrubbing Bearers and nasty Grave-makers. . . . Fear and Trembling (the two Catchpolls of Death) arrest everyone: No parley will be granted, no composition stood upon; But the Allarum is struck up, the *Toxin* rings out for life, and no voice is heard but *Tue, Tue, Kill, Kill.* (*The Wonderfull Yeare*, ed. F. P. Wilson, 1925, p. 31.)

The journalism of repentance which Nashe and Greene were practising in the 1590's is borrowing back from the stage in reviving a derivative of the preaching-tradition. But the strange *toxin* in the English blood is the same as it had been when the Totentanz was to be seen in Pardon Churchyard beside old St. Paul's, with the verses John Lydgate made for it from the famous model of the Holy Innocents' at Paris (painted *c.* 1424).

The earliest Totentanz was, as the name suggests, a dance of the dead in the churchyard, striving to entrap the living. By the fourteenth century this piece of pagan superstition was converted to a christian end. It joined with the literature of the terrors of death and of world-contempt which can be traced back to the eleventh and twelfth centuries. The word 'macabre', which we apply to such things, dates from 1376, when the poet Jean le Fevre wrote: '*Je fis de Macabree la danse.*' It was only in the fifteenth century that the plain skeleton replaced the thoroughly macabre figures of hollow tattered corpses, often with the 'channering worm' coiling in the putrescent flesh. The original dancer, as surviving stanzas often tell us, was not Death but 'the dead man' or 'woman'. Not seldom they speak directly and dramatically to the living.[25]

Now in the thirteenth century there already existed those *vado mori* distichs in each of which a type (pope, knight, doctor, pauper, etc.) says: 'I go to die (*vado mori*). I am so-and-so. My place (or art) availed me nothing. *vado mori*.' As in:

> Vado mori logicus; aliis concludere novi.
> Conclusit breviter mors mihi: vado mori.

This Doctor of Rhetoric who says that he made short work of others, but Death makes shorter of him, is on the verge of being dramatic. Though Emile Mâle's thesis of the dependence of the visual arts on the drama has not won the acceptance of the learned, both Chambers and Huizinga allow that the Totentanz may be related to a ritual of mortification, in which contemporary figures pageanted in the garb of their status or calling, each to be led away by the Leveller, perhaps to a Tomb, with the appropriate *vado mori* speech. A 'dance of the dead' was certainly performed before the Duke of Burgundy at Bruges in 1449, but it does not follow that the pictures did not come first.

The essence of the connection with the morality-play can, however, be seen in Holbein (printed at Lyons in 1538 and at Basle as *Icones Mortis* in a sixth edition of 1554). There bony hands lead away representatives of all estates of the realm, and where the skeleton-attendant waits on the proud lady or lurks behind the cheating lawyer or the haggling merchant, or snuffs out the candle behind the nun whose devotion is all to her lover, the antic is often ironically appropriate as a clash or travesty-parallel to the manners of his victim. Over the king, death 'keeps his court . . . scoffing his state', his clawed phalanges on 'the golden rigol', the epitome of Shakespeare's humouring humorist who:

> Comes at the last, and with a little pin
> Bores through the castle-wall, and—farewell king!

But with less distinguished persons, the sworded nobleman, the knight, the titivating bride, the newly married pair led with the drum, or the fool danced along with his own bagpipe, the types of human-kind are entirely contemporary: factual, life-like and vivid in dress and habit. The *memento-mori* idea is not only made visual, but also *present*, of today: pinned down to contemporary life. This is of the essence of the Morality. The general abstract notion (as of conflict between Virtues and Vices, of the *Ars Moriendi* or Holy Dying, etc.) takes the form, dress, and tongue of the world about. To see Moralities only as the contest or warfare or duels of abstractions is indeed to make them 'colourless': it is not to *see* them at all. As with the crudities of language in the Miracles, one must remember that these things were made to be *shown*, not read. The Miraculists and Moralists, like their Elizabethan descendants, knew all about the manager's view in Goethe's *Faust:*

> Besonders aber lasz genug geschehn,
> Man kommt zu schaun, man will am liebsten sehn.[26]

Like the Totentanz figures, the persons of the Morality have a doubleness about them. A competent artist gives the former the 'dramatic' quality of visualized suspense, by catching an act as it is just about to happen or to be completed—as with Holbein's Knight, thrust through with a knight's spear by a Death in bits of armour. But the two figures exist on quite different planes. The skeleton only *stands for* the concept of dying or death: belongs solely to an allegoric, image-making plane; but the knight (or merchant, fool, or lawyer, etc.) exists on two. In dress, etc., he is a type from contemporary life—perhaps even an individual, like 'Maister John Rykell sometime tregitour', who was juggler to Henry V, and who appeared in Pardon Churchyard and remains in Lydgate's verses. But in allegoric significance he is the type or exemplar of man, or man's mortality. With the Totentanz the shift of attention from plane to plane seems imperceptible, because we are used to it. In the Morality it is easy to stick on the allegoric plane, oblivious to the original effect, viz. of real people 'in modern dress' going through a complicated plot, the meaning of which was partly left for the audience to see.

It was this particular characteristic of the Morality which fathered the Elizabethan taste for seeking 'applications': that is, morals and topic references together, preferably of course of a 'confidential' sort. Ben Jonson's works are full of complaints about this—how disingenuous we are never likely to know. But the simple habit of mind which the Morality bred as a result of its 'doubleness' or bi-planar nature can be seen at once from the notes which Simon Forman made in 1611 after going to *The Winter's Tale* and a play on Richard II. On the first he warns himself: 'Beware of trustinge feined beggars or fawninge fellouss'. Autolycus has been shifted back to the world of New Gyse, Haphazard, Iniquity, or other such figures of sixteenth-century drama. On the other play, having seen how Gaunt hanged a soothsayer who told him his son would be king, Forman notes: 'Beware . . . of noble men and of their faire wordes, and sai lyttel to them . . .': extracting a useful moral for soothsayers because he was one himself.

These crude examples show how, to our unromantic ancestors, didacticism was itself an attraction. The allegoric method has, however, far more subtle possibilities. It is easy to see how the contemporaneity of presentation made immediate room in the Morality for satire and social criticism; for something like the real-life scene is presented, *and* in a play whose business (if it has a moral) is *judging* the ways of the people it presents. This duly appears in quite early plays of a kind which can still be called religious (e.g. the so-called *Mind, Will, and Understanding* of *c.* 1460).

But allegory can be of at least two distinct kinds. In one—which is the kind you immediately think of if allegory bores you—a prefabricated and preformulated code is naïvely demonstrated to be the right one, by an action predetermined to that end; and you may very reasonably object that life is not quite so simple as all that, nor the distinctions made by the code so infallibly distinct. But if one follows the development of the 'allegorical tendency' from Roman to Roman Catholic civilization, as examined in C. S. Lewis's *Allegory of Love*, the personification of abstractions, to which the era of the *Roman de la Rose*, the preachers and the Moralities seems so unreasonably addicted, appears in a very different light. It appears as nothing less than an instrument in the process of the evolution of self-awareness; and in that process the discovery of visualized (or visualizable) projections of mental events or states clearly played a major part. For some purposes the half-evanished Roman deities provided a 'form' under which the mind could literally 'see itself': as its own Mars (*Ira* or Anger) or Venus (*Voluptas*), or its own conflict as a war, a duel or a siege. This is approximately half-way between our modern capacity to think quite abstractly of abstracts ('desire' in 'conflict' with 'fear', or simply 'conflict' as such) and the primitive limitation of being able only to 'think' in terms of affecting or afflicting gods or spirits, each a pseudo-human superhuman. To take an example which is, I hope, new: In his famous invocation to Venus in the *De Natura Rerum*, the lines which Lucretius writes on Mars and Venus refer, in passionate particularity, at once to those individualized Olympians in their olympian remoteness *and* to human lovings ('this noble *circumfusa*' as Montaigne said). But on the plane of the real thinking of the poem, Venus is *Voluptas:* the joyous fulfilling amative urge in men, beasts, birds, and all nature, and *Religio* is superstition, the religion of baseless fear, always ready to *suadere malorum*, an evil which sound philosophy will destroy.[27] In other writers, both pagan and Christian, this untroubled 'metaphysical-poetic' equilibrium of different 'planes of reality' is disturbed. The mitigated monotheism of a Christianity which (for untheological minds) starts with three gods and a goddess and includes steadily-increasing armies of sub-divinities—to say nothing of the hierarchies of the anti-gods—was very near to the paganism in which the separate divinities had come to be regarded as limited or localized and subjected to Fate or to a Jupiter whose functions were not easy to distinguish from those of Fate. Simultaneously, the European mind becomes increasingly aware of the divided will: the *bellum intestinum* or war of the mind within itself, about which both Stoic and Christian use the same metaphors. As C. S. Lewis shows, Seneca's 51st *Epistle* anticipates the exact terms of the *Psychomachia* of Prudentius (*c.* 400), the epic Holy War or Battle of the Soul, to which Creizenach long ago traced back the Moralities. It presents the battle of the virtues and the vices: exactly what our earliest completely surviving Morality is about (i.e. *The Castle of Perseverance*). Owst's examination of the evidence from the sermons takes the emphasis off the direct dependence on Prudentius. Long before him, Tertullian, arguing vehemently against *Spectacula*, had thrown out one remarkable blue-print for a Christian future he could not have imagined, when he wrote: 'If gladiators you must have, then behold Shamelessness hurled down by Chastity, Perfidy slain by Faith, and Cruelty crushed by Pity.' (*De Spec.* xxix.) Here C. S. Lewis misses the interplay of 'planes' when he complains of the absurd contradictions involved in presenting the *triumph* of Humility or the *vengeance* of Mercy. The battle or sieges with their crushings, revenges, and subsequent triumphs merely represent the *superiority*, on a moral and abstract plane, which the trial-by-arms allegorizes. The victory is only an image of a 'betterness' in the mind, and unless a reference is evoked there, the morality fails of its moral effect. A modern cult of Humility and a literary expectation of consistency of character may prevent our seeing that these images worked well for those truly humble Christians of whom Walter Hilton wrote: '*By a certain carnal reverence* their mind is stirred to adore *with bodily humiliation* that image rather than another';

arguing that this 'sensual and carnal emotion' is a necessary stage in religious education for ignorant men. (Owst, p. 138, but my italics.)

It may be admitted that Prudentius seems prophetically aware of Mr. Lewis's admonitory eyebrow, and therefore attempts to save the patience of Patience by presenting that undramatic virtue as a kind of moral pachyderm, passive before the darts of rage, but totally impervious.

A more important point is that made by T. S. Eliot in a breif but brilliant digression on allegory in his essay on Dante. Not thinking of allegoric drama at all, still less of pictures, he there remarks how allegory demands clear visual images, and that what we must consider is 'the type of mind which by nature and *practice* tended to express itself in allegory'. He adds: 'Clear visual images are given much more intensity by having a meaning—we do not need to know what the meaning is, but in our awareness of the image we must be aware that the meaning is there too.' (*Selected Essays*, 1932, pp. 228-9.) I take this to be relevant to the kind of allegory which became the common currency of the medieval world *because* it showed (made seeable) the mind to itself: *because* its 'sensual and carnal emotion' was a picture-thinking, often in visions, deeper than what we commonly think of as 'thought'. When it is effective, thinking or contemplation is itself visual: there is an intuitive apprehension of significances, rather than an intellectual de-coding. Indeed, intellectual formulation may be difficult or impossible; or at least seems crude, tentative, and unsatisfying. We substitute a plotting of marks on a moral target for the jab and rip of the bullet.

I would not for a moment suggest that any Morality-play is capable of stirring that 'certain carnal reverence'. But that was, I believe, what they were meant to do. They appear towards the fag-end of the preaching-tradition, and much of their allegory is stereotype, lacking the vitality of the genuine *apprehensive* thing; so that whereas the Totentanz pictures, or Bruegel's engravings of the Deadly Sins, still give a taste of the original sting, the appeal of moralities to their audiences, which apparently preferred them to miracle-plays, seems mysterious. Possibly one reason for it was that the authors were committed to the devising of a plot, the changes in which could not be foregone conclusions like those of a Bible-story. For the rest, there was the appeal of the 'doubleness' of the action, which often involves seeing through the equivocation of appearances: as, for instance, in following the tricks of plausible vices, engaged by their rascality, but *morally* certain that the pot must go too often to the well, that pride goes before a fall, that fine feathers don't make fine birds—or some other such evergreen platitude.

Much has been argued about the Deadly Sins and the Vice; but after noting the comic and always undignified devils of the Miracle-plays, the derivation of the Vice as riotous clown and his (usual) supplantation of the other six—or all seven—needs little explanation. With the setting of entirely contemporary situations, often in part from low life, the infiltration of fooling and horseplay was rapid: the taking-up of the Morality by professional companies made it even more so. But even in the pre-dramatic stage of this kind of didacticism the corrective use of derision and caricature had prepared the way for a 'Vice' to be a comic. A preacher might have as sharp a tongue as Chaucer's Pardoner and the same gift for picking on people—left unnamed though everyone knew whom he meant—without being anything but zealous and disinterested. Men are, after all, more often impressed by being made ridiculous than by being called damnable. The Pardoner's thumbnail caricature of Drunkenness is an example of what any preacher might produce, if he were a sarcastic humorist. Langland's Accidia in *Piers Plowman V* gives a more extensive reportage-in-caricature: as do his Glutton (*Gula*) and ex-brother Wrath (*Ira*). Modernize a few lines on Slouth and you have a draft for a 'dramatic monologue' of self-exposure which is comic and moral at once:

> Then came slobbering Slack the Parson, with two eyes like poached eggs. "I must sit myself down," said the sot, "or I'll drop off to sleep. . . . If I once got to bed, no bell 'ud disturb me till Belly said 'Dinner'." He began to say grace with a gurk, and his guts grumbled. He yawned with a roar like a horse and started to snore. . . .

Woken up, he burbles on about himself complacently thus:

> "I've never poked round my parish pestering poor folks, nor yet prisoners in gaol. I'd sooner hear a smutty story or a shoemakers' May-game, a spicy yarn to laugh at or a smart bit of scandal, than all Mark said, or Matthew, or all the rest of 'em. . . . I've been priest and parson here thirty years past, and I can't sing these sol-fas nor read saints' lives; but I can find a hare in her form inside a furlong and better than I could construe a line of Latin or explain it to the parish. . . ."

We can see here how the Improving (on the moral plane) is one with the Amusing (on the mundane). The hateful, presented as ugliness, becomes the grotesque: one type of which is 'the obscene' for its affront to human dignity. Landland's Slouth is an obscene creature; but if he is put on a stage to belch and leer and be knowing, the audience will respond with laughter. This gives the opening for the clown; and when the 'vice' has become a jester's part, both playwright and audience will have a weak spot for him. At the end of the play, when the moral ritual wants him hanged or otherwise punished, the comic wants him to get away with it—and often has its way, in defiance of sound doctrine.

In this there is again an ambivalence, though less searing than the inner clash of the Miracles. It shows why the Moral Play tends to split into 'layers' rather as slate does, one set of *laminae* still concerned with morality, the other with mirth and immoralities, or mere farce and horseplay. This begins very early in its career: the Elizabethan consequences are of the greatest interest. Though C. M. Gayley questions the descent of Vice from devil, saying he is only 'a riotous buffoon', there is plainly some kind of interaction, and the farcical-grotesque of the terrifying black-faced demon is not entirely separable from the grotesque farce of his analogue.

This is seen in the morality called *Mind, Will, and Understanding* (*c.* 1460, otherwise *Wisdom*), where Lucifer appears himself as 'a prowde gallant' who corrupts all three, as Pride should. Mind turns to ambition and tyranny, Will to lust and idleness, and Understanding to double-dealing and avarice. Very intriguingly, each achieved seduction is presented as a *dance*, each main evil in turn leading up a ballet of six associated ones, the resulting catalogue of twenty-one vices being of close historical application to the anarchical fifteenth century.[28] Maintenance (graft-with-intimidation) leads six evil red-bearded fellows wearing lions-rampant; Perjury leads six jurors; and only with Lechery's ballet of three gallants and three 'matrons' (Greed, Fornication, and Adultery) are we on familiar Christian ground. The debasement of *Anima*, the Soul, is 'visualized' by a decidedly Spenserian spectacle when she appears fiendishly ugly and with little devils running from under her skirts. Yet though Lucifer is *The* Devil, he has a sudden descent to slapstick. Having said how he wins many a soul to hell, he makes his exit with a stage-direction, 'taketh a shrewd boy with him and goeth his way, crying'—the little victim being either a 'stooge' or some fidgeting and troublesome (*shrewd*) brat near at hand, 'unconscious of his doom' until his 'cryenge' was required for practical purposes.

Ever since the eighteenth century historians the text-books have made far too much of the Vice's lamming the Devil with his 'dagger of lath' and at last riding off on his back. This was certainly an *Elizabethan* show, as is demonstrated by *Friar Bacon and Friar Bungay;* but the passage which—if any—the middlemen of literary traditions have had in mind does not really support the favourite generalization. It runs:

> It was a pretty part in the old church-playes, when the nimble Vice would skip up nimbly like a Jack-an-apes into the Devil's necke, and ride the devil a course, and belabour him with a wooden dagger, till he made him roar, whereat the people would laugh to see the Devil so Vice-haunted.

Its date, however, is 1603; and though a little black soul is thus removed in *The Castle of Perseverance* (p. 98) the effect is nothing like that described by Harsenet.

The Vice, when he is *the*, begins roughly where the Miracle-devil leaves off: where devilish jocularity, as in Tutivillus of Wakefield, goes over to the impish mischief-making of the born *mauvais sujet*—there are such beings, despite the *Problem-Child* school of thought—the human scamp who is an example of vicious failings *and*, like 'old J.B.' in Dickens, 'tough and devilish sly'. Thus the standard Deadly Sins drop out of the picture by degrees, leaving a being endowed with the qualities which make a simple matron call a lad 'a terror' or (in the West Country) 'a Gall'us': meaning one 'as full of tricks as a wagonload of monkeys', and with about as much social sense: probably born to hang, and in the meantime alarmingly addicted to ruthless practical joking. No such being is in the earlier Moralities, though in *Mankynd* (*c.* 1475) there is the beginnings of the type which we shall follow to Shakespeare's day. I observe in passing that if such a one is given to double-crossing and mischief-making *in matters of fatal consequence*, he is the germ of a 'villain', and one of a peculiar sort—knave and savage comedian at once. Incidentally, too, *The Seven Deadly Sins* is an Elizabethan play-title. The 'plot' or stage-production schedule of one part survives and shows that it was a series of 'historical' episodes, each apparently exemplifying one sin, presented by the poet Lydgate before Henry VI, who is, I take it, having a medieval nightmare throughout.

But before considering the earlier and more nearly devotional morality, we must return to the theme of Death and indicate a certain persistent doubleness there too. In the terms of chemistry, the Skull is, as a symbol, *amphoteric:* that is to say, it can be the eating 'acid' or its opposite the 'base' according to its context. Just so it reached the reigns of Henry VIII and Elizabeth. In Holbein's picture *The Ambassadors*, in the National Gallery, the distorted reflection of a skull, as seen in a concave cylindrical mirror, is put on the floor in the foreground. Another skull is worn as a jewel in the bonnet. His portrait of Sir Brian Tuke which was formerly at Munich shows a very fearsome death's-head gaping at the nobleman, over whose other shoulder appears a fleshless hand grasping a scythe. By the sitter's hand is an hour-glass, and his finger points out the Vulgate text of Job x, 20, which runs in English. 'Will not my short days be soon ended?' Similarly, from Elizabeth's time, the Fitzwilliam Museum at Cambridge has a portrait of her favourite, Leicester, by Zuccaro (1562), in which a singularly bestial little chapless skull thrusts itself against his cheek, between the words RESPICE and FINEM. The earl's age is given—thirty-two—but at no time were his the meditations of Donne or Jeremy Taylor.

The *memento-mori* must, in fact, often be taken as an amphoteric symbol: like the fading rose which says: '*Carpe diem, quam minimum credula postero*': pluck the flower of today, my dear, never trust tomorrow—or, more simply, the antithetic *memento vivere*. As such, presumably, skull-rings were popular with English whores: a taste which somehow survived among American soldiers till the 1940's (as I accidentally discovered by asking in a shop who made them and why). But the fashion was not restricted to the disreputable, and Shakespeare touches on it several times. To Byron, Holofernes' face is like 'a death's-head set in a ring': Portia would prefer the whole show to either of her suitors; while Falstaff not only observes that Bardolph is as good a penitential picture to him as another man's *memento*, but also bids Dol Tearsheet not to speak like a death's-head, not to bid him remember his end.

Immediate light on this contradiction between the Elizabethan vitality and life-lust and the surviving medieval mortifications of proud flesh is given by the accounts of the Innocents' Churchyard in Paris. There, beside the Dance of Death in the cloisters, was the most famous of burial-grounds. Bodies were said to rot to bare bone there in nine days; and so many parishes had rights of sepulture there that on three sides the cloisters were decorated with confused stacks of bones in charnels, as old graves were made vacant for new tenants. Yet despite all this, the very atmosphere of mortality, *there* was the most popular rendezvous in Paris. Booths stood beside the bones, and prostitutes vaunted there the flesh they hawked: silken and velvet life brushed the yellow labours of mortality; and behind all the silent dancers danced, mocking with their lipless grin the state and pomp and laughter of the living.

Though Huizinga comments, 'To such an extent had the horrible become familiar', the explanation is surely to be found rather in what he elsewhere calls 'the sensual note': where the 'grave' *memento-mori* tone is crossed by the 'regret for lost beauty', whose symbols are the woman's beauty fronting chiselling time, the summer flower, the full-blown rose.

The *Totentanz*, then, like the clown, is amphoteric; and death, like laughter, ambivalent.* To Elizabethan manhood 'remember your end' could also be a reminder to live: to end with a certain uncertain impudence in what Gray called 'trembling hope', perhaps; but certainly with Petronius':

> Pervixi, neque enim fortuna malignior unquam
> Eripiet nobis quod prior hora dedit.[29]

Plague, civil wars, anarchy, and the dissolution of the old faith strengthened such tendencies. But the mortification-mongering of the Elizabethans, their drawings-towards-themselves of the little pin that made all castles seem futile, and yet set them so greedily agrab despite the moral warnings: all that belongs to one great picture, of which the two-sidednesses of the medieval drama are only a small detail in a corner.

* The perfect example of this ambivalence is the Death of the closing lines in the *Copa* (Dancing-girl) poem sometimes ascribed to Virgil:—

> "Down with your wine and your dice, to hell with thoughts of tomorrow!
> Here's Death twitching my ear-lobe: "Live, lad," he says, "I'm coming."

CHAPTER VI

# THE MORALITY GENUS

IF Moralities are broadly defined as 'allegorical plays with some formulable "moral" point'—where 'moral' need imply no more than 'which could be called a lesson'—then all can be classed under two heads. One class, generally speaking the earlier, takes a complete conspectus of man's life, often divided into 'ages'. The paternoster plays can be included in it with *The Castle of Perseverance*, because particular vices were commonly associated with particular ages. In calling Avarice 'a good old-gentlemanly vice', Byron was as traditional as is the Old Shepherd in *Winter's Tale* on the age when there is 'nothing but getting wenches with child, wronging the ancientry, stealing, fighting'. This type continues into the sixteenth century with *Nature* (p. 103) and *Mundus et Infans*, though with a difference. Whereas *The Castle of Perseverance* is 3,650 lines in length (50 per cent longer than the average Elizabethan play) and has thirty-five speaking parts, the six ages of man in *Mundus et Infans* (*c.* 1509) are compressed into 979 lines, with only five speaking parts. The big plays of this kind are related to the cycles in that they are meant for outdoor production; but the earlier theory that they *derived* from the Miracles is now abandoned. The very long *Mary Magdalene* in the Digby plays (EETS, ed. Furnivall), which uses allegorical figures to present psychological changes, is an attempt to combine the attractions of both types of play. The same is true of the allegorical devices in some of the N-town plays, where the Debate of the Heavenly Virtues (p. 81) is prefixed to *The Salutation and Conception*, and death himself appears at Herod's court. Apart from its obviously strong—though to our minds very puzzling—attraction, the allegorical figure can make play-making much easier: as witness the Norwich *Creation*, where at the Fall, Dolor and Myserye enter and take Man by both arms. (Adams, p. 88 f.) We shall note even naïver things in much later plays written under Elizabeth (see p. 142).

The other class of Moralities deals only with some one age or other restricted problem: as in *Everyman* (which is about dying), in the various youth plays (e.g. *Hickscorner* and *Lusty Iuventus*), and those on Wit. Many are like one single sequence from the bulkier pieces they tended to outmode as the exigencies of playing demanded less lines and fewer actors. But the King-and-Death theme of the fragmentary play called *Pride of Life* (*c.* 1410) suggests a derivation from the Dance of Death and the débats or contentions between Death and Life, rather than from an extracted episode from something like the *Castle*. The derivation of the whole-life type, on the other hand, is plainly from the sermons and the *Psychomachia:* the one essential difference being that the Virtues and Vices now battle *for man*, presented as a *persona* (*Humanum Genus*, *Mankynd*, etc.), though it is usually also true that some at least of the powers of evil tend to become comic. One important thing about the 'whole-life' Morality is that, like *Dux Moraud* (p. 73), it does provide an approximate first-idea of the kind of play which was later entitled 'The Life and Death of X': a point to which I return later.

The outline of *Pride of Life* is given in the Prologue, which shows what the extant speeches led up to. The King of Life (*Rex Vivus*) boasts of his invincibility and his two henchmen Strength and Health; and when his Queen rebukes him, bidding him think on his end, she is treated rather worse than is usual with hortatory wives and gets about as much notice as they. The King calls his messenger, a flattering fellow called Mirth and Solas, and sends a challenge to Death. But when he has retired (into some curtained alcove on the stage), the Queen sends the messenger secretly for the Bishop, who comes, lamenting the world's wickedness and the oppressions of the rich; but only to have his sermon ill received and himself called 'babbler' and 'chagler' (which may be 'cackler' or 'gabbler': in short the King thinks he natters, and indeed he does). The Prologue shows that Death sent a terrible dream of the King's relations dead, which was apparently fact as well as vision, for Life and Death fight, and the King's soul goes to the fiends. Our Lady, however, prays that the Soul and Body shall dispute, and with her intercession it is to be supposed that the King was saved.[30]

With *The Castle of Perseverance* (*c.* 1425) we reach the maximum of size and content: a gigantic compendium of moral themes. An annotated diagram shows that it was staged in a circular area, with a 'castle' in the middle, five 'skafolds' about for *Deus*, *Caro* (Flesh), *Mundus* (World), Belyal, and Covetyse; the whole being either barricaded against the crowd or, 'if any dyche may be mad', insulated by a water hazard. The 'skafolds' are drawn outside the ring, but I take this as diagrammatic only. The producer is warned to keep spectators off the 'castle', and informed that when Belyal goes to battle he is to have gunpowder burning in 'pypis in his hands and in his eris and in his ers'; but it is hard to decide whether this primitive kind of jet-propulsion was only funny, or mainly alarming. In what looks like an archway beneath the 'castle' was Mankind's bed, under which some poor soul—probably a boy—lay hidden till his cue came (at l.3009!); and by its foot was 'Covetyse copbord'. (These scenic arrangements are like those of the Digby play of *Mary Magdalene*, which requires a workable ship.)

The play includes all the sins. World is attended by Folly and Lust (i.e. pleasure, *Voluptas*), and has a messenger called Backbyte (*Detractio*): Flesh by Gluttony, Sloth, and Lechery (*Luxuria*); and Belyal by Pride, Envy, and Wrath. Covetyse has a place to himself, but is World's treasurer. The performance is introduced by Banns, and the whole cycle-like show amounts to four Moralities in succession. Borrowing from film-criticism, I shall call these 'sequences'.

The first is a sequence on birth and youth, with Mankind's fall to vice and his (first) conversion (i.e. it includes more than makes a complete play in *Mankynd*, *Hickscorner*, and *The Interlude of Youth*). The evil ones present themselves, and then Mankind or *Humanum Genus* enters from birth, feeble, faint, and naked, between a Good Angel and a Bad. The Bad leads him away, and after 'pipe up music' World boasts as Rex Vivus had boasted, and Folly cries all about for men to serve the World. Mankind is taken to World's stage and then sent off to be richly dressed by Lust and Folly, and then passed to the backbiter (otherwise Flepgebet) for further education in what the medievals plainly found one of the supreme social pleasures. On the stage of Covetyse he meets (and gladly) all the Vices; but the sequence ends (and the next begins) with his abrupt collapse into virtue on meeting Shrift (*Confessio*), sent by the Good Angel.

No. 2, the castle-sequence, is a battle-of-life allegory. After homiletic from the Seven Virtues (all ladies), Mankind enters the castle which is then besieged by the mobilized Vices, all of whom have been flogged for negligence by their respective masters. They brag a lot but are beaten both by argument and the original weapon of a red-rose barrage, standing for 'a rose that on rode was rent' (i.e. on the rood). Backbyte runs about being staff-work, intelligence (military), and a bit of a clown. The war is won by diplomacy, however, Covetyse parleying with Mankind and seducing him with offers of sound investments for his old age, including real estate. In Sequence 3 the Virtues plead in vain, and he goes to Covetyse's 'bower' under the archway, where the 'copbord' is. (I think here of Bosch's picture of the man with Death's dart approaching him, and all his wealth in a chest in the foreground, under a vaulted roof which suggests a cradle.) He will forswear heaven only to be rich; but Death comes with the pitiless and poignant allusion:

> Against me is no defence;
> In the Great Pestilence
> Then was I well known.

Mankind's appeals to World are now in vain, and he is derided by being sent his heir, aptly called 'I-wot-never-who'. He dies, the main symptom being prolixity and assuredly not shortness of breath; and from under the bed creeps the concealed *Anima* (the soul) in a pretty little surprise, neatly followed up. For the Bad Angel takes leave with the winning line, 'Have good-day. I goo to helle' and exits with the small soul pickaback.

The fourth and final sequence is the Contention of the Four Heavenly Virtues or Daughters of God before His throne (see p. 81). All are in mantles, red for Righteousness, 'sad green' for Truth, white for Mercy, and black for Peace; and the soul wins forgiveness, with much scriptural citation. The moral is pointed in the last fifty lines, where a list of estates of the realm—beginning 'King, kaiser, knight, and champion, Pope, patriarch, priest, and prelate'—receive warning to think of their end, for all must give their 'count of conscience'.

In *Everyman*—which I take to be familiar to Everyman and therefore do not describe—it is obvious that Sequence 3 has been shaped to a unitary play of some 900 lines length. Death there is less violent, more sardonically grim than this armed terror with a dart. Indeed he, like the whole play, is too simple and dignified to be representative. The tight-woven treatment of Holy Dying, where the way to salvation is allegorized as a journey on which Everyman finds the worth of Good-deed and the vanity of Good-fellowship, Kindred and Goods, may seem at first sight 'seraphically free from taint of personality'. But its grave concentration, no less than its earnestness on priesthood, are really the marks of an individual mind, not those of the Morality. It is quite untypical in far more besides the lack of Vices, devils, battery, squibs, and jocularities; and if for its time (*ante* 1495?) it is a highly artistic achievement, it must also be said that it is an artistic cul-de-sac. It could be repeated in the stronger words of a Marlowe or a Tourneur: it could not serve as germ for further growth.

With *The Castle of Perseverance* it is otherwise. It may—it does—demand a wealth of the virtue it names. Not one episode in its sprawling bulk is worthy to be set beside Everyman's 'recognition' (*anagnorisis*) of God's 'myghty messengere'. Yet it has one great potentiality. It is—what no previous play had been—a potential frame for a life-story: not of mankind as *Humanum Genus*, but the human-kind as revealed in One Man. I do not see how the Miracles could ever have led to that. The descent from the life of Christ is too great, even were that a tragic story, which it is not. And the incidental bits of human life-stuff in the Miracles are too incidental.

Moreover, the *Castle* has a plotted action, and one concerned with a conflict whose result the audience must go on awaiting. It subsumes all the usual patterns of Morality plotting. In *Mind, Will, and Understanding* and in *Mankynd* the sequence is (1) innocence, ending in a fall: (2) an exposition of ill-living, with Vices: and (3) repentance and conversion. In *Hickscorner* there are still three sequences, but (1) is merely a display of virtues (Pity, Contemplation, and Perseverance), followed by a display of their near-opposites and (2) the maltreatment of Pity; the whole concluding with (3) the conversion of the two roughs, Freewill and Imagination—Hickscorner himself vanishing in the middle, so that one is left to guess whether by allegory F plus I equals H, or whether something is missing. In *Nature* (p. 103) the Innocence-Vice-Repentance pattern is twice repeated, so that it resembles the *Castle*, except that it has no castle or siege; though Reason plainly has the old play in mind at the beginning of Part 2, where this image of man's life in the world is used, and immediately followed by short paragraphs on the World, the Flesh, and the Enemy.

The Morality-writer had to have a plot. His moral gave a point towards which his action must point, and in that way *débat* was slowly urged towards logic-of-events: which is true plot. For unless a 'fable' *is* an argument, the structure is episodic and lacks true form. Here, in time, the 'whole-life' kind of Morality was to lead to better things: through the handling of what at all events *purported* to be 'real-life' stories by ordering them on a moral framework—or 'frame-up', as you may prefer to call it, (e.g. *Kynge Johan*, discussed later, is a manifest frame-up). The Morality not only got at the dramatic essential of protracted conflict in a world of jarring wills, but also arrived at one of the simple formulae for play-making. It is put well enough by Dryden:

> 'Tis the moral that directs the whole action of the play to one centre; and that action or fable is the example built upon the moral, which confirms the truth of it to our experience. (*Preface to Troilus, etc.*)

To see how nominal the homiletic or conversional aim could become, even before the end of the fifteenth century, we need only glance at *Mankynd* (*c.* 1475). It is extremely low in parts, and often just dirty: written for inn-yard amusement and East Anglian—not to say 'Cambridge'—bumpkins. But though Professor Tucker-Brooke was scandalized by it and Professor Adams' text suffers from spots and footnotes which say 'unprintable', an abstract of its plot would make it sound pure Morality. The Vices, New-Gyse (i.e. new-fangledness), Naught (-iness), and Nowadays are all buffoons, and in the knockabout turns indelicate places are hit and crude comments follow. They stand for smart good-for-nothings who deride and molest the unheroic hero, Mankynd, an artisan with a spade. Mercy and Mischief contend for him, and when he gets bored with spade-work, he is bedevilled by Titivillus, falls to despair, and is minded to hang himself. But Mercy saves him, with a homily on the World, etc., which 'explains'—not too convincingly—that the three scamps are 'the World'. To compensate for a wealth of 'unedifying' comments, improper terms and obscene suggestions, the audience are very properly reminded in eight lines at the end to search their consciences and to remember that 'the world is but a wanite'. (This accidental Wellerism is not alone. The genuine type of 'as the man said to the boy when he swallered a varden' appears in the mouth of New-Gyse, but in a specimen too feeble to quote.) The Vices' buffooneries have no relation to their symbolenda: e.g. there is no meaning behind New-Gyse's attempt to show Mankynd the art of hanging oneself, in which the demonstrator nearly goes through with the experiment on his own.

*Hickscorner* (*temp.* Henry VII), another crude piece, adapts itself to a London environment, with a strong smell of Newgate. Freewill and Imagination are Tudor gangsters, and Hickscorner a nautical tough, whom I suspect of having served under the *Narrenschiff* pennant, though he only claims to have been in a great shipwreck when Truth, Patience, Humility, Meekness, and a lot more virtuous persons were drowned. On shipboard he ran a bawdy-shop, and Falsehood, Favell (?graft), Jollity, and many other undesirables have come ashore with him—along with his prize piece Sybil, who, however, no more appears on the stage than the rest do. The only action in the play is a dagger-fight between the Vices, with Hick trying to keep them apart, and the baiting and stocking of Pity; who has a long lament on the wickedness of things, with the refrain 'worse was it never', before his release by Contemplation and Perseverance and the final conversion. Hick went off to Shooter's Hill and, as noted above, 'is heard no more'. The whole is indeed somewhat 'a tale told by an idiot'; but it 'signifies' its morals at the end, and gains its little place in dramatic history as example of the trend towards the 'characterization' of 'low-life'.

The class or group of Moralities which picks on one phase of life, or on some one restricted 'problem' such as Wit-and-Wisdom or Money lives on in the sixteenth century by close adaptation to environment. The basic pattern goes on almost unchanged, and can be picked up at Court as late as 1600, when *The Contention of Liberality and Prodigality* (printed 1602) was played before the Queen. If this was the sort of thing that Gloriana really liked, it makes our traditional term for the drama of *c.* 1586-1625 quite the greatest compliment that that much-flattered woman ever received! In the play referred to, Money (a promising lad till first 'spent' and then 'bloated') is first entrusted to Prodigality—a courtier-type—and then to an old, rustic-spoken churl called Tenacity, who is the only amusing person in the whole dull show. Both fail with him, and he goes to Liberality who (like Her Majesty?) rewards only the deserving: ex-Captain Somebody and his trusty ex-soldier. The play is only worth mentioning as an example of quite unambiguous Morality in the highest of high places in Shakespeare's mature manhood. The line of evolution and survival of the really important *developments* of the Morality-pattern will concern us in the next two chapters.

## CHAPTER VII

# INTERLUDES

POLONIUS: "This is too long."
HAMLET: "It shall to the barber's with your beard. Prithee say on—he's for a jig, or a tale of bawdry, or he sleeps. . . ."

THOUGH 'Interlude' and Morality are often synonymous, a distinction can be drawn between the graver and more nearly devotional pieces and those which show an approach to a *kind* of comedy of manners by emphasizing the contemporaneity of the types of wickedness. As a rule this is incidental. The Vices turn into recognizable scoundrels in a London comedy of ill-manners, but without losing their place in the allegorical pattern. Usually there is a jarring and quite inartistic incongruity of tone between the 'virtuous' framework and the 'vicious' intervals, and the severer the moral, the greater this is likely to be, in plays where changes of heart are clumsily sudden and devoid of all finesse of language. The traditional criticism of such 'transitional' plays is that Tudor drama is straining towards the gestation of a true comedy of character 'for its own sake', the implication being that the dramatists really *wanted* to be rid of allegory, though they had to keep some appearance of it to justify their artistic indulgences in scenes of 'low life'. There is a shadow of truth in this, for, from Henry Medwall to Jonson and Middleton, comic drama can be watched getting nearer and nearer to the seething life of the London streets; but it entirely misses the continuity of the morality pattern both as structural in plays and as a Tudor habit of mind.

This we can demonstrate by following the 'educational' Morality from the reign of Henry VII (d. 1509) into that of his son, when the polemics of rival churches begin to pervert it.

Henry Medwall, as the title of *A goodly interlude of Nature* records, was chaplain to 'the right reverent father in god Johan Morton', Cardinal, Archbishop of Canterbury, and the witty deviser of 'Morton's Fork', who died in 1500. The 'sometyme Cardynall, etc.' therefore dates the play as earlier. Medwall has a certain distinction as the first importer of an Italian comedy in his *Fulgens and Lucrece*. It is suggestive that Thomas More was of Morton's household, for John Bale and Roper's *Life* say that in his youth the great humanist acted and wrote plays. His sister, Elizabeth, married

John Rastell (d. 1536), lawyer, printer, and playwright: his niece, Elizabeth Rastell, married John Heywood—whose plays were printed by William Rastell, Elizabeth's brother (d. 1565)—and, to follow the line further, a third Elizabeth, Heywood's third daughter, married a London ironmonger and became mother to John Donne. A suggestively 'Elizabethan' lineage.

*Nature* is a Morality, on how Sensuality is opposed to Reason, Man's true guide. It retains the 'ages of Man' pattern, for Man is naked with his nurse Innocency till World gives him dress; and towards the end we learn that he and Reason are no longer at odds, because age is 'now com in place', though Covetyse is still in favour. The two-part plot shows Man corrupted by Sensuality and Worldly affection and entertaining all the Deadly Sins in turn after Pride has traduced Reason to him and he has fallen with one Margery in a tavern. There is much brothel-talk in both parts, and all the vices are presented in a lively manner as London types—Wrath as the quarreller, Envy as the slanderer, Pride as a dressy popinjay with a boasted bastard in attendance, and Glotony who, anticipating Falstaff, has a 'botell' for his 'harnes' when a fray is threatening. (Part II, 775 f.) The Vices all give themselves 'respectable' names to delude Man. Pride is 'worship', Covetyse 'worldly policy', Wrath 'manhood', Gluttony 'good-fellowship', and Sloth is 'ease'. This equivocation by titles reappears in a number of later plays, including *Magnyfycence* and *Respublica* (p. 115–6 and 124–5).

The first part ends with the unexpected appearance of Shamefastness after Man's debauches, and a return of Reason to favour. The second opens with Reason comparing man's state to 'the assyege agayn a strong town or castell' and with warnings against worldly vanities, the flesh and the devil. But soon Man, who is weary of abstinence, is drawn back to his old company, led there by Sensuality, who reminds him of Margery—now in a 'nunnery' where entry is 'fre for every body' and they 'can wed theym selfe alone' with short ceremony. Bodily Lust starts a scheme to lure him to a brothel, but this comes to nothing, beyond showing the vices in low-company intrigue. There is some goodish characterization in this part, especially when a 'fray' against Reason is plotted, Wrath appears, and Gluttony and Sloth back out of any dangerous exertions. The switch via age to Reason and repentance comes suddenly, and there is a longish rounding off of moral allegory as Man wins favour with all the opposites of the Vices. Meekness, Charity, Patience, Good Occupation, Liberality, Abstinence, and Chastity all join him—though without as much emphasis on the last as the earlier incidents would seem to require. The contrast with earlier Morality is marked in the way sin is made the result of unreason, and in the allegorizing of moral lapses in terms of servitors (the Vices) being taken into a gentleman's favour, and again in Medwall's allusions to the London of his day. As compared with *Everyman* or even *Mind, Will, and Understanding*, it is far nearer to Charing Cross than to Jacob's Ladder. But it is no less a Morality for that.

True, Medwall called it 'a goodly interlude'. But its two parts, each of some 1,400 lines, make it longish for playing as a kind of 'cabaret-show' at a feast. In any case the general sense of the term 'interlude' is only *ludus inter personas* (a play between persons)—a vague term best interpreted as 'a shortened Morality-product, commonly with more stress on entertainment than on morals.'

This use of interludes as intermezzi in social occasions is amusingly side-lit by the Elizabethan play *Sir Thomas More*. More is entertaining the Lord Mayor, and the Cardinals' Players are engaged to do *The Marriage of Wit and Wisdom* (though their lines are mainly from *Lusty Iuventus*, which the real More would not have endured). Calamities start at once. Young Wit's beard has been forgotten, and though they begin without it, hoping that one Luggins can fetch it for Scene 2, all that happens is an awkward hiatus: Good Counsel is due to enter—and Luggins is Good Counsel. More steps into the breach and does the part impromptu, playing up to actors and guests at once. Then the beard and Luggins arrive; but the banquet is now ready, so the play is put off; and before its turn comes, More is called to Court and the show is off—leaving the players a trifle short-tempered with one another.

Nor is this the only suggestion of the kind of necessity which made brevity the soul of profitable wit. According to a paper copied by Collier (so he said), Medwall's *Finding of Truth* was played at Court at Christmas 1514-15, but was 'so long yt was not lykyd . . . the Kyng departyd befor the end to hys chambre'. The veracity of Collier is suspect, and—with ironical appropriateness—*The Finding of Truth* is itself lost; but Chambers accepts the report, which is in any case supported by the sad note on the title-page of *The Nature of the Four Elements* (*c.* 1509-17). The piece, it says, will play in an hour and a half; 'but if ye list, ye may leave out much of ye sad matter, as the Messenger's part, and some of Nature's part, and some of Experience's part, and yet the matter will depend conveniently, and then it will not be past three-quarters of an hour in length.' (*Dodsley's Old Plays*, ed. Hazlitt i.) One can feel poor

Rastell's heart bleeding at the cuts; but if the king (who was Henry VIII) was likely to exit with 'Give me some lights. Away!', it meant a bad night for the interlude-makers. This kingly gesture of boredom was a sign that the take-it-or-leave-it improvingness of such moral megatheria as *The Castle of Perseverance* was a thing of the past. Tudor interludes do show some slight fear of boring their audience—though *we* may wonder much rather at our ancestors' astonishing *endurance*!—and from that laudable weakness comes, in time, a totally non-instructive kind of entertainment, meant for the early-Tudor Poloniuses who wanted less 'matter' and more 'art', even if not quite the brevities of jigs and bawdry. It was there that John Rastell's son-in-law, John Heywood, was able to say: "I'll fit you."

The names in the paragraph above suggest another important contrast. Of the More-Heywood group, only Medwall was in orders. By the earlier sixteenth century the writing of plays was getting into the hands of the kind of educated layman who was produced by the grammar-schools (often founded by the guilds, it should be remembered, the title 'King Edward VI Grammar School' signifying only that his ministers refrained from suppressing some of them, stealing only the credit for earlier benefactions). The names of Rastell (later a celebrated legal authority) and Heywood (a semi-professional court-playwright), not to mention the humbler John Redford, are all evidence that the interludes were not only the productions of starveling hacks and itinerant mountebanks. We may find their fun crude; but where they touch the ethic of the New Learning, or propagand naïvly for Education—still more when these themes get involved with the inky wars of the Reformation—it is an error to measure their importance only by æsthetic standards. The issues they debate are the foundations of the Elizabethan world and, in many ways, of our own. The old fideistic moulds were cracking, and in the dramatic confusion of the century between Medwall and Marlowe (*c.* 1493-1593) the play-of-abstractions is part of the struggle to establish new ones, to arrive at values applicable to the individual life, to man as subject in a state, and as member of a church no longer integrated in an authoritarian and indivisible Christendom.

Looked at this way, the dull or naïve 'educational' Moralities stand for the voice of the 'new men'; the common-lawyers, financiers, civil servants (laymen or erastian clergy), and schoolmasters who were coming to have 'a stake in the country'. The opposition of an 'old' learning to the 'New' leads logically to the state of things where Idleness, the vice in *The Marriage of Wit and Wisdom* (printed 1579) is a *priest;* but in an earlier stage, idleness and ignorance are pilloried simply as bars to sound learning, taken to be good in itself. The old model of the assault of the frailties on man-the-frail serves the new turns of propaganding for the New Learning, of teaching things which the New Learning thought important (e.g. geography and, later on, history), and of allegorizing 'the struggle for knowledge' as an analogy to the old battle of the Soul against worldly temptations. The results often look to us as if written for the problem-children of backward actors who could only be taught 'the play-way'. Not seldom they were indeed written by schoolmasters, as indoctrination-pieces or allegorized pep-talks, intended to inculcate the academic virtues and to show the dangers of idleness, the nastiness of ignorance, and to throw an adventurous glamour over the trials of the scholar in pursuit of a degree—or at least the imaginary Tudor equivalent of a 'full-house' of achievements in the General Certificate of Education or a pair of aces at Advanced Standard. This aim is shown in the amusingly light *Wyt and Science* (?1530, *ante* 1548) of John Redford (Adams, p. 325 f.). The other aims mentioned above must first, however, be briefly inspected, in John Rastell's *Four Elements* (*c.* 1509-17?).

In it Humanity is mercilessly lectured to by Natura Naturata, Studious Desire, and Experience, mainly on elementary geography: how the earth is round, hangs in the firmament, has a circumference, and other such novelties; and as the note on cutting hints (albeit by a misprint?), it is 'sad matter'. We stir from near-slumber a little when Studious Desire displays a map with the new-found lands of only twenty years ago marked on it and is sorry that the glory did not go to Englishmen. Momentarily we touch on the thrill of Columbus, Da Gama, and Vespucci: on what Drake and Raleigh were to mean . . . on what underlies Donne's line to his mistress:

'O my America, my new-found-land,'

no less than the geographical bombasts of Marlowe. But alas, *our* studious desire hardly stirs at all when Humanity—most understandably—runs off with Ignorance, Sensual Appetite, and a Taverner: unless to note that this touch of *Nature* (even if it is only one touch of Medwall) is a bit less dull than the rest. Yet the scholastic moral is there. Studious Desire is virtue, Sensual Appetite is danger; no longer to spiritual salvation, as in *Nature*, but to right knowledge, which is secular and intellectual. Glance back to

*Everyman* and observe how Five Wits leave him before the end while Knowledge remains, and you are back in another world: one where Bacon's 'sense and particulars' support no valid knowledge, for that belongs alone to faith. Return to the *Four Elements* and you stand somewhere in the vicinity of a turning-point of time: between the Age of Theology and the nascent Age of Science. For Rastell is taking a stand for *all* Science (as we understand it) when he says in his prologue that it is not good to study *invisible* things only, and not care for this *visible* world. The play, which is very incomplete, does not live up to that hint. When not a compendium of stale information, it is all tedious low-life traffic with the vices; and Humanity is left at the cut-off end still in company with Ignorance (a fool who sings nonsense-verses), and how he escapes we do not know or care.

*Wyt and Science* is quite a different matter. It is an allegory of the undergraduate life, in which Wit, a nice young freshman, woos Miss Science, the daughter of Dr. Reason and his wife Experience, and seeks to vanquish Giant Tediousness and attain Mount Parnassus. Dr. Reason, whom I take for his tutor, is a reasonable person. He gives him a 'mirror of reason', but does not expect him to work all the time; and so a decent woman, Honest Recreation by name, is sent to take care of him. (We gather from another lady's abuse that she includes dancing, music, and gambling—but not 'organized sport'). But Wit is not a reasonable student; he is too keen. He goes to Study and Diligence before seeking help from Instruction (whom Cambridge would call his supervisor), and when Study succumbs to chronic headache, Giant Tediousness has an easy victory. The influence of the Mummers' play (p. 22) is evident here, for after the stage-direction, 'Here Wyt falleth down and dyeth', there enter Honest Recreation, Comfort, Quickness, and Strength, to kneel about him and sing. The song, restored to its right place by Adams, is about the need for a little proper relaxation:

> When travails great in matters thick
> Have dulled your wits and made them sick

and it works like a charm. Wit revives, and his patient tutor starts him off once more. Now (which may be taken as his second year) he overdoes it the other way. He forgets his engagement to Miss Science, is impudent to the honest woman Honest Recreation, casts off his gown, and dances—and falls exhausted into the lap of Idleness, a strumpet. She has a half-wit boy called Ingnorance, whose lines look like a verbatim report from a mental-deficients' school;

and while Wit sleeps his face is blackened and he is attired in the fool's cap and coat. After a pretty allegoric interlude in which Worship, Favour, Riches, and Fame sing to Miss Science, only to be sent away (because Learning as such gets none of these things), Wit approaches her. He is taken for Ignorance and snubbed; and when he sees himself in Reason's glass, he submits, first to a flogging from Shame, and then to all the academic virtues together. Giant Tediousness is slain by policy, Parnassus is gained, and the entertainment ends with nuptials, part-song, and the prayer for the King and Queen usual at the finish of the Interlude.

Almost exactly the same course of events is followed in *The Marriage of Wit and Science*, which was licensed in 1569-70, at least twenty years after Redford's. In short, what Rastell called '*A dyalogue . . . compilit in maner of an enterlude with divers toys and gestis addyd thereto to make mery pastyme and disport*' had very considerable stage-possibilities. As *Wyt and Science* serves to show, a light and rounded-off little tale is quite compatible with what can quite properly be called a 'moral play', since its business was to teach boys the right management of their wills, and to suggest to them the rights and wrongs of academic discipline. This intention of pleasurably suggesting moral self-management connects it with *Nature*, which is marked off from the older and graver Morality by its 'divers toys and gestis' in the extensive by-play of the vices. Given controversial matter, as it soon was, the 'educational' interlude became a debating-piece on the rights and wrongs of the Reformation, and ultimately of state-discipline. But in the meantime, by emphasizing the aim of *pleasure*, the farces of Heywood had shown a new development.

## II

Their neatness and brevity, with their more-than-occasional touches of a Chaucerian spirit, have tended to win for Heywood's plays rather more notice than they really deserve in histories of drama. From the reign of Henry VIII (1509-47) to that of Elizabeth, the dramatic world is like a seething primordial swamp in which local time is, so to speak, accelerated, and a confused wealth of forms emerge, few of which last long. The historian picks his way among the fossils, patternizing, simplifying—and, of course, falsifying, if only by dancing his ghosts to the accredited tunes of his own palæology. It is always tempting to point to Heywoods' neat little dramatic anecdotes on contrasted points of view and say: 'Here at last we have English comedy (if you won't accept the *Secunda Pastorum*), and this is what the Moralists were unwittingly striving towards.' But though Heywood is a relief, it will not do to say that he 'dispenses with allegorical machinery'—as Dr. F. S. Boas does in the *Cambridge History* (V, p. 91). As with that other misunderstood merryman, Jack Point, it has been discovered that some of Heywood's jokes were 'imported from France'; and even in literary criticism:

> It's a general rule, though it comes with a wrench,
> If the family fool tells a joke that's too French—
> —Half a crown is stopped out of his wages.

Behind *Johan Johan* and (to a less extent) *The Pardoner and the Frere* lie *sotties*: a kind of play of fools presenting the universal domination of folly, and related to both the burlesque *sermon joyeux* and the *Festa Stultorum*, which here made a definite contribution to the types of comedy. A similar derivation of plays somewhat like Heywood's is seen in Germany, where Hans Sachs' work descends from the *Fastnachtspiele* (Shrovetide plays) which in turn derive from the sword-dance as a Spring *v.* Winter ritual with a Fool in it. In England the sword-dance with a fool (usually 'the Bessy', and sometimes in a woman's clothes) long outlasted Elizabethan times; and the Spring-and-Winter contention can be seen in *Summer's Last Will and Testament* as well as the end of *Love's Labour's Lost*.

But however derivative some of Heywood's work may be, and though it is true enough that he dispenses with 'didactic aim' (Boas), the marks of the Morality are plain enough if we are not blinded by an imaginary opposition of the 'artistic' (aiming at real comedy and characterization) and the 'didactic'. In *Wit and Folly* and *The Play of Love* he goes back to the *débat* stage behind the Morality, and neither has any structure beyond that given by conflicting viewpoints. The first shows James and John arguing whether it is better to be a fool or a wise man, and then Jerome forcing the winner—the fool—to admit that a reasonable man is better than a beast, whereas a fool is not. *Love* is a more elaborate contention between types: lover loved, lover-not-loved, loved-not-loving (a woman) and a 'vice', one of the earliest to be formally so named, called no-lover-nor-loving, who is a clown who mocks and plays a prank with fireworks. It ends, as Boas admits, with 'religious moralizing'. The last speech is rather like Chaucer's 'O younge fresshe folkes, he or she' at the end of the *Troilus*, in which the Heavenly Love is recommended. This seems to me a plain example of 'primitive survival': the unexpected, somewhat disharmonious moral is a 'vestigial structure' at the end, like the human *os coccyx;* which also tells an evolutionary tale. The tiny clash of tones, with the implied ambivalence, is medieval. But the habit of turning 'moral' belongs to the dramatic tradition; and though we may perhaps think of Chaucer as thinking out the ambivalence implied by his palinode and pondering the estimate of human sensual love in the universal scheme, we cannot ascribe any such profundity to Heywood.

Even plainer marks of the Morality are on *The Play of the Wether.* Jupiter has decided to oblige humanity by asking their advice on this perennial English theme, and sends his cryer Merry-reporte (the 'vice' and a court-jester) to half a dozen voters. Naturally, everyone wants something different. The Water-miller wants rain without wind: the Wind-miller wants wind and less rain. The Gentlewoman, who dislikes sun-tan, wants the opposite of the Laundress's requirements. The Hunting Gent wants it dry and windless, the Ranger likes blustering winds; the Merchant requires no storms or mists, but 'mesurable' winds nicely adjusted to commercial enterprises; and the Boy (scheduled as small—'the lest that can play') who approaches Merry-report with 'Syr, I pray you be not yon Master God', wants hard frost for birding and plenty of snow for snowballing. In the end, Jupiter arrives at the decision common to Royal Commissions, that things had best remain as they were. Each will get his turn, and, as Boas puts it, 'in the didactic vein of a lecturer on economics, he points the moral of the mutual dependence of all classes'. I agree entirely; but the comment is totally incompatible with Boas' rejection of 'the traditional view.' If the moral is this, it seems a good one: for those who expect more than a humorous contention of types about something which nobody can alter. Once again, both pattern and conclusion show that the audience—and the writer—*did* expect more. And what moral a play on the weather could have, beyond 'It's an ill wind that blows *nobody* good', is not easy to see without Jupiter's assistance.

*The Four PP* (4 pees) develops a trait from the *jongleur*-minstrelsy tradition, namely the farcical conflict of scurrilous abuse. In the *Wether* the Laundress and Gentlewoman have a nice 'fytte' of this, and it goes even further in *The Pardoner and the Frere*. In the Moralities slanging-matches are often part of the fun; and as 'flyting', a regular duel of dirt between experts in abusive, scatological, and other obscene language, they were long a recreation of the gentry, especially in Scotland. In part they represent the abiding human interest in volubility—which is Merry-report's quite as much as Mercutio's, or Prince Hal's in flyting at Falstaff—and in part they show 'dramatic conflict' in debate at its lowest level: where neither can argue, but both can call names and extend coarse invitations.

The 'four P's' are a Pedlar, a Poticary or quack, a Pardoner, and a Palmer, and the whole piece is a contention by competition in the one thing all are good at—namely lying. The Pedlar is made judge, after each has introduced himself at length and they have sung in chorus as well as squabbled. As hors d'œuvres the Pardoner has produced some remarkable relics, including 'a buttock-bone of Pentecost' and one of the Seven Sleepers' slippers. The poticary's comments equal Harry Bailey's in Chaucer, and the Pedlar 'thynketh your devocion is but small', which is putting it mildly. The Poticary plays back with an exhibition of *materia medica*, most of it admittedly deadly, even by Tudor standards, and then they get down to solid lying. The Poticary tells a very crude tale of a wonderful cure by 'glyster': the Pardoner, how he visited hell in the interests of Margery Corson, arriving on the anniversary of Lucifer's fall. There he is told that he can have her and welcome, provided that he will apply his pardoning activities to ensure that no more women come there; for two women are more trouble than all hell together. This profound piece of human wisdom lays the way open for the Palmer's ace. He doesn't question the journey for a moment (the Pardoner has indeed been quite Chaucerianly circumstantial); but what he cannot understand is the bit about women. He has been everywhere, he has known half a million women, but never once has he seen one out of patience. The others are caught at once. Thinking there is a tale coming, they exclaim on this 'great lye' and the Palmer wins hands down. The 'immoral' against women is rubbed in, and the Palmer slides right back into the Morality world with a long homily, before the final speech, which I take for Heywood's own apologia:

> To passe the tyme in thys without offence
> Was the cause why the maker dyd make it;
> And so we humbly beseche you take it.

It seems an adequate explanation. Amusement is the aim: coarse, Chaucerian (some of it), and spirited, if but little dramatic. The Tudor Polonius has his jig and tale of bawdry. But the morality is still there, both in the well-known truthlessness of three of the 'four P's' and in the equally medieval theme of their views on women —always excepting the gallant Palmer's!

Of the pieces mentioned, *Wit and Folly* is the shortest with 739 lines: *Love* has just over 1,500, and the *Wether* and *Four PP* somewhat over 1,200. The two pieces of French extraction are both under 700. Heywood seems to have worked to write plays for a company of only four, limiting his material (except in the *Wether*, with ten speaking parts) so as to eliminate the awkward poppings in and out which are very noticeable in Medwall's *Nature*, as the result of much doubling. *Johan, Johan* needs only three, and is in every way the terminus of his art. It is on one of the world's oldest themes—one ancient in Rome's decline—the meek but jealous deceived husband who is not even deceived. Johan Johan the husband, is fooled before his own eyes by Tyb and Syr Johan, the priest: who hears her confession in what moderation would call 'compromising circumstances'. It is straight, low domestic farce, with much humour in Johan's resolutions (while alone) to play the marital lion, immediately followed by abject collapse when confronted with her who is only most nominally his match. The framework is, of course, all accepted 'moral' views of wives and clerics. But the end, where Johan beats them both up and kicks them out, only to be forced to run after, to see what they are up to (which he knows already), reaches the edge of genuine low 'high comedy'.

The structure in Heywood's plays is anecdotal. Their typical form is preserved in those stories which start with an Englishman, an Irishman, and a Scotsman together, where one says this, the other says that, and the third caps the lot, all the points of view (or actions) being 'in character': i.e. in agreement with a popular superstition of types. Both by this neatness and by his remarkable reduction in the cast, Heywood stands rather by himself, contributing but little to subsequent comedy. If we could seek his true descendants among the Elizabethans, they would be found, I believe, among the writers of jigs, of whose work—still close to the libellous and naughty tradition of the minstrels—Dr. Sisson has collected some relics from the papers of the Court of Star Chamber. The rank low-life humours of *Roister Doister* or *Gammer Gurton's Needle* owe him no more than they do to the Morality at large; in their *form* they owe him nothing at all. As his plays were mainly printed in 1533, it seems probable that the requirements of controversy cut across any general acceptance of his particular legacy from the Feast of Fools.

CHAPTER VIII

# INTERLUDE OF CHURCH AND STATE

O Father Abram, what these christians are! (*Merchant of Venice*, I, iii.)

The meaning of words had no longer the same relation to things, but was changed by men as they thought fit. (THUCYDIDES, Bk. III, 82, 4.)

UNSTABLE as water, the Morality was the fitter to prevail amid the rapidly changing conditions of the reigns of Henry VIII and his three children, of faiths as distinguishable as their mothers. Its method, 'forensic rather than dramatic' (Boas), made it potentially as useful an instrument of open discussion as the Platonic dialogue: its derivation and its diabolical cousinships in the Miracles gave example to a 'freedom' approaching that of Lucian, or the Christian controversialists of the time of Arius (p. 32). The paper-warfare of the Reformation made it inevitable that the morality should become immoral, an offence against Christian charity: that there should be a diversion of its allegorical, principle-hunting dogmatic machinery in the interests of rampaging Reformer and counter-checking Catholic. We may even say a perversion; for it is obvious, whatever one's creed may be, that if the Pope is made Antichrist, if Iniquity is his son, or if the old sanctities are lauded by Hypocrisy, then the established field of Virtues and Vices has been perverted. In such a world there is small room for the ladies of *The Castle of Perseverance:* for Meekness, Patience, Charity, or Generosity. The offences to Chastity in the slanderous libels of sectarian antagonists require even less comment.

It would be inadequate to say only that the propaganda-play of abstractions teaching the Christian virtues was diverted to the interests of Christian vices: of hatred, malice, sectarian spite, sexual slander, and all uncharitableness. Were this true, the 'controversial Morality' could be quickly passed by, leaving only the same sort of nasty taste in the mind as the correspondence of Henry VIII, Cranmer, and others *in re* their unhappy Queen, Catharine of Aragon. But after 1533, when Clement VII excommunicated Henry, there remained a wider purpose for polemic drama, and one man at least to see it—Thomas Cromwell. The wider developments of this wider purpose leave their mark on much later dramatic writing.

Thinking over the principles of warfare while he lay fever-sick in his tent at Abu Markha, T. E. Lawrence fixed his attention on the moral strength of bodies of men, such as an army or a population, and, to name some such thing as 'an adjustment of its spirit', readying it for activity, he 'went to Xenophon and stole, to name it, his word *diathetics*, which had been the art of Cyrus before he struck'. He continues: 'of this our "propaganda" was the stained and ignoble offspring.' Diathetic purpose means the recognition of the changing spirit of a mass of men and 'the pre-direction of this changing spirit to a certain end'—an end, in this case, of action. Now what the older text-books call the 'patriotic' motive of the Elizabethan history-plays can be seen as a matter of diathetics. 'Patriotic' is a queer name for whatever it was that sent them to King John, Edward II, Henry VI, and almost all the discreditable reigns in history. 'Diathetics' is at least no worse. It calls attention to important factors working down the lines which connect history-play writing with Protestant polemic. It is for these lines of communication alone that the plays mentioned in this chapter are worth consideration: at any rate in a world already prepared to write off Reformers and counter-Reformers alike with Mercutio's 'a plague on both your houses!' To pick up the threads of Elizabethan 'diathetics'—as implied statement of accepted notions making for coherence of thought and political solidarity—we must begin with the times of Thomas Cromwell and his astute recognition of the need to get a determined policy backed by the opinions of those who were amenable to propaganda.

In 1531, as Trevelyan phrases it: 'Convocation acknowledged with a sigh that Henry was Supreme Head of the Church of England, with the scrupulous addition, "so far as the law of Christ allows".' With that, the revolution, 'anti-Papal, anti-clerical, Anglican, and Erastian all in one was launched'. In 1534 the Act of Supremacy 'contained no proviso about "so far, etc."'.

Looking at events from the point of view of the historian of drama, this means two things. First, between *c.* 1525 and 1543, the interlude shifts sail according to the wind, as Henry flouts Luther, flirts with Luther, makes himself Pope in England, takes up Cromwell in place of Wolsey, and throws him down: first encouraging polemical dramas, then blowing hot and cold, and finally suppressing them altogether (1543). This *va-et-vient* can be continued for Edward VI (1547-53), who released them (and John Bale) from bondage; for Mary (1553-November 1558), and for Elizabeth—who came to the throne twenty-nine years before the 'accession' of *Tamburlaine the Great*. Recounting the death of the unhappy Mary,

A. D. Innes produces a happily symbolic phrase when he writes: 'the sun had not risen when Mary passed away'. The suns of Elizabethan drama too. Thus polemic Morality is 'Elizabethan' as well as 'Tudor', and there is no break in the diathetic continuity.

Secondly, Pope Henry the First and Eighth meant that polemic of sect merged into polemic of state, till the two were indistinguishable. The old allegory of man's duty towards God, within His Catholic and universal Church, was narrowed towards the allegory of men's duties as subjects under a God-representing King. Thus the Morality became the vehicle of Tudor propaganda; and thus the contentions of Protestant polemic came to shape and determine the Tudor view of history—and specially that of the ninety years between Richard II's reign and Bosworth Field. If the King supreme is *justified* by the allegoric debate (or if that position is attacked) then necessarily the theme becomes *political:* comes to be about the rights and wrongs of rule: about statecraft: about man in ordered society, which means the clash of will with will in the lists of power. Since this is very near to Aristotle's 'men in action', it results in the dramatic treatment of much wider human considerations than were to be met in the fields where mansoul was the standard in set battles of Cardinal Virtue and Deadly Sin. It positively invites the use of historic examples to justify by past experience the moral—a moral of State. This, in fact, is what John Bale did.

But Tudor playwrights need not have reached the allegorical debating of questions of government by going via Protestant propaganda. The general unsettling caused by the Renaissance as a 'new' learning must sooner or later have brought Rule and Policy upon the stage, just as they brought Ethics, in the opposition of Reason and Sensuality under Nature. In fact, as Chambers says: 'historically it was politics rather than religion with which the interlude first claimed to interfere' (*MS.* ii, 219). 'The instinct of the drama . . . to mix itself up with politics is incorrigible.' (id., ii, 64, on *Antichristus.*) I find these s atements far sounder than the same writer's verdict that there was no room on the Elizabethan stage for topics of political controversy (*William Shakespeare*, i, p. 67), which seems to fly in the face of many facts assembled in his *Elizabethan Stage*. However that may be resolved, the facts about some pre-supremacy plays on government are not in question.

The first to consider is Skelton's *Magnyfycence* (*c.* 1516), whose hero, the name-part, is a prince. It falls into five sequences, like acts, but is of course 'scene indivisible'. In the first, Magnyfycence is in prosperity, and Felicity (meaning riches and richness) debates against Liberty on the true aims of statecraft: are they gratification of the (princely) will, or preservation of wealth? Measure, an old counsellor, supports Felicity, and Liberty is put in his control. Follows (2), conspiracy, beginning with the arrival of Fancy with a letter of recommendation, which gets him in and opens the door to four Skeltonically named rascals, Counterfeit Countenance, Crafty Conveyance, Cloaked Collusion, and Courtly Abusion. These are all presented under false names, and when Fancy has been joined by his little brother, Folly, Measure falls from favour. The vices get offices, and Felicity (now the exchequer) goes to Liberty and Fancy. Measure comes with humble supplication, but Cloaked Collusion (i.e. graft and lobbying) gets him rejected. The sequence shades off into (3), calamity. The Prince is persuaded to make the four court-vices his vice-gerents; he falls into the power of Folly, and learns that they have run off with his Felicity. In unallegorical terms, he is bankrupt from prodigality and parasites. The fourth sequence is Magnyfycence in misery: despoiled by Adversity, passed over to Poverty, he is left in rags and mockery; and when Despair recommends suicide the end seems near, for Mischief promptly enters with rope and knife. But this is no tragedy, for in a fifth sequence Good Hope arrives in time to take the knife and, watching over the crisis carefully, goes on to administer the Rhubarb of Repentance. The royal purgation includes confession to Redress, submission to lectures from Circumspection and Perseverance, and final admonitions from the last—to Mass-going, fear of God, and contempt of the world: all three rather unexpected in so secular a play.

Here, as R. L. Ramsay pointed out in his E.E.T.S. edition (1908), the Renaissance appears in the taking of the idea of Measure —moderation—from Aristotle's *Ethics*. Not only is the play not concerned with the conflicts of the devotional Morality: it presents 'measure' as right because it is 'reasonable'. Human judgment is appealed to, not revelation or authority. Looked at thus, it gives an individual morality, quite applicable to Everyman. But there is more behind.

Taken with Skelton's other writing and with the passage from Halle which I shall quote later, there is reason to suppose that *Magnyfycence* was aimed against Wolsey and the policy of luxuriousness and ostentation which his opponents thought corruption. It had, therefore, a temporary 'application' in being meant to 'sketch' the actual historical scene in shadow-show of conflicting principles ('Sound Finance' *v.* 'Squandermania'). The motif of world-contempt and 'mutability-ethic' at the end merely hints 'in my end is my beginning'—i.e. in the Morality proper—and with Professor Farnham as guide, we can follow this heirloom right through the century. But the moral about rule and misrule is new, and its nearness to that of a 'goodly disguising' by Master Jhon Roo, which 'sore displeased' the cardinal when acted at Gray's Inn at Christmas 1527-8 cannot be missed. We know of this from Halle (I supply capitals to pick out the 'characters' clearly):

> . . . the ffect of the plaie was that Lord Governance was ruled by Dissipation and Negligence, by whose misgovernment and evill order, Lady Publike Wele was put from governance; which caused Rumor Populi, Inward Grudge and Disdain of wanton sovereignty to rise with great multitude, to expel Negligence and Dissipation, and to restore Publik Welth again to her estate, which was so done. (Reprint of 1809, p. 719.)

The cardinal was not mollified by Roo's explanation that it was all written twenty years ago and therefore could not have been meant for him. . . . But quite apart from the *allusive* side (where we can leave Wolsey judging that the cap fitted), there is here, as in *Magnyfycence*, a morality of rule, which says that kings *ought* to refrain from prodigality, and look after publike wele or welth (felicity): i.e. this world's goods. (Contrast *Everyman!*)

Moreover, allusiveness in allegoric 'disguisings' also provides a link between plays and politics. Here again Halle can be cited, for in a show of 1521 he describes something which is plainly related to the Court Masque: as a sort of charade, behind which the quick-witted saw an 'application', by treating the entertainment as a guessing-game or cross-talk puzzle. And here we may remember what Hamlet expects of *his* entertainment. The chronicler writes:

> on Sonday at night in the great halle (i.e. at Windsor) was a disguising or play, theffect of yt was (*that*) there was a proud horse which would not be tamed nor bridled, but amitie sent prudence and pollicie which tamed him, and force and puissance brideled him. The horse was ment by ye Frenche kyng, and amitie by the king of England and themperor, and the other prisoners were their counsaill and power. . . . (1809, p. 641.)

Here is no Morality: merely an allusive charade. But that others beside courtiers could use—or misuse—the drama politically is shown by the 1537 report of a seditious May-game in Suffolk, 'of a king, how he should rule his realm'. It was seditious because 'one played husbandry, and said many things against gentlemen, more than was in the book of the play'; but what more there was to it, we do not know.

Briefly, then, we may say that humanism must, sooner or later, have come to discuss man-political. Outside the drama there was the growing historical industry which includes the Italian, Polydore Virgil, whom Henry VII encouraged, More, Halle, Grafton—and the Holinshed omnibus. There was also the fairly extensive literature of 'governorship' and the doctrines of princecraft, with the counter-checks of the Catholics and, later, the Calvinists: in all of which the literary man essays to become the governor's governor. Such theoretic discussions might have produced their own allegoric treatments in a morality-of-courts, quite apart from the peculiar conditions generated by Henry VIII as a result of what a good Elizabethan would ascribe rather to divine providence than, say, Anne Boleyn. . . .

In any event, the Tudor autocracy itself made the king-figure doubly interesting: first, it is a kind of man-absolute, with the greatest of 'degrees of freedom'; and secondly, it is the determinant of states:

> the massy wheel . . .
> To whose huge spokes ten thousand lesser things
> Are mortised and adjoined, which, when it falls,
> Each small annexment, petty consequence,
> Attends the boist'rous ruin.' (*Hamlet*, III, iii, 17 f.)

Either of these interests might lead towards kingly life-histories' and thence towards an idea of tragedy: as something more than those tales *De Casibus Illustrium Virorum* (of the falls of the eminent) which were tragic to Chaucer's tedious monk, as to Philip Sidney and his contemporaries, the authors of the *Mirror for Magistrates*.

* * * * *

The sectarian 'war of the theatres' began in England in 1527 at latest, for under that year Halle (p. 735) tells of an anti-Luther play given in French and Latin by the Paul's Boys and before the French ambassador. It is said to be related to the German Hasenberg's *Ludus ludentem Luderum ludens* (roughly, 'a lusty interlude of Luther loose' or 'Luther's lewdness') of 1530, the title of which is quite as suggestive as that of the *Monachopornomachia* ('monkstrumpeting' or 'monkswarmongering') of 1538. It showed 'the Captivity of the

Pope', and included 'the herretyke Lewtar' and a 'frowe' (Frau) in the dignified company of Religion, Veritas, Ladies Peace and Quietness, Dame Tranquillity, Ecclesia, three saints, and a cardinal (Wolsey). As opponents to these virtues were Heresy, False Interpretation, and Corruptio Scriptoris. The Dauphin and his brother also appeared from 'current affairs', and there was a poet as presenter—perhaps John Ritwise, the author himself.

The answer to this kind of thing was also provided in Germany in a play called *Pammachius:* an *Antichristus*-derivative by the violent Kirchmayer, translated by the no less energetic Bale, to whom—as in the play—the Pope was simply Antichrist. Though a proclamation of 1533 tried to put a brake on interludes 'concerning doctrines', this was played at Cambridge, at Christ's, in 1545; when the Chancellor, Bishop Gardiner, called some parts of it 'so pestiferous as were intolerable'.[31]

By then the stage was set for the entry of John Bale: almost literally, for Baleus Prolocutor is a figure in his own plays. Born in 1495 he had been educated as a Carmelite before his conversion, and then at Jesus College, Cambridge: a pre-Reformation house, established in 1497 by the suppression of a nunnery for reputed immorality and proven incompetence. Thomas Cranmer was there as Scholar from 1503 and as Fellow till 1528, except for a short interval of marriage; and it seems likely that Bale drew from his environment both his Protestant determination and his marked taste for tales of monastic 'abhominable living'—as his follower Wever was to call it. He became Cromwell's man, and from 1538 was a paid propagandist who—unlike the earlier contestants—wrote *in idiomate materno*, his native English. Ultimately he listed forty-six pieces, of which a few survive, and one only needs notice here. A title such as 'A Comedy concerning thre lawes, of Nature, Moses, and Christ, corrupted by the Sodomytes, Pharysees, and Papistes' tells its own tale: though actually it is almost entirely about the last item. The employment under Cromwell went on till that minister's fall (1540), when Bale went into exile. That it was a deliberate attempt to influence policy is clear enough in *Kynge Johan*. Others too were in it, for in 1537 another clergyman, Thomas Wylley, wrote to Cromwell for support for three plays of his which 'preche the trewthe': this being exactly Bale's claim, not only in his plays but in the very plain terms of the pseudonymous *Epistel*, which he wrote after the suppression of controversial interludes by the Act of 1543, under the name of Henry Stalbridge.

The contrast between the terms of the *Act for the Advancement of True Religion and for the Abolishment of the Contrary* and those of the *Epistel Exhortatory of an Inglyshe Christian* is not only amusing, but gives an insight into the Tudor world's own way of classifying its dramatic activities. The Act permits plays 'rebuking and reproaching of vices' and 'setting forth of virtue', but will have none of those touching 'interpretations of scripture' unless authorized. The rejoinder of 'Stalbridge' jabs back to the point, and makes one wish he had used prose in his plays:

> None leave ye unvexed and untrobled—no, not so much as the poore minstrels and players of enterludes, but ye are doing with them. So long as they played lyes, and sang baudy songes, blasphemed God, and corrupted men's consciences, ye never blamed them, but were very well contented. But sens they persuaded the people to worship theyr Lorde God aryght, accordyn to hys holie lawes and not yours, and to acknoledge Jesus Christ for their onely redeemer and saviour, without your lowsie legerdemains, ye were never pleased with them.

As Ben Jonson said: 'speake, that I may see thee.' There speaks the man. Tiresome, contentious, dogmatic, and scurril as Bale may be, the rapping, rasping courage of his rebuke—directed at God's vice-gerent—is one with his adventurous life. In 1553 he was back from exile and Bishop of Ossory; and when Mary was proclaimed, he improved the occasion of his second exodus by having his plays done, 'to the small contentation of the Prestes and other Papistes there'. He was fifty-eight that year. Thereafter he was an exile at Basle till Mary died; but he had five more years to live as an aged prebend of Canterbury under Elizabeth—satisfied, one may hope, that 'that Duke Josue, whych was our late Kynge Henrye' had indeed 'clerely brought us in, to the lande of mylke and honye', and that, like his own hero, he

> 'Johan, as a faythfyll Moyses
> Withstode proude Pharao, for his poore Israel
> Myndynge to brynge it out of the lande of Darknesse.'

Those lines really summarize the treatment of history in *Kynge Johan*. First made by 1536, and altered to the form played before Cranmer in 1539, the text survives only in a still later revision of 1561; but no alterations could bedim the *tour de force* of making John a Christian hero. The reason is simple enough. John stood up against the Pope, and was victimized by the papal interdiction which made Commonalty submit to (Cardinal) Pandulphus after Nobility, Clergy, and Civil Order had been undermined by Sedition in the disguise of religion. Thus John must yield his crown; and all England's troubles were caused by Usurped Power (the Pope) and by Sedition, who (or which) says that Popes may depose kings. John denies this doctrine, and stands for the view that kings are divinely appointed, 'the good for the good, the bad is for ill-doing . . .' (ll. 101 f.); so that he who condemns a king condemns God, just as he who resists him resists God. All this is 'proved' from Scripture, and one main point of diathetics in the whole is that an English Bible is essential in the English State, if men are to know God's regulations about obedience (see ll. 2311 ff. in Manly's *Specimens* i). John's England was brought to despair through treason and rebellion, and these are due to ignorance of the Bible (ll. 1579 ff.).

All this is, of course, totally inapplicable to the reign of John, who might have jumped, in every sense of the word, at the solution offered—had the Tudor situation or Wycliffe's Bible been available by 1213. But it is all what Bale—and his long-sighted Machiavellian master, Cromwell—wanted about 1539; as well as an excellent prognostication of the principles of good order laid down by the *Homilies* under Edward VI and strongly reinforced by the additions *Against Disobedience and Wilful Rebellion* under Elizabeth (after 1569).

From the dramatic viewpoint, we observe that the rights and wrongs of rule are demonstrated by 'using' history: taking events which serve that purpose and ignoring the rest. (Magna Charta and Arthur are as much 'in the picture' as Trotsky was in the Soviet film *Lenin in October*, or as the first item is in Shakespeare's *King John*—where the 'history' is quite as odd.) The thesis is a religious-political moral-of-state, and, as Dryden said, 'tis the moral that directs the whole action'. Bale's 'moral' is incidentally the essential iniquity of all Papists, but more pressingly that Royal Supremacy rests on the infallible rock of Holy Scripture, and that England needs The Book to tell them so. The play, in short, is directed at Bale's own times—as Roo's or Skelton's were at theirs: only now the 'lesson' is given a local habitation and a name in the historical reign of an English king.

In comparison with this it is chronicling very small beer to note, as all the text-books do, in the watch-this-space manner of advertisers, that during the course of the action Sedition becomes Stephen Langton, Usurped Power is named Pope, and Private Wealth, Pandulphus; while Dissimulation is first Raymundus and then (he dead) the wicked monk, Simeon of Swynsett, who poisons John—the vice being of course as catholic as indestructible. To rejoice over this first faint—faint indeed!—foreshadowing of right royal characters is to miss the point. The point of *Kynge Johan* is that it suggests a method by which any not-wildly-unsuitable 'chronicle' stuff can be made into a history-play: by beginning with 'what you want to prove' and patternizing history in accordance with set dogmas about all the personages named in Bale. These include Widow England (cf. *Respublica* later), Nobility, Clergy, and Commonalty—estates of the realm: political 'forces' such as Sedition, Treason, Private Wealth, and Civil Order; and the collection of state-moral homilists including Verity, Imperial Majesty, and Civil Order again. Their true function in a moral-historical whole is not altered by giving them names out of the history-book or even individual traits of character. As 'the good Duke Humphrey' or 'old John of Gaunt' they can be just as referable to a framework of accepted moral ideas, which still provides a pattern in which they have an allegorical place: to which, indeed, their character may be subservient.

Somewhat aside from the English dramatic world, but with an influence on it, and also too accomplished a play to pass over is Sir David Lyndsay's *Ane Plesant Satyre of the Thrie Estaitis*, played at Linlithgow in 1540. It is a long, very lively, two-part political Morality directed sharply at contemporary Scotland, and its main 'message', apart from slashing satire of 'Spiritualitie'—the clergy, represented also by an abbot, a parson, and a lady prioress—is that John the Commoun Weill should take his due place in government.

The first part follows *Magnyfycence* in plot, though this is obscured by Lyndsay's wealth of morality-cum-interlude detail, in which his French masters have taught him to turn Heywood's kind of farce to the purpose of derisive comical satire.[32] Rex Humanitas is misled by Sensualitie, brought into court by Wantonness, Placebo, and Solace; and as Gude Counsell arrives too late, three court-vices establish themselves. Flatterie calls himself Devotion, Falset and Dissait become Sapience and Discretion; and the Skelton plot is followed again when the three try to run off with the King's box on learning that Divyne Correctioun is arriving. Before this, Veritie has appeared with the New Testament, but only to be put in the stocks by Spiritualitie; and when Chastitie follows, her fate is no better. Lyndsay here interrupts his action with the vigorous coarse farce of the misfortunes of Chastitie with the Tailor, the Soutar and their termagant wives. At the end of Part I the stocked Veritie and Chastitie are released, and restored to due place, with Gude Counsell.

Part II is preluded by the complaints of Pauper (a farmer reduced to beggary by ecclesiastic greed), followed by the detailed comic-satirical interlude of the Pardoner—who has learnt his business from Hypocrisie, a friar. He sets up his board and discourses on his trade with more than Chaucerian 'freedom', and when the Soutar sees his chance to get a separation decree and his wife proves unexpectedly amenable, the Pardoner devises a ritual—appropriately indecent—for the usual considerations. The interlude ends with his taking Pauper's last groat, only to get his shop wrecked by that unfortunate, who thinks—not without unimpeachable evidence—that pardoning is indistinguishable from robbery.

The parliament of the Three Estates follows, where Spiritualitie, Temporalitie, and Merchant appear, each in bondage to his vices; and after the complaint of John the Commoun Weill, all are stocked. The latter two, representing lords and burghers, make their amends, but Spiritualitie is impudent, together with his 'members', the Abbot, the Parson, and the Prioress. A general debate follows, in which Pauper and the two clowns take part, and after this a doctor preaches, heckled by the Abbot and the Parson, until a whispering friar is detected and found to be Flatterie in disguise. The ecclesiastics are then unfrocked—the Lady Prioress coming out in a silken kirtle and with abuse for her parents for denying her the common rights of a woman. John appears in state to take his place among the governors, and all the vices are realistically hanged. Flatterie saves himself by turning hangman. As a kind of epilogue or after-piece a clown appears as Follie, to preach a burlesque sermon full of cynical wit on the universal folly of mankind, from kings to clowns.

Lyndsay's position is shown by the utter derision for the Spiritualitie, by the Pardoner's cursings of the New Testament, Luther, Melanchthon, and even St. Paul, and by the triumph of the Commoun Weill. This last makes its mark on the later *Respublica*, in which the 'democratic' idea reappears in a piece which counters Bale's propaganda with several of his own devices.

With the accession of Edward VI dramatic controversy burst out again in England. According to Bale, who enjoyed a brief Red-Indian summer just then, the boy-king was himself the author of an improving Latin play on the Whore of Babylon. Protestant morality is, however, adequately represented by R. Wever's *Lusty Juventus*, and to say it casts both a baleful eye and Bale's-full of dirt at the old religion is not excessive. In it Hypocrisy, Satan's child, brags of the pains he has taken to ensnare mankind, and his

Skeltonic catalogue of 'trim-trams' skips along nimbly for some forty lines of:

> 'Holy skins, holy bulls,
> Holy rochets and cowls,
> Holy crouches and staves,
> Holy hoods, holy caps,
> Holy mitres, holy hats;
> Ah, good holy, holy knaves!
> Holy days, holy fastings,
> Holy twitchings, holy tastings . . . etc., etc.'

The plot shows Iuventus enter singing a nice little song with the refrain 'In youth is pleasure' (*bis*), to be converted by Good Counsel, who gives him knowledge and a book for companions, and informs him how his elders have been 'deceived with blind hypocrisy'. The Devil agrees with this is the next scene, adding the specific complaint that the (Protestant) Youth-movement is ruining his kingdom. But Hypocrisy talks Iuventus round, calling himself 'Friendship', and brings him together with Fellowship and 'little Bess', otherwise Abhominable Living—but to her victim 'Unknowen Honesty'—who is the usual strumpet, but not otherwise catholic. Hypocrisy is somewhat of a low comedian, but the only knockabout is verbal. When they have sung a catch, the third and last sequence shows the reconversion of the sinner by Good Counsel, after Iuventus has tried on him the rejoinders of Hypocrisy: which are very much what any conservative father might say to a son turned New Gospeller. The final conversion is patently dyed-in-the-wool, for Iuventus grows 'improving' as an 'Oxford-groupist' in dwelling lovingly on his own mild wickednesses, aiming it all at 'people which be here present'.

Religious controversy and morals appear again in *Respublica*, played in the first year of Mary (1553). Though this is from the Catholic side, the otherworldliness of the earlier Morality is almost as lacking as in *Magnyfycence*, which it closely resembles in theme. Respublica is a lamenting widow, and she and her servant People (a quasi-clown who speaks West-countrified) have been sadly maltreated by Avarice, alias *Policie* (the Vice), aided and abetted by three 'gallaunts' whose aliases show the whole game up. Insolence is known as *Authoritie:* Adulation as *Honestie:* and Oppression as *Reformation*.

We met this first in *Nature*. But though there is a hint for it in Prudentius, where *Avaritia* calls herself *Parsimonia* (i.e. Greed alias

Economy), one reason for its steady persistence in the drama until it becomes stock-in-trade of equivocating villainy is the moral confusion which the Renaissance and Reformation caused, and which the 'moral' interlude did much to increase. The contemporary confusion, with its atmosphere of 'propaganda' and misrepresentation, made the equivocator the logical symbol for the spokesmen of the other side. "The old religion *looks* all right," said the Protestant, "but beware of covert evil. I'll show you." The Catholic replied in similar terms about the new; and if *Respublica* is representative of its kind, the reply was more decent and moderate than the charge. To ascribe insolence, oppression, and avarice to the Reformers is nearer the truth than writing of 'the knaveries of Thomas Becket' (Bale), even though not all of the Church's riches were 'poured in the laps of parasites and whores' (T. S. Eliot, *Murder in the Cathedral*). For the confused Tudor man-in-the-street the fellow with a double name, the possessor of the original Serpent's double tongue, brought the slipperiness of evil down to Cheapside terms; and it is this *lingua franca* which Shakespeare gives to *Richard III* when he says:

> 'Thus, like the formal vice Iniquity,
> I moralize two meanings in one word.'

The 'ambidextrous' vices of the interludes written between 1560 and 1570 link Hypocrisy, the Devil's son, and Dissimulation, the monk, with this developed type of equivocating villainy.

*Respublica* hovers between two worlds, one dying, the other struggling to be born. The advent of the Four Daughters of God (Truth, Justice, Mercy, and Peace) belongs to that of the *Castle of Perseverance;* but the wholly secular salvation which follows, when the Vice and the Aliases are brought before Nemesis—whom the title-page describes as 'the goddes of redresse and correction' and the Prologue identifies with Mary Tudor—is down on the political level of Lyndsay. Avarice-Pollicie is to be squeezed: Adulation-Honestie repents: the rest are left awaiting promulgation of sentence; but as in *Magnyfycence* 'felicity' is identified with what Avarice can grab. If Magnus is right in ascribing the play to Udall, this would add to its interest: directly, because of *Roister Doister*, and ironically, at the expense of the only headmaster of Eton to be suspected of complicity in robbery—and of the college plate at that.

From Mary's time classical matter—of a kind—begins to be adapted; and here the feeble braggart-warrior farce *Thersites* must be mentioned, along with the more interesting *Jacke Jugeler*. The latter is an undistinguished crib of Plautus' *Amphitruo*. Jack disguises himself as his fellow-servant Jenkin Careaway and persuades him—mainly by *argumentum ad baculum*—that he isn't himself. This duly gets Jenkin a thrashing for suggesting to others that he can be in two places at once—which is Gilbertianly logical enough, if 'he' isn't where he is—and may be a sly gird at Transubstantiation, which Mary's ministers were 'persuading' her subjects to accept, by arguments mainly different from Jack's in using more sticks.

The further influence of Bale is shown in the later plays which use Biblical stories on the Protestant side: among others, *Goodly Queen Hester* (1561?), *King Darius* (1567?), and L. Wager's *Life and Repentance of Mary Magdalene* (1567), which last demonstrates the principle of salvation by faith (as distinct, theologically, from works). His personages or close equivalents to them appear in *New Custom* (printed 1573), *The Trial of Treasure* (1567), and *The Longer thou livest the more Fool thou art* (1570), in all of which his *Three Laws* has been drawn on. Avarice, Sensual Suggestion, and Hypocrisy, all from *The Three Laws*, are used as vices in *Conflict of Conscience*, (1581) a 'founded-on-fact' personal-history of a man who turned Catholic and ended by committing suicide.

In the interim *Hester* and *Darius*, bad plays as they are, show some interesting connections with the 'tragy-comedies' to be examined in Chapter X. *King Darius* shows a complete dichotomy in structure, a Bible-history being so diluted with an independent Morality, in which Iniquity stands for Catholicism(!), that Darius gets little above a quarter of his own play. *Goodly Queen Hester*, where the complimentary intention to Elizabeth is as evident as in *Darius* (in the passage about the strength of a woman, taken from I Esdras), is in form a Morality on the *Magnyfycence* pattern, but about the aspiring upstart and misgovernor Aman. Pride, Ambition, and Adulation attend him, but the Vice is called Hardy-dardy: a variant on Lear's 'handy-dandy' when he asks how one can tell the Justice from the Thief. (It was the name for the children's game of guessing in which hand a coin or toy is hidden, and has the same implication of 'double-crossing' or 'ambidexterity' in both places.)

Aman seems to me an early example of the wicked and aspiring man with whose successful ambition the audience is half sympathetic so long as he is on the up-grade of Fortune's Wheel—only to take it all back as soon as the turn begins. The *De Casibus* ethic made even a thoroughly bad man 'tragic'—in defiance of Aristotle—since he so beautifully illustrated both mutability and morality together:

combining the half-pagan conception of fortune with the not-very-Christian expectation of retribution here-and-now, as symbol and foretaste of the Christian damnation to follow. Thus stage-exhibitions of naked villainy need have nothing a-moral about them.

Sir Philip Sidney, writing about 1580, thought it the business of 'the high and excellent tragedy' to display 'the ulcers that are covered with tissue', so that by seeing 'tyrants manifest their tirannical humors' kings might be instructed, while mankind at large was taught 'the uncertainety of this world'. Sir Philip was high-principled in no disagreeable way, but he failed to see that persons less judicial than himself must develop a two-faced attitude towards attractive villains: handy-dandying with their sympathies, as they did with those Vices who are at once obviously wicked by moral standards and obviously engaging rascals by mundane ones. A conscientious Christian knight might sit back in firm disapproval and Christian expectation; but the Protestant knave had a more exciting moral experience for his penny. To put it in text-book terms, the knave took a 'renaissance' attitude towards 'aspiration', and then, after a stirring debauch of wish-fulfilment, recollected his principles and went all 'medieval' by Act V: to come away with just the kind of moral that Sidney would approve, and no doubt saying that he always knew such fellows came to a bad end—totally unable to see that some of his deeper human impulses had enjoyed their crowded hour of glorious life in the company of the Devil's disciples.

The importance of the polemical Moralities is that they show some of the moves in that Elizabethan direction. The specific importance of John Bale is that, by an historic accident, he extended the Morality-pattern to treat one (ostensibly) real-life story; and not in terms of the psychomachic conflict but of order and disorder within the State. From this trend in the controversial Morality there derives the writing of histories by patternizing the chronicles (in which the same State-moral patterns are often evident already); and from that, an impulse towards a greater subtlety in the presentation of motive. For State is supremely an organism where

> There is no vice so simple, but assumes
> Some mark of virtue on his outward parts.

Thus Bale and his kind, though their hard, determined, uncharitable minds did not care a tinker's cuss for the æsthetic 'world of profit and delight' that was to follow, had done much to form the later drama. Bale had pointed to the vast treasure-house of human experience in history. The sectarian rivalries had made Christian faith itself equivocal: thereby assisting in the splitting of man, as well as of Christendom. The evils belong to history, not here. But if we follow to the Elizabethan world the dramatic results of this splitting-process, whereby all such once-standardized abstractions as Pride, Ambition, Glory, Avarice, Lust-of-Life become equivocal—and therefore ambivalent, with the admirable and the damnable juxtaposed if not comeddled—then we must look on the whole battle of the spitting Churches with Henry V's eye:

> There is a soul of goodness in things evil
> Would men observingly distil it out.

From that division in the soul sprang not only Elizabethan 'glorious villains' but, with the pouring in of richer ores thrilled with veins of complicated human mettle, the Elizabethan tragic experience itself.

CHAPTER IX

# THE STAGE OF ACADEMIC IMPORTS

We doe it to recreate owre selves, owre house, and the better parte of the Universitye, with some learned Poeme or other; to practyse owre owne style eyther in prose or verse; to be well acquainted with Seneca or Plautus. . . .

So wrote William Gager of Christ Church to John Rainolds of Queen's, in a letter dated 31st July, 1592, answering the theologian's objections to stage-plays after he had refused to see Gager's *Ulysses Redux:* a Latin tragedy, against which he not only brought forward a decree against actors from Roman times, but also the ancient objection that Gager's men had assumed the dress of women, and on a Sunday too. Puritan attacks of this kind lasted far longer than the academic drama whose purposes Gager describes so well, but they must be passed over here.[33]

Academic tragedy, still more academic comedy, made important contributions to the Elizabethan theatre, though the attempt to foist rigid 'classical' standards on England was a complete failure. For this reason we turn aside from the native tradition for a superficial glance at another kind of play-making, before returning to the development of the interlude in the next chapter.

The term 'academic' covers two differing aspects. On one, it indicates the existence of play-acting and play-writing in schools, colleges, the Universities, and the Inns of Court. In schools this meant that Latin comedies were recited, though 'non-academic' interludes were also given, because, as Richard Mulcaster, Spenser's teacher, said of his boys at the Merchant Taylors' School, playing 'taught them good behaviour and audacytye'. Gager says as much about undergraduates. School plays existed continuously from *c.* 1520, and the Westminster play with its topical epilogue and ingenious punning on the old English pronunciation of Latin still, I hope, survives. Plays done for what the Elizabethans called 'children' are important in connection with Lyly, Marston, Chapman, and others; but they only touched Shakespeare as dangerous competitors with his own—as recorded in the familiar passage in *Hamlet.*

The other aspect of the 'academic' play concerns dramatic form: though the pieces were written for academics, as above defined. It includes on the one side, the translations and imitations of Roman

Comedy, and especially Plautus; on the other, the later development from *acting* Seneca through *imitating* him in Latin to the third stage of *applying* his rigid form to original matter, and in the native language. Here highbrow England was the cultural borrower from the more theatrically erudite world of Italy and France, the latter already converted by Italian example.

On comedy there is little to say. Nicholas Udall's *Ralph Roister Doister*, played by his Eton boys about 1553, is quite patently the braggart-soldier theme of Plautus done again in English; if with more than a touch of those later Tudor translators who, in their own terms, did not so much 'translate' works as 'Englished' them. But Matthew Merygreke is not only the knavish 'parasite' or servant who makes the wheels go round (as he continues to do in Jonson): he is also the Vice, an impish antidignitarian leg-puller, whose prank with a mispunctuated letter Shakespeare stole for *Midsummer Night's Dream*. (The juggling with equivocal language links the Roman punster and the old Tutivillus, whose business was the collecting of dropped syllables and misused words from careless pray-ers. The presumable theory is, that whatever you *say* can be 'used as evidence against you'.) *Gammer Gurton's Needle*, by William Stevenson of Christ's, was written for his college by perhaps 1563. Here the 'Englishing' is complete, and the play deals solely with low-life types in a village rumpus which makes a very well-plotted farce. All the works are Plautine, but beautifully assembled and concealed. But once again the Vice is there in Diccon the Bedlam, who is a rustic good-for-nothing and mischief-maker. Though rustic humours continue on Shakespeare's stage, there is too much in the interludes to make *Gammer Gurton* of major importance (though Harry Porter's *Two Angry Women of Abingdon* is, I think, in a continuous line with it). The strict imitation of Roman comedy, however, continues to *The Comedy of Errors* (played at Gray's Inn, 1594), which is really much the best of the English derivatives.

George Gascoigne's *Supposes* (Gray's Inn, 1566) is later than *Gorboduc*, but must be treated here to continue the comic importations. It is a close rendering of Ariosto's *Gli Suppositi* (1509), a comedy of Italian intrigue, bright, brittle, and shallow enough, but touched with that exotic and sophisticated grace which made Italy a wonderland to innocent English eyes: a land of theatrical marvels of wit, crime, colour, glamour and revenge far surpassing what the most naïve of modern film-fans might dream of a combined Los Angeles, Paris, and Chicago. *Supposes* owes enough to Plautus, but—as the author would undoubtedly say—no one reading it casually would suppose so. The plot turns on the mistaken suppositions which arise from the favourite tale of the ingenious young man, with an even more ingenious servant, who is sent by his father to study at the university in another place, but who there falls in love, and so comes to pursue his studies by becoming a servant in appearance (as well as that of the lady), while the real servant becomes the apparent student. There is always an undesirable suitor, in this case old and absurd; and the real fun begins when he is ousted and the supposed student, with the hero's real name of course, is accepted by the lady's ingenuous father. A sham father must then be produced to settle the marriage-contract; and although this is well within the scope of their combined ingenuities, a nice confusion of supposals and counter-suppositions arises when the real father appears on the scene. Hence the title. In the lines, Gascoigne torments the word with far more equivokes than I have been able to hint, even falling back on *sub* and *ponere* to wrest a bawdy twist from it, till the poor word finishes as exhausted and strained as a Wyckhamist's 'notions'.

Gascoigne uses prose, and in this, as in his imported plotting, he indeed 'brake the ice for our quainter poets', as one R.T. wrote in 1615; or, as Nashe put it, 'beat a path to that perfection which our best poets have aspired to since his departure.' Considering the use of the *Supposes* theme in the Bianca part of the *Shrew*, and the line of Italianate comedy of smart intrigue in highly wish-fulfilment settings which runs through Greene's *James IV* (a sham history) to *The Two Gentlemen of Verona*, *The Merchant of Venice*, and the triumph of *Much Ado*, there is every reason to accept these contemporary compliments, and to set the bright play beside *Gorboduc*.

On the face of it, no two plays could be much more different. But just as Gascoigne's use of prose anticipates one of the essential media or instruments of comedy, so does *Gorboduc*, with its introduction of blank verse to the tragic stage. Both were Inns of Court productions, and in both an alien and 'academic' form was adopted, of which the literary purists (such as Philip Sidney) strongly approved. But whereas English practice, almost always wiser in its empiricism than 'the bookish theoric', adapted the comic form in a variety of manageable compromises, the tragic it utterly rejected. The line of *Gorboduc* was as foredoomed in this respect as that of the undistinguished monarch whose fall it sang with burdensome Senecan solemnity. The strictly 'regular' classical-pattern play, with its five-act divisions, its scrupulous avoidance of violence on the stage—even of action, save in a most restricted sense—its messengers and commentatory choruses: all that was too far from English tastes, too high and dry, too bloodless in every sense. Yet with all these items the Elizabethans picked and chose: little as most of them heeded Sir Philip Sidney's grumble that despite the play's 'climing to the height of Seneca his style', it was 'defectious' in respect of the unities of time and place—though decorum itself as compared with average English practice, on which he had some very amusing things to say. It is therefore an important piece, for we can see from it and its successors exactly what classical imports offered to the dramatists of the 70's and 80's, and what they made of them. In 1561-2, when Thomas Sackville's and Thomas Norton's *Tragidie of Ferrex and Porrex* (the original name) was presented, first at the Inner Temple and then before the Queen at Whitehall, there was at least a chance that English drama might have taken the way which Sidney, then a boy of seven, and the unborn Jonson earnestly wanted it to take. For excellent reasons it did not; and accordingly the theatre of Racine and Corneille has never meant much to the average literate Englishman. But between 1560 and 1590 it is conceivable that the practice of a single major tragedian might have tied down the malleable spirit of Shakespeare to a dramatic form as cribbing as cribbed, and as confining and cramped a cabin as Prospero's knottiest oak for fretful Ariel.

The *Gorboduc* story comes from what Professor Schelling regarded as mythical or legendary history, but what Elizabethans took for fact. The preposterous patriotic myth of the Line of Brute (the great-grandson of Pious Aeneas, and also father of Locrine, from whom Lear was eighth in line and Gorboduc sixteenth) duly appears in Tudor chronicles, and was to them as historical as Troynauvant (New Troy) for London, or for that matter, the fall of Jericho. Grafton's chronicle, which Schelling ignored when he classified history-plays, does its best to include these unlikely monarchs and those of the Bible in a single time-scheme. Gorboduc, therefore, was as real a person as King John, and was apparently Regan's great-great-great-grandson—as in *The Faerie Queene*, Book II, Canto X—though Grafton is none too clear on this.

The only interesting thing about him was that he divided his kingdom between his two sons, Ferrex and Porrex, who then fell out: with fatal consequences to themselves, the line of Brute and England at large. Porrex slew Ferrex and his aggrieved mother then killed *him;* whereat the people rose against the unnatural family, destroyed the survivors, and the country was left to civil war until some Duke either of Albany or of Cornwall, established order again.

That, in outline, is the tale. It would not seem to provide a very firm basis for a demonstration of 'divine right'; but that is what Sackville and Norton end by making it. The division of the kingdom was 'unkindly' (unnatural, against law of kind), as Queen Videna says, and the kingly self-will is also very wrong, but in the good counsellor Eubulus' words:

> Though kings forget to govern as they ought,
> Yet subjects must obey as they are bound.

The doctrine of non-resistance is as plain as in Bale, though the authors do not grind an axe for an Ancient-British Bible, merely stating the duty of passive obedience thus:

> That no cause serves, whereby the Subject may
> Call to accompt the doings of his Prince,
> . . . In act nor speech, no; not in secret thought
> The subject may rebel against his Lord,
> Or judge of him that sits in *Caesar's* seat.

This is precisely the doctrine of the *Homilies* of the Church of England on this subject. For instance, the sparing of Saul by David is improved on thus: 'Here is evidently proved, that we may not withstand, nor in any wise hurt an anointed king, which is God's lieutenant vice-gerent, and highest minister in that country where he is king.' (1811 ed., p. 131.) And again: 'all subjects are bound to obey them as God's ministers, not only for fear, but also for conscience' sake.' (p. 128.) And although the same homily says that we may not obey kings and other magistrates if they command us contrary to God's ordinance, yet 'nevertheless, in that case, we may not, in any wise, withstand violently, or rebel against rulers . . . either by force of arms or otherwise, against the anointed of the Lord, or any of his officers; but we must, in such case, patiently suffer all wrongs and injuries, referring the judgment of our cause only to God'. (*Homily X* of 1547, ed. cit., p. 133.)

In a sense this was controversial matter, for Goodman's *How Superior Powers Oght to be Obeyd*, published at the safe distance of Geneva in 1558, took the very different view that a king was only a 'lieutenant', and the subject's conscience gave him a right to resist. But if Sackville, the courtier, did not see eye to eye with the Puritan-leaning Norton on this, he had the last two acts in which to state his own (and the orthodox) moral-of-state; and it is to this that the whole play works up. Considering that the Queen had ordained that 'common interludes in the English tongue' should not touch 'either matters of religion or the governaunce of the estate of the common weale', it is mildly surprising that no objection was taken to *Gorboduc*. That it is aimed diathetically is beyond reasonable doubt. Besides the general moral, which Eubulos makes at very great length, there is the additional point that the succession ought to have been settled. It is no good leaving such things to Parliament:

> Which though it be assembled by consent,
> Yet is not likely with consent to end—

when the general state of affairs will be a conflict within the State, which 'shall fill ambitious minds with gaping hope'. The intention here is patent when we know that Norton used some of the *Gorboduc* arguments in 1563, when he was responsible for a petition from a committee of the House of Commons, on this very question of the succession and to the Queen herself.

In short, though all the form-contrivances of *Gorboduc* are either imported or influenced from Italian senecanizings, the play is a Moral History. It is followed, in time, by many other civil-war-and-chaos plays, in which catastrophic reigns are chosen, not for their 'patriotic appeal' but their excellent morality. These do not, of course, *imitate* this play: they use the same methods as led in *Gorboduc* to the most unexpected retention of a 'Morality-pattern' within the sophisticated art-for-art's-sake form.

None the less, the formal aspects of *Gorboduc* deserve attention. The chorus 'foure auncient and sage men of Brittaine' performs after each act except the last, where Eubulus takes its place. The line which says that this great king 'A mirror shall become to princes all' reminds us that Sackville had his hand in the *Mirror for Magistrates*, and that this is another *De Casibus* tale, not without its Senecan reflections on fate and human will. The 'patterned speech', as T. S. Eliot neatly christened it, which is the main characteristic of the verse—apart from flatness—derives its echoic technique from Seneca; and this immediately caught the logomaniac Elizabethan and gave a quondam literary distinction to the punnings of Kyd and of Shakespeare (in serious passages, understand). True to classical rule, all violent action occurs off-stage, and is reported in messenger-speeches. The characters are of Morality-like flatness, and the attachment to the King and both his sons of Good and Bad Counsellors is very much 'on the side of the angels', though they are given barely symbolic names and the Princes' pair are 'parasites'. By an Italian innovation, very popular in that country, each act is preluded by what Hamlet rudely called 'inexplicable dumb-shows and noise': the latter being of course *music*, not mere row. The instruments are varied, violins going with the fable of the faggot which is easily broken stick by stick (Act I) and oboes (hautboys) with the Furies and a parade of infanticidal royalties before Act IV.

The same paraphernalia was used in 1566 in *Jocasta*, played at Gray's Inn and affecting to be from Euripides; though Gascoigne, assisted by Francis Kinwelmershe, had 'imported' it from Dolce's *Giocasta* (1549)—itself lifted from a Latin translation! It is in blank verse, has musical pantomimes, and a chorus of four 'Thebane dames'; and Gascoigne at least thought it moral.

Next year, 1567-8, came the more interesting *Gismond of Salerne*, the history of which 'fable' should be compared with that of the Promos-Angelo story in the next chapter. It is dramatized from the Decameron; but after it had been played at the Inner Temple, to the contentment of Her Majesty and the notable applause of 'the whole honourable audience', as William Webbe put it, the whole was reshaped from rhymed to blank verse by Robert Wilmot, who has thus a claim to be taken for the deviser, though the original work was shared by at least two others. (For this and Webbe's letter, etc., see Hazlitt-Dodsley VII.) The Boccaccio story, one of violent southern passion, has been frozen into moral patterns suitable to a climate where the authors come within an inch of anticipating the famous 'people don't do such things' of *Hedda Gabler*. Wilmot's dedication states the aim as 'commending virtue, detesting vice, and lively deciphering their overthrow that suppress not their unruly affections'—a moral he hopes will be 'acceptable to the wise'. Comment is needless: unless I suggest that when he goes on to gird at 'the *tragedian tyrants* of our time, who are not ashamed to affirm that there can be no amorous poem savour of any sharpness of wit, unless it be seasoned with scurrilous words', we are receiving direct from 1591 the objections of the defeated and importing purists to the kind of tragic drama which had killed all the 'Gorboducklings' by then. (The last, apart from closet-drama, was *The Misfortunes of Arthur*, of 1588, which carries Wilmot and Co.'s Seneca-pillagings to a final excess. Like *Hamlet*, it is 'full of quotations'; but there the resemblance stops.)

*Gismond of Salerne* or *Tancred and Gismunda*, as the later version is called, has a four-man chorus and dumb-shows; but these rather anticipate the action than allegorize in parallels. By 1591 'decorum' was so far undermined that one show brings in a golden cup 'with a bloody heart reeking hot in it'; and at the end Tancred bursts out in a dozen lines of true 'English Seneca read by candle-light', in which he takes Oedipus' example with his eyes:

> Unworthy lamps of this accursed lump,
> Out of your dwellings!

and then stabs himself with the Romeo-like: "Daughter, I come."

Meantime Marlowe had come and Kyd, and Shakespeare was already successful enough to be annoying Greene. The *Tenne Tragedies* of Seneca had been englished by Jasper Haywood by 1581, and his prologistic *Vindicta*-shrieking, corpse-cataloguing ghosts had come to haunt the stage where the horrors which he merely reports—albeit with sickening circumstance—were played out in well-dyed villainy. The horridness of Alabaster's Cambridge Latin *Roxana*, which sent a lady mad in 1592, was really quite endurable in comparison with the bloody horrors of *Titus Andronicus*.

If we want to see why the strict academic-senecan form would not do, it can be done without leaving the Line of Brute. In *Locrine* (after 1591, printed in revised form 1595) we still find the dumb-shows, the music, and the Senecan themes and tags; but this British history of a troublesome reign has been broken up by the incursions of a clown named Strumbo. The moral-of-state is still there, in a warning against 'usurpation and ambitious pride' put into the improbable mouth of Ate; and the theme of Albion's impregnability also appears, in a speech of Corineus. All these can be pursued through the *Trouble some Raigne* (print 1591) to *King John* and the other histories.

This was to be the English way. It appears again in the old *Leir*, where Mumford is a very free-spoken clown *and* a gentleman at the same time. The immensely vital English stock, though strengthened *verbally* by 'climing to the height of Seneca his style', retained its irresistible humour and the urge for 'notable morality' —in a more inclusive sense than Sidney meant in writing those words. Indeed, inclusiveness was the supreme Elizabethan requirement, and the true inner demand which left the high and doleful tragedy of the academics as a dead-end. To live on the inn-yard stage of the 'Cross Keys' at Newington Butts or the 'Rose', drama had to hold in it more of the full gamut of human life than was recreation for the Inns of Court or 'the better parte of the Universitye.'

CHAPTER X

# MUNGRELL TRAGY-COMEDIE

. . . all theyr Playes be neither right Tragedies, nor right Comedies, mingling Kings and Clownes, not because the matter so carrieth it, but thrust in Clownes by head and shoulders, to play a part in majesticall matters, with neither decencie nor discretion . . .

SIR PHILIP SIDNEY, whose *Apologie for Poetrie* provides the title and motto above, was an idealist. As such, he did not quite inhabit the world about him. The heroic ending when—like so many other brave fellows—'he was presently carried to *Arnheim*' (as his friend Fulke Greville wrote) had in it a touch of the Don Quixote. So, too, his delightful assaults on the drama of his day. The 'gentle knight' who cast off armour and rode in the mist against an ambush of entrenched musketeers saw himself as 'pricking on the plaine' in a different kind of adventure; and a similar inability to appreciate the dramatic world-as-it-was appears in his impetuous chargings at the windmills of the stage. There is nothing to show that he would have mitigated his verdict on 'tragy-comedie' if he had lived to the age of forty-four and seen *Faustus*, *Locrine*, *Woodstock*, and *Henry IV;* still less that as a man of fifty-plus he would have been more enlightened than Coleridge on whether 'the matter so carrieth it' where a clown is 'thrust' into *Macbeth*. Nor does his criticism of *Gorboduc* augur well for *King Lear*.

All this makes him an invaluable contemporary witness: he points out things which *he* regarded as very wrong, but which *we* regard as having led to something very right, in Shakespeare at all events. The most important item among these is the mingling or juxtaposition of genres, which we have seen in the Miracles and again in the clown-vice interludes of the Moralities, which leads towards the generation of a 'play in two tones'. This Sidney calls 'mungrell', affirming that one reason for its lamentable existence is that his contemporaries had no idea of 'right comedy'; and so packed their nominal tragedies with 'scurrility unwoorthy of any chast eares, or some extreame shew of doltishness, indeed fit to lift up a loude laughter'—the last being a human failing on which Sidney leant towards the views of Lord Chesterfield and our contemporary 'classic', Mr. T. S. Eliot. (*The Use of Poetry*, etc., p. 41.)

Now on comedy *c.* 1550-90 I believe that Sidney is for once entirely right. For that reason I have not discussed its 'evolution'. Despite items of comical farce and sporadic importations—Medwall's *Fulgens and Lucrece* (*c.* 1500), the '*new commodye in englysh in maner of an enterlude*' printed by Rastell (J.) about 1530 and usually called *Calisto and Melebea:* despite even *Roister Doister*, *Gammer Gurton*, and all the other Roman-comedy derivatives—English 'right comedy' comes into existence only in Shakespeare's lifetime. Its shaping influences are, even then, predominantly Italian, for which reason *Supposes* (1566) is a landmark in a way that *Misogonus* (*c.* 1560) and the other importations from the Prodigal Son plays of the Dutch humanists are not. If you start looking for 'the first English comedy', you can find it all over the place: only it is either not quite English (after all, Hilarius was an Englishman, so they think) or not quite comedy.

One reason for this is simple, provided it can be allowed that when we reach the 1590's and what Shakespeare made of Lyly's court-entertainments in *Love's Labours Lost*, we all say: "That is the real thing." Love is very largely the subject-matter of comedy: apart from the 'corrective' kind which can be traced very easily to the Moralities, with an unmistakable junction in *Roister Doister*. Love demands a certain subtlety both in treatment and in language: the 'corrective' kind of comedy much less so. It follows that the 'right comedy' of sentiment and sophistication, of romance and apt (if naughty) wit had to wait until other things had evolved. The first is the essential grace of language, without which the second—a given degree of 'internality'—of self-marking interest in telling changes of sensibility—cannot express itself. Without these, love is either limited to the poignant but no less simple simplicities of *The Nut-brown Maid*, or is a crude game altogether. It seems to me that the 'pre-Shakespearean comedies' show a certain tact in making it approximately 90 per cent harlotry.

Another reason can be educed in support of Sidney, helping to explain the time-lag between *Supposes* (1566) and the true comedy of the 1590's: one which justifies the separation of the 'tragy-comedie' class. As everyone knows, the dramatic significations of the terms tragedy and comedy were quite lost in the Middle Ages. A 'tragedie' was defined as Chaucer's Monk defined it (taking it all from Boethius), a 'comedie' was just the opposite—a tale with virtue rewarded and a happy ending.

Now if a tragedy is a *De Casibus* tale about the fall of an illustrious but *bad* man, it is plainly easy to get muddled about whether it isn't also a *comedy*, so right-and-proper is the end, so happying to the virtuous. This, I take it, is the reason why the running-title of one such play is *A Comedie of King Cambises*, while the title-page calls it (with unwitting candour) *A Lamentable Tragedie mixed full of plesant mirth*. Even if the virtuous are killed, but thereby escape a fate traditionally 'worse than death', their drama can properly be entitled, *A Newe Tragicall Comedie of Apius and Virginia*. Thomas Preston, the author of *Cambises* (registered 1569, reprint after 1584), obviously wanted the term 'tragical comedy' which Richard Edwards invented in his Prologue to *Damon and Pithias* (print, 1571) as 'a just name' for 'matter, mix'd with mirth and care'. Despite this, the play went down as a 'tragedy' when played at Court in 1564–5, though it ends with both the friends escaping execution and the 'parasite' Carisophus getting nothing worse than a beating, plus a homily on flattery, which court-vice he represents. The one sure thing in all this is that everyone is in a muddle. Sidney's explanation that they don't know what 'right comedy' is hits the mark. His own 'tragy-comedie' points to these plays as a class, though what he is mostly deprecating is the mixing of farcical stuff where he wants maintained 'a well raised admiration'—presumably as in *Gorboduc*, the only tragedy we know he knew.

For all these reasons we shall connect the 'Tudor' scene with the Elizabethan by considering what I have elsewhere styled 'the dramatic atrocities of those very amateur humanists Edwards, Pickering, Preston, and R.B., whom I am sometimes tempted to call "the University half-wits".'[34] Temptation returns, and inclines me to include Udall and Stevenson at least in a 'circle'—rather long and narrow, like most literary circles—which is quite as well defined as that which includes Lyly, Green, Nashe, and Lodge among 'the University wits'. Like those, the older group compromised between life and letters, and acted as middlemen of learning—often classical and somewhat ostentatiously displayed. Moreover the tragicomedians distinguish themselves by always getting something wrong with their spelling, as in *Apius*, *Pithias*, and *Horestes*, though to call them academic half-wits for that is too severe. Rather, they earn the title because they were probably all university men who 'descended' to the stage for a time.

Richard Edwards (1523?–66) was at two Oxford colleges, and produced the lost *Palamon and Arcite* for the Queen's entertainment there in 1566. From 1561 he was in charge of the singing-boys of the Chapel Royal, by whom his *Damon and Pithias* was played in 1564. It is the famous story of devoted friendship, enlivened with songs and the antics of Snap, Jack, Will, and Grim the Collier (of Croydon), who is put through a shaving process and robbed, and then forgotten. The Prologue says it is a tragical comedy:

> Wherein, talking of courtly toys, we do protest this flat:
> We talk of Dionysius' court; we mean no court but that!
> . . . Lo, this I speak for our defence, lest of others we be shent,
> But, worthy audience, we you pray, take things as they be meant.

But despite this protest, in verses of quite remarkable flatness, the piece ends by praying 'true friends' for 'most noble Queen Elizabeth'. The Vice-parasite replies to his thrashing with: "There shall be found within this court as great flatterers as I," adding that he hopes to spy a time when he may creep in again. It is, in short, a moral-backboned piece on true friendship and flattery, and decidedly appropriate to the position of a young queen who needed the one almost as much as she received the other.

*A Newe Enterlude of Vice, Conteyninge the Historye of Horestes* by John Pikeryng, printed 1567, nicely brings together the three terms followed in Chapter VIII: vice, interlude, history. It is about the revenge of Orestes on his mother and the paramour 'Egestus', and one is unprepared for the first scene, where the Vice, Revenge alias Courage, sets two rustics at loggerheads by malicious tale-bearing and then beats them both. The revenge is carried out with full military honours as you might say, for Horestes borrows a complete army from King Idumeus, with which a castle wall on the stage is assaulted and, as a direction says, 'your lively battel' is to be made. Egestus is taken and hanged *coram populo*, and Clytemnestra brought in to see. After fourteen lines of 'suspense' the body is removed; and one thinks of the Miracles, and of the Judas of Oberammergau who had trained himself to hang thus without lasting hurt.

The Vice exactly combines clown and allegoric figure throughout. He is the tempter in the mind when Horestes wavers over his unnatural revenge on his mother, and when the story is ending Revenge appears as a rascal out-of-work, sacked, but confident that the vengefulness of women will soon restore him to service. More than once he addresses 'cosen cutpursse' in the audience, just as the Vices do in *Cambises* and *Apius and Virginia*. With Lady Fame, who enters with iron and golden trumps, he is the vulgar buffoon, and between-whiles he sings. Song plays a fair part in all these plays. Here the duet of Egestus and Clytemnestra is not without its aching little touch of dramatic irony when the lover sings, to the charming 'Lady, lady' refrain, of one 'that ventured life to purchase ye, my dear ladie'; for he sings it in the very hour when the payment must be made.

The allegoric apparatus includes Nature, pleading with Horestes against matricide, and the crowning of Horestes and Hermione by Truth and Dewty. The pair deliver homilies on 'a kyngdom kept in Amyte', not divided against itself, and on the strife, dissension, and ruin which follow if 'dewty' is neglected by 'aney estate'. Some obscure lines at the end suggest that the whole was intended for 'application' to the murder of Darnley by Bothwell, with Mary Stuart's connivance, in February 1567. The classical story is completely declassified by conversion to interlude, but it leads to a political moral. The only quite irrelevant turn is knockabout by two roughs, Hempstringe and Haltersicke; but if we look into it, we observe that some sideshow must go in there, to give Revenge time to change his dress and reappear as Nature! Others fared far worse; for of the twenty-six parts, one man must play seven, and two others five each.

That *Horestes* is no mere 'popular-stage' hack-stuff is shown by the wealth of classical information it contains. Nature reminds Horestes of Oedipus, and gets a reply from Pythagoras; and when Clytemnestra adds Nero, the well-educated son repiques with Socrates and Juvenal. The Vice knows that Socrates was 'cround with a pyspot' by his wife 'Exantyp': the last alarming spelling being really no worse than Gabriel Harvey's *fisnamy*, from a scholar who indubitably knew Greek.

*Apius and Virginia* (printed 1575) by one R.B., who was probably Richard Bower, Master of the Chapel before Edwards, is put together on a similar plan. Virginius and his wife are introduced with their daughter Virginia, and after they have sung together the Vice Haphazard appears, in a below-stairs turn with the servants Mansipulus and Mansipula, which also includes part-song. Then he becomes true vice, the tempter of the judge Apius. But in both layers he represents 'taking chances' or 'gambling on it, trusting to luck', and his gabbling word-play on 'hap', 'hazard', and his own name appears everywhere. When Apius is determined to force Virginia, Haphazard suggests a scheme; but the fall from grace is also allegorically underlined by the dumb-show of Conscience with a lamp and Justice with a sword, followed by a quaint anticipation of Expressionism when Conscience is directed to 'speak within' (i.e. behind the scenes). A striking bit of stagecraft is required when Virginius sees that only death can save his daughter's honour. The stage-direction bids him: 'Here tie a handkercher about her eyes, and then strike off her head.' The head is duly produced before Apius, who is exposed and condemned by Justice and Reward; and Haphazard is sent off to be hanged—with a warning to Cousin Cutpurse as he goes. Haphazard turns are interlaid with the 'tragic' throughout, but the inter-relations are firmer than in *Horestes*, since the Vice shows two aspects of the same devil-may-care recklessness which his name signified to Elizabethan gamblers.

In the 'lamentable tragedie' of *Cambises*, which was probably the 'huff-suff-and-ruff' played at Court at Christmas 1560-1, another classical story is melodramatized by strata. The tale comes from Herodotus, but via Erasmus's *Apothegmata* as pillaged in Taverner's *Garden of Wysdom;* but it is laminated with performances by the Vice, Ambidexter, who is a spirit of double-dealing in the 'lamentable' strata and a slapstick clown in the 'pleasant mirth' layers. He too makes much of his name and its meaning 'with both hands to play', and in the betrayal of the king's honest, outspoken brother Smirdis, his doubling is plain villainy. Smirdis is dealt with by Cruelty and Murder, the latter coming in proleptically red-handed; but lest the audience should miss anything, 'a little bladder of vinegar prickt' ensures the stage-effect.

The play is a museum-piece for these naïve allegorical labour-saving devices and violent sensationalisms. Cambises determines to be a warrior, and leaves the judge Sisamnes as regent. His rule of extortion is denounced by Small Hability, and when the king returns —preceded by Shame 'with a trump black' to say how wicked *he* has become—first Commons-Cry and then Commons-Complaint appear, with two other persons called Proof and Trial. With a touch of the 'humane Mikado' and his 'object all sublime', Cambises has the fleecer fleeced. Execution manages the exacting stage-direction: 'Flay him with a false skin.' There was no room for '*Ne pueros coram populo Medea trucidet*' in the Elizabethan treatment of stories from the classics.[35]

Towards the end, the pace becomes furious. The king forces a match on a reluctant cousin, finds himself imperfectly married, and when Cruelty and Murder have provided the obvious solution and even Ambidexter thinks him 'akin to Bishop Bonner', our capacity for surprise is so exhausted that it seems a matter of course for Cambises to enter 'with a sword thrust up into his side, bleeding'. So he dies, with 'quake and stir' insisted on; and Ambidexter, after his usual fashion, first laments and then laughs. It is crude stuff, and yet at the same time the first outline of the cynical double-crossing villain. And that the Elizabethans saw it that way is shown in *Edmond Ironside*, where the double-dealing Edricus says:

> 'Yet I can play an *Ambodexters* part
> And sweare I love, yet hate him with my harte.'[36]

That play is Anglo-Saxon history from Holinshed; but once again broken up with slabs of fooling by Stitch, the clown, who is also a comic executioner. The rather empty vessel Ambidexter, with his repeated addresses to the cutpurse in the audience and his bouts of slapstick, is, in fact, ready for the infusions of Marlowe, of extract-of-Seneca, and misunderstood and bedevilled Machiavelli. The step to *The Jew of Malta* is not so great as from that to Iago.

The other side of the vice cannot be neglected, since the abrupt switches from gory melodrama to farce are what Sidney most condemned. Roughly speaking, Ambidexter either beats up or is beaten up by all the minor characters below princely rank. Cambises' decision for war is immediately clowned by his appearing in a grotesque parody of armour, rather like the preparations of Tweedledum and Tweedledee for their battle. This introduces a knockabout turn between Ruf, Snuf, and Huf in which a lady called Meretrix is first auctioned, and then does some knocking-down on her own, defeating and disarming Ruf—an episode paralleled in *Horestes*—before departing with him to the tune of 'kisse kisse kisse' (stage-direction). Towards the end the Vice has a set-to with two yokels, Hob and Lob, followed by another with Hob's wife, by the revealing name of Marian May-be-good; and here the stage-direction reads: 'she gets him down and he her down, thus one on the top of another make pastime.'

The whole is a lamination of the murderous and the farcical, and yet purports to be a kind of history. Nobody knows what the comic episodes once inserted into *Tamburlaine* were like, for they were never printed, but if the build of *Dr. Faustus* is considered, it is plain that almost exactly this same process has been applied to the 'history' translated from the *Faustbuch*. The clowns may vary in the two editions; the critics do very much want to say that that gross fooling was never Marlowe's. The fact remains that Wagner at least is in the source; and he has been staged as a comic, whose conjurings burlesque those of the doctor, his entirely tragic master. Pass on to *I Henry IV* with Shakespeare's 'mingling kings and clowns'—its immense buffoon playing *his* 'part in majesticall matters', and you are in a fair way to see what could be made of this apparently hopeless jumble of absurd incongruities and double-faced see-saws.

Since *Cambises* derives from interlude, it ought to have a moral, as well as this 'pattern' of mood-switchings. Read the Prologue and Epilogue, and you see that it has. The one starts with three advices of Agathon to *princes:* how they should practise law and justice, and recognize their mortality; and this is endorsed from Cicero and Seneca, with the 'Sisters Three', Icarus, and Jove thrown in—though Preston is not usually so lavish with his classics. The Epilogue returns to the theme of state—which one has excusably forgotten—and in praying for the Queen and her council does mention all the virtues which, if we glance over the play, *Cambises* illustrates *per contra.* Thoroughly adapted as it may be to the penny-stinkard environment, this 'historical' tragedy of divine retribution does still bear the marks of its evolutionary derivation—on its appendages. The Dancer's prayer for the Queen at the end of 2 *Henry IV* is, as 'Q' told us years enough ago, a similar 'primitive survival' or 'vestigial structure'—(though I am sure that he would have condemned my terms as jargon).

Despite the scepticism of Chambers and the arguments of Manly, I find nothing amiss with Boas's accepting Thomas Preston of Eton and King's as 'afterwards author of *Cambises*'. (*C.H.E.L.* VI, 298, and cf. p. 285. Adams' ref. p. 638 is wrong.) Preston was B.A. in 1557, M.A. in 1561, and in 1564 not only played before the visiting Queen in *Dido*, but 'did so genteely and gracefully dispute before her' that he won a £20 pension. Later he was made Proctor: later still (1572) was directed to read Civil Law and became LL.D. —which no doubt assisted in his final promotion to the Mastership of Trinity Hall (1584). But Cambridge dons have been comedians (and good ones) before now, and the advantages of a humorist in the proctorial office are so great that I see no reason why the B.A. of 1557 should not have written the robust farrago—which would not embarrass his unexpected dignity ten years later. Manly quotes his ballads, one of which is entitled—

> 'A Lamentation from Rome how the Pope doth bewayle
> The Rebelles of England cannot prevayle'

—with a 'surely the Preston of Cambridge would not have published these things.' But the reference to Bonner, the Marian bishop, in *Cambises* was not beyond any learned controversialist; and I am afraid that the ways of learned men under war-conditions often fall short of Manly's expectations.

The mixtures of learning and loutishness in these plays contemporary with *Gorboduc*, *Supposes*, and their derivatives could be followed up: in Fulwell's *Like wil to like*, Anon's *Common Conditions* and *Syr Clyomon and Syr Clamydes*, and Wapull's *The Tyde taryeth no Man*. Not one of them has 'literary merit'; but in the queer hybrids which resulted from taking a 'classical' story and processing it after the fashion of the moral-interlude or 'interlude of vice' there was a vitality and popular appeal utterly denied to the imitations of classical form. The Elizabethan stage—Shakespeare's stage—was the 'popular' stage: it grew great because it became London's and England's, not the preserve of a class or 'highbrow' clique of Sidneys and their tame poets. Accordingly, the old dramatic patterns passed on to the new men: to be transformed and translated to subtler uses, but often still remaining quite apparent. The serio-comic, derisive or satirical, clownish and farcical *intermezzi* persist, and the greater writers learn to use them—to make plays more comprehensive and daring than the classical limitations allow. And often enough the Morality-pattern is still to be seen, in plays which still debate, still present the war of opposed abstractable qualities within the theatre of the human consciousness.

Space lacks in a book of this size for detailed examples. But the case of the 'fable' in *Measure for Measure* is too pretty to pass by. In the first instance the tale of the unjust authority who seduces a woman by promising to pardon her brother belonged to Giraldi Cinthio, who used it in a tragedy, *Epitia*, and then in prose, in his *Hecatomithii* (1565). The story was dramatized by George Whetstone in 1578, and, like Cinthio, he too made a prose tale of it later, in his *Heptameron of Civil Discourses* (1582). The play was called *Promos and Cassandra*, and as Whetstone held views on play-writing, he prefaced it with some adverse comments on contemporary ways, and an explanation that 'decorum' required a two-part play in this case. One thing, however, he does not explain: viz. why he should have supplied his classical five-act contrivances with a sub-plot centring in a harlot named Lamia—but for which ten acts would not be needed. This sub-plot dwells on the general corruption of the world beneath Promos (Angelo) and Cassandra (Isabella), and it grins at classical *Decorum* by being comic. On the long title the marks of the Morality are written so large that I need do no more than quote it:

> The Right Excellent and famous Historye, of Promos and Cassandra; Deuided into two Commicall Discourses. In the fyrste parte is showne, the unsufferable abuse, of a lewde Magistrate: The

> vertuous behaviours of a chaste Ladye: The uncontrowled leaudenes of a favoured Curtisan. And the undeserved estimation of a pernicious Parasyte. In the second parte is discoursed, the perfect magnanimitye of a noble kinge, in checking vice and favouringe Vertue: Wherein is showne, the Ruine and overthrowe, of dishonest practices: with the advancement of upright dealing.

Other examples of this kind of thing could be given. The Italian 'humanist' story has, so to speak, been 'medievalized' by the Germanic mind: the artistic babble and tale-telling from which a man can learn how the world works and perhaps a smatter of practical psychology, has been turned to a narrower aim and a moral point. But the moralizing brings its companion gene with it, and the result is a double-theme play, which a classicist should condemn on that score alone.

In Shakespeare, sometime after 1603, the 'morality-pattern' is not only evident, but has been developed to an amazing extent. The whole is still in two 'layers', one including Angelo, Isabella, and Claudio, the other the denizens of the brothel-world of Pompey and Mrs. Overdone. Lucio, a gentleman as well as whoremonger, belongs to both. The drama is concerned with justice and with lust; and the sexual urge which causes the downfall of Angelo as of Claudio, and which equally grasps and entangles Isabella, as an aversion, is just as much the basis of Lucio's jokes as of Mrs. Overdone's profession. One and the same thing is thus doubly presented. In Angelo it is tragic: in the stews it is smutty quip at lightest, and even at that, as Pompey says: "it does stink in some sort, sir". At lowest it is case-hardened jesting about syphilis, where fear expresses itself in devil-may-care words, and the pretence of familiarity supports the pretence of contempt. Yet all this is shown as—what we find it in life—coarse comedy. The underdogs and underbitches are funny, and although some of it can be shuffled off Shakespeare the scheme of the whole remains; *and*, moreover, is such that the filthiest and nastiest jest is appropriate to it. The play is a searching analysis, an *empirical* moral investigation—not an application of ready-made Christian *a priori* moral-schemes where all the answers are known. Shakespeare does not know the answers. He pokes and probes around, a duke of dark corners. He observes that the medieval text-book conflict of Reason and Sensuality (or 'Instinct') means Claudio and Juliet, and that that is a joke for Pompey. It means Angelo's confusion at the seething of his own blood; and Lucio's loose life and looser tongue. Everything is multi-faced, and at the end we do not know what justice is, or virtue either. The gospel moral which some critics read into it is as hollow as Angelo's marriage—or Isabella's.[37] Such is Shakespeare's employment of the ambivalent pattern which his drama inherited. The underworld belongs to the devils of lust and hardness of heart; but it is comic, as the Devil's world must be—since it is the negation of human dignities. In *Henry IV*, Part I, Shakespeare took it humorously, since it only undermined honour and glory and left the very shaky criterion of successful action in command of the field. But in his later Moralities the ambivalences of experience made his writing take on a more deeply troubled tone. To meet that demand within himself, he relied on 'mungrell tragy-comedie' with its hereditary splitness, its clashes of tone between the worlds of Good Man and Goodman Devil, its innate Gothic incongruities, its cackle of laughter which is more undermining than damnation. Nor, when he wrote his tragedies, was that comic spirit absent from them. For the final stroke of the Spirit of Negation, *Der Geist der stets verneint*, is the turn to farce; which empties meaning and dignity out of all the fine speeches, the fine attitudes, and even the final suffering, to leave even a hero alone 'in the small circle of pain within the skull'; and beyond that, perhaps even within it, as the mordant irony eats in—a nothing in a world of nothings.

# EPILOGUE

THE further growth and triumph of English drama lies beyond the scope of this book. It must suffice here to mark some of the continuities between the 'medieval' and the 'Shakespearean' stages, and to sketch a few of the scenes towards which the earlier Elizabethan sign-posts point.

By the year of the Armada, 1588, two dramatic events had occurred which provide some justification for starting 'Elizabethan' drama at the twentieth year of Elizabeth. The stage had sounded to the drums and tramplings of *Tamburlaine the Great*, with Edward Alleyn in the name-part, declaiming what Nashe was soon to decry as 'the swelling bombast of a bragging blank-verse'; and Thomas Kyd had brought forth Old Hieronimo in *The Spanish Tragedy*, striding on wildly in his nightgown, to open his complicated tale of murder, intrigue, and revenge with the famous line: 'What outcries pluck me from my naked bed?' In all probability Kyd had also written a blank-verse tragedy in which a ghost cried: "Hamlet, revenge!" and "Blood is a beggar," and made himself a measure for Shakespeare in the mind of Ben Jonson, who was to bracket these two innovators in setting his friend's superlative merits against those of 'sporting Kyd, or Marlowe's mighty line'.

Within five years of the Armada, the University wits had come, and almost gone. Marlowe was murdered: Greene dead of dissipation: Lyly, Nashe, and Lodge turning to more profitable occupations: Peele the same feckless clever 'George . . . of a poetical disposition never to write so long as his money lasted'; and the future lay predominantly in the mind of the man from Stratford who was just a month past his twenty-ninth birthday when Marlowe was killed (30th May, 1593). Kyd was finished, with about two years to live, in a mysterious obscurity. But though neither he nor Shakespeare was a university man, it is right to insist that one of the main shaping forces of the Elizabethan theatre was the advent of what Nashe called the 'idiot art-masters': the lightly associated group of Oxford and Cambridge men who turned, if only for a time, to professional play-writing for the popular companies who catered not for the Court alone, nor for the Inns of Court, but for the world: the little world of London, which was then the microcosm of England. But for that there could have been no Globe.

Here the growth of drama is conditioned by the evolution of

the 'permanent' theatre and the professional company. Had the play-damning London *bourgeois* had his way with either, the line of *Gorboduc* would not have petered out with *The Misfortunes of Arthur* (1588), and Shakespeare would presumably have been forced into writing the kind of academic synthetic-Senecal plays which pleased the Countess of Pembroke (Sidney's sister) and her cultured friends. The 'meer English' tradition of comedy, still more of comic-plus-serious would have been written off as a 'mere gallimaufrey' (the phrase was More's in *Utopia*) or 'a goodly hotch-potch' (Joseph Hall, 1597–8), and *King Lear* could no more have been produced than *Bartholomew Fair* or *The Changeling*.

It must be therefore marked 'with a white stone', in the Elizabethan phrase, that one John Brayne, who had put up the money for fitting a stage and seats in the Red Lion Inn at Whitechapel in 1567, did as much and more to assist James Burbage in 1576, in a building which called itself *The Theatre*, in Shoreditch. It lasted till 1598, when Richard Burbage's name was made, and Shakespeare moved with the Lord Chamberlain's Men to the *Globe*, on the Bankside. Meantime their great rivals, the Lord Admiral's Men, had established the *Rose* (1587) and were planning the *Fortune* (1599), backed by Philip Henslowe—financier, money-lender, and brothel-owner—who was Alleyn's father-in-law and the author of a singularly soulless business diary which has accidentally preserved for us a gold-mine of information on the theatrical business of the period. If we add that the *Curtain* opened in 1567, the *Swan* in 1595, and that by 1600 the Paul's Boys (active in the 1580's with Lyly's plays) were co-rivals with Shakespeare's men and the Children of the Chapel at the Blackfriars (private) theatre, there is no need to emphasize further the *demand* for drama in the Elizabethan world. The number of playhouses in so small a city is as good evidence for it as are the energetic blasts of Puritan vituperation, in which a prim, precise godliness is not seldom mingled with a more human and fallible envy: as, e.g. when a would-be popular preacher complains that 'when the bells toll to the lecture, the trumpets sound to the stages'.

By this time the theatrical company had taken shape, as a kind of co-operative enterprise somewhat like merchant-venturing on the high seas. The professional entertainers who inherited the minstrel tradition as 'waits' (musicians) and other attendants on nobility and gentry became gradually detached from liveried service; and after a period in which they were in grave danger of being scheduled permanently as able-bodied vagabonds, 'caterpillars of the commonwealth' (Gosson), had established a certain position for themselves, in that they had the right to perform in places outside the jurisdiction of the City. (This included such special enclaves as the Blackfriars and Whitefriars.) Towards 1600 acting was becoming 'respectable' or, at least, no longer disreputable; but from what we know of players and playwrights we must regard the enrichment of Alleyn and of Shakespeare as entirely exceptional. The great majority of both were exploited, not less by the 'sharers' in a co-operative company, we may suspect, than by such enterprisers as Henslowe. But it is impossible to overlook the fact that Marlowe was singularly lucky in getting his plays into Alleyn's hands; and that the exact personnel of Shakespeare's own company is a shaping force in much of his writing. To notice the effect of different styles of playing we need only consider Pistol, whose mouth and manner are filled with parodies of the Admiral's Men, with whom the tradition of 'thundering threats' in the Marlovian style lived on. In Marston, or in Chapman's *Bussy d'Ambois*, we are in yet another world of shadows: that of the 'private' theatres, where a better-class audience expected difficult thought and recondite or libellous allusion, and where a somewhat recherché entertainment was derived from hearing 'bloody bawdry' in the mouths of children.

These considerations make it difficult to generalize about 'the Elizabethan audience'. But we can insist that there *was* such a thing, and that it was of major importance in shaping its own drama. Plays ran but a matter of days, and where constant fresh appeal is required, *breadth* of appeal is essential. And breadth means that we should not permit too much to be made of that well-worn distinction between what (Shakespeare) wanted to put into his (superior, for-the-judicious-only) play, and what he had to stick in, or let be stuck in, to catch the ears of 'the groundlings'. His audience is belied and traduced by that old-fashioned abuse, which the romantics (the great Coleridge among them) inherited from the mass-despising eighteenth-century editors. Much rather, the mind of his audience was like Falstaff's good sherris-sack: 'apprehensive, quick, forgetive, full of nimble, fiery, and delectable shapes.' All its tastes and quiddities were there for him to play on: from City pageants to May-games and Whitsun pastorals: scaffold-eloquence to sermons at Paul's Cross: from singing-boys to fencers, wrestlers, and even performing dogs and bears; from 'merry conceited jests' to 'notable morality' from Seneca, to be jotted down in the courtier's 'tables' and used as his own fine wit at the 'ordinary';

from the old-fashioned moral interlude with its abstractions to the new-fangled Court Masque with its subtler insinuations and 'silken terms precise' . . . all these, and more besides. At one end of his career, the *Errors* invited its auditors to see what smart sham-Plautus it is, while *Titus Andronicus* settled down in popular favour (to Jonson's annoyance) as a terrifying out-Kydding of Kyd. At the other, the ancient fertility-ritual glides magically into *The Winter's Tale*, and the medieval skull-symbol appears with as complete a naturalness in *Hamlet* as in *Cymbeline*. Midway in his course of development, such plays as *Henry IV*, *Troilus and Cressida*, *All's Well* are not to be understood without some awareness of the developed and refined tradition of moral interlude in which they are conceived. With his clowns the same. In all he, like his fellows and rivals, is using his rich native material, not as he finds it in his isolated consciousness, but as that consciousness is an outgrowth and symposium of the varying degrees of consciousness and appetency in the 'imaginary forces' of the audience. Thence springs that astonishing inclusiveness of the Elizabethan drama which so contrasts with the classical (Greek) and neo-classic (French), which must have given the patterns for a Court and connoisseurs' drama: which might have had its excellences, but could not have accommodated the English spirit. It does not matter whether Shakespeare does or does not speak consciously through his Prospero in the famous 'farewell to the stage'. When he tells his then audience how:

> 'Gentle breath of yours my sails
> Must fill, or else my project fails,
> Which was to please. . . .'

he writes what he was always aware of. Nor do the derogatory observations on the mob contradict it; for Tudor society was hierarchical, and the low position of those who are punningly called 'the under-standers' is taken for granted on both sides. Admittedly, Shakespeare shows an unusually keen fear of the rebellious and disordered forces of the mob broke loose. But there is nothing in his writing to suggest the attitude of Webster in the *White Devil* preface: where he whiningly complains of how he *would* have written in a high sententious style if it were not for his tough-gutted hearers; and where Master Chapman heads the list of contemporary excellencies, while Shakespeare comes only on the tail, with Dekker and Heywood, and an unconvincing apology. The answer to all those sophisticated persons who talk and write as if Shakespeare were only to be appreciated by the most finely adjusted 'sensibilities', and equally to those who doubt if the rag-tag people of the Bankside could have understood his plays is to be seen—if in plan only—at Stratford on Avon. His audience gave him New Place. The author of the most intellectual of Elizabethan plays—which I take to be Chapman's *Charles, Duke of Byron*—was ill-rewarded. So too Lyly: the appeal of whose courtly comedies to the polite world cut them off from the common stages.

Between this miscellaneous audience and the dramatist there grew up a body of unwritten conventions: a communicative code which often seems to us naïve or silly because we are not used to it. The convention of black-and-white 'realistic' appearances in the cinema is one we do not notice until we are jogged into observing that it is a convention. The Elizabethans plainly found the conventions of the long soliloquy, the unlikely or impossible messenger's speech, and the aside no more troublesome than we cinema-goers find a colourless world where all the persons apparently speak through tin trumpets or out of water-tanks. Nor were they disturbed at what strikes us as an abrupt change of technique, or even of type of play, when morality personages mingle with or interrupt the realistic action. This is where a knowledge of the earlier Elizabethan or Tudor drama is of great value.

At least until the period of Shakespeare's maturest tragedies the different genres were by no means as distinct as we consider them. True, the allegoric figures of Tragedy, History, and Comedy all appear in the induction to *A Warning for Fair Women* (printed 1599). But in *The Gull's Hornbook* (1609), where the smart young man is ironically given advice on how best to misbehave himself in the theatre, he is told how effective it is 'if in the middle of the play (be it pastoral or comedie, morall or tragedie), you rise with a shrewd discontented face from your stool to be gone'. How 'moral' remains firmly established as a genre is evident not only from the plain morality-plays given late in Elizabeth's reign (p. 101), but also from occasional evidences that the convention of abstract personages made no unusual or difficult demands on the popular audience. In the *Warning for Fair Women*, which was played by Shakespeare's company, Lust, Chastity, and other abstractions appear in symbolic interludes of dumb-show; and this in a story of a realistic middle-class murder. Between Captain Brown's determination to seduce Mistress Sanders and its success, leading to the murder of her husband, the audience saw Lust lead Mistress

Sanders in, with Chastity plucking at her sleeve to draw her back; and finally, when Chastity has fled, allegoric figures and real persons sit down together to a banquet given by Murder. All this to music, and with dancing Furies as attendants. Such a convention was perfectly understood: was, so to speak 'common talk', *lingua franca* between an artist and his understanders. He could slip a real-life character into an allegoric mode with perfect confidence, and call the shadow of a devilish spirit from the dark uncertainties of his hearers' minds with every assurance that it would indeed come when he might call for it. Thus Barabas, the Jew of Malta, Aaron in *Titus Andronicus*, Richard III, and Iago has each his devil's shadow; and the tricksy malice and jocularity of each of them derives from the tradition of the old Vice, but for whom no villain need have been a comic. That the miracle-play grotesque of Herods, Pilates, and the Devil himself was still in contact with the London of the 1590's is a contention impossible to demonstrate, in spite of Hamlet's condemnation of the ranting player who 'out-Herods Herod'. With Morality-play devices and expectations, however, there is a wealth of material to hand as soon as we look for it. Its effectiveness is not only shown by the frequency of its use: as, for example, when *The Taming of the Shrew* is made to end with a 'legend for good women' and a homily put into Katherine's 'reformed mouth'. Willis's *Mount Tabor*, or *Private Exercises of a Penitent Sinner*, which was published when the author was seventy-five, in the year 1639, contains an account of a Morality which the sinner saw with his father, at a time when he was so small that 'he made me stand between his leggs, as he sate upon one of the benches'. He sketches the plot, which sounds very dull indeed, explains how the Prince stood for the wicked of the world, three ladies for Pride, Covetousness, and Luxury, and two old men 'the end of the world and the last judgment'. And to this he adds, as if to make the man and his age come alive for us: 'This sight took such impression on me, that when I came towards man's estate, it was as fresh in my memory, as if I had seen it newly acted.' This R. Willis was born in 1564 (1639 minus 75). He was, therefore, Shakespeare's exact contemporary. If we wish to see all that Shakespeare is doing when a new character, Mercade, enters at the end of *Love's Labours Lost*, apparently with nothing but news of the King's death, the situation must be referred to the imagined minds of such men as Willis. He saw two old men approach '*the Cradle of Security*', one in blue 'with a serjeant at armes his mace on his shoulder', the other in red 'with a drawn sword in his hand',

and at once the first was 'the fell sergeant Death' and the other bore the sword of divine justice. In Shakespeare's play the serious and dramatically deepened tone of the ending comes in with the suggestion that Mercade not only speaks of death, but brings Death with him. It is a magical transition, only matched by the final one, where the sophisticated court-comedy is turned off to the age-old traditional stuff of the Contention of Spring and Winter: using now the convention of the fertility-rituals, as preserved in the German *Fastnachtspiele* (Shrovetide plays), but again transformed by Shakespeare's touch.

Less difficult to observe than allegoric insinuation, but really harder to estimate critically, is the English refusal to exclude some kind of comic effect from serious plays. As late as 1597-8 the satirist Joseph Hall is still deriding this in *Virgidemiarum*, and no defence is offered, except for the persistent practice of the dramatists. In the University Wits' plays we can observe the constant effort to combine a variety of different tones and interests. We know that comic episodes were foisted into *Tamburlaine*—presumably to make it conform to London tastes, of which Marlowe was possibly still ignorant—though the printer cut them out when it was published. The farce in *Faustus*, the mingle of novelettish sham history, comedy, and social-moral allegory in Greene's *James IV* and in *A Knack to Know a Knave* (1592) can escape no attentive reader. But between *Tamburlaine* and Shakespeare there is *The Troublesome Reign of King John* (1591) in which some steps have certainly been made in the direction of capitalizing the necessity of comical side-plot or secondary character and turning them into an implied commentary on the rest. It remained for Shakespeare to maintain *and transform* the 'tragy-comedie' tradition by compelling the divergent tones to yield a new and greater unity. In 1 *Henry IV* he triumphs in this kind (1597). The irresponsible and irrepressible spectator, Falstaff, is no more 'The Vice' than was the Bastard Falconbridge in *King John* (written perhaps four years earlier). Yet both have hereditary genes from equivocal figures in straightforward moral interludes. By accredited critical theory among the Elizabethans, both plays should have been condemned. The terms are given in a dialogue by Florio, printed in 1591. One speaker says that the plays played in England are 'neither right comedies, nor right tragedies', and when the other asks: 'How would you name them then?' he is answered with: 'Representations of histories, without any decorum.' The playgoers were unmoved by such theoretic stuff. They agreed with Lodge that the dramatists 'dilucidate and well explain many darke obscure histories, imprinting them in men's minds in such indelible characters that they can hardly be obliterated.' The suggestion of an allegoric shadow-show behind the historic characters, on another plane than the clash of transient personalities, was an essential part of that 'dilucidation'. Shakespeare was a great and original writer in seeing what untapped resources of irony lay in the comi-tragic history-play where 'many times (to make mirth) they make a clowne companion with a kinge' and 'in theyr grave counsels, they allow the advice of fooles'. But if the traditional expectation of such incongruities had not lain to his touch, the subtle opal-twinkling ambivalences of *Henry IV* would have been beyond his invention. As much might be said of the interplay of appearance and reality, delicate or bitterly ironic, in *Midsummer Night's Dream* and *Troilus and Cressida*. 'Comic relief', as tonal contrast in tragedy, becomes farcical, satiric, or sarcastic discordance in comedy; and we can observe these phenomena as well in Jonson's *Volpone* or Middleton's law-comedies as in Chapman or Shakespeare: to name only major writers of the best period. In Marston and Tourneur the contrasting themes are often a kind of loathsome farce, like an antimasque of Yahoos; and as late as Caroline times John Ford still seems to strive for some such effect with his extremely unfunny sub-plots. It would be exaggeration to say: 'Scratch any Elizabethan and you find a Medieval'; but whenever an Elizabethan dramatist is frightened or worried or plunged suddenly into the depths of himself and his universe, the medieval heritage is likely to come out strongly. The Tudor-Jacobean drama is of the English Renaissance, no question. But in it the Middle Ages became dramatically vocal on their death-bed. If 1588 is taken as a reference-point, it is one from which to look, and far, in two directions. For England at all events, a world conquered a world in the narrow seas then, as completely as West conquered East at Actium. But in that same invasion-period a woman fell in labour, and, as her son said later: 'she brought forth twins, myself and fear.' That son was Thomas Hobbes.

If we seek an imaginary dividing-line somewhere about 1588, we can, while still marking the medieval continuities, give some proper indication of the differences made by Marlowe and by Kyd. This necessitates some reference to Seneca, whose drama can hardly be said to touch anything discussed in this book except *Gorboduc* and its descendants, though there are a few lines from the *Octavia* in *Damon and Pithias*. As Mr. T. S. Eliot has insisted, the Elizabethan Seneca is not quite the Roman closet-dramatist. Much rather he is, in Nashe's phrase: 'English Seneca read by candle-light': that is to say, misread a good deal, and decidedly mistaken—for the classic that he really was not. Seneca's plays are moral melodramas of violent passion—always including some kind of revenge, usually intentional—and their morals are stoic. By English standards revenge was murder; and for that reason the earliest of revenge-plays—Pickeryng's *Horestes*—shirks the death of Clytemnestra. It followed that, for most Elizabethans at all events, a revenge-play was a villain-play, even if the villain economically became the hero. This is the state of things in the most impressively horrific of Seneca's tragedies, the *Thyestes:* in which a monomaniac revenger feeds his brother on the flesh of his murdered sons, and his hearers on the niceties of artistically satisfying retribution. (This Thyestean banquet is 'put on' réchauffé in *Titus Andronicus* and *Antonio's Revenge*, as well as in a Cambridge Latin play of the 1590's, *Roxana.*) But Seneca also has a striking collection of thoroughly bad men, of the sort known as 'tyrants', who utter neat formulations of the principles and delights of tyranny, either as a complete self-sufficiency or as a naked power so complete that it can make the sanctions of right and wrong rest only in its will. In the latter case the superhumanity of the tyrant is clearly best demonstrated by his *inverting* the established moral order, and making his people choose to do or be or say exactly what nature, conscience, law, or tradition would have them refuse. These are Atreus's principles of rule in *Thyestes*, and in the *Agamemnon* the adulterous usurper Aegisthus formulates them just as briskly. 'Kings deem the supreme jewel of domination to be the power to make unlawfulness their sole law.' Here will goes beyond the self-sufficiency of the mere tyrant, and becomes an ambition of restless self-conscious evil, in which a Christian reader can only see an adumbration of the Devil himself.

No such tyrant appears in *Gorboduc*. The king is wrong-headed and ruins his state by wilful will, but nothing is made of it as a force of passion in himself. The psychological interest of Seneca in tearing passions was left alone by Sackville and Norton. But in Marlowe the terrifying force of will speaks out. All his heroes are invertors of the accepted moral order. From the traditional English viewpoint, his plays are moralities, only by an immoralist of genius. Each shows an heroic figure whose comet-blaze of transitory glory is a violation of the universal moral law. Of other glories he has none. His characters move in the mind like the cloudy outlines of ambitions so vast that they have no substance but desire. They speak in gigantic hyperboles, or in such a vaulting sequence of terms as:

> 'O what a world of profit and delight,
> Of power, of honour, and *omnipotence*,'

where the imagination experiences some analogue of the pilot's indescribable sensation when his machine takes off, and the 'little world of man' is launched into another element. Nothing is too difficult for the superman:

> 'Nil mortalibus ardui est;
> Caelum ipsum petimus. . . .'[38]

Tamburlaine, born a Scythian shepherd, does exactly this. And whereas Horace adds '*stultitia*' to make the line mean 'We assail heaven itself *in our folly*', in Marlowe it is glory. For it is not *Weltmacht* that the king-killer Tamburlaine aspires to, but divinity itself. His only limitation is that he is mortal. In the end he dies; but undefeated: indeed, surprised and shocked at his mortality.

The humanist vision of man as a dream-figure limited only by time is as evident in his conquests of all the realms of power as in the famous passages beginning: 'Nature that framed us of four elements' and 'What is beauty?' In both Marlowe goes clean outside the character of the conqueror, and his hero steps triumphantly into a frame of allegory where 'Energy is eternal delight.'

This adumbration of a demonic figure of human will 'beyond good and evil' (*Jenseits von gut und böse*) derives from Christopher Marlowe the man: in Beddoes' phrase, 'a bold trampling fellow', a 'reviver' of the drama such as no academic 'peerer into wormholes' could ever be—or ever can. But in the shaping of this revolutionary conception due measure must be allowed to two imaginative sources, both of which Marlowe absorbed as a Cambridge undergraduate. The first is the impact of the demigod Hercules in Seneca, like Tamburlaine amazed at his own suffering mortality. Through that image the other Senecan superhuman motives become current; and they are mainly criminal—just as Faustus, Barabas, the Guise, and Mortimer are criminal: on a huge scale, if only in their own estimation.

The second imaginative foundation is the conception of The Prince, as Marlowe dreamt it from his readings in Macchiavelli. We know from Gabriel Harvey that *Il Principe* was among the brightest and wickedest of the dons' naughty reading of those afar and politically innocent times. But the infamous Florentine was already a myth before Marlowe brought him on the stage as prologue to *The Jew of Malta* or made his principles a text-book for the Guise. The myth was of a superhuman sub-man, a creature of heartless, cool-headed, pitiless intellect, with a tool-steel will, indomitable in resolution, infinite in cunning faculty, inhumanly free from all the natural restraints of conscience, religion, law, and decency—and, moreover, utterly convinced that in this freedom lay his whole claim to be made of finer mould than other men.

The diabolical tyrant of Seneca fused with this myth to provide the Elizabethan stage with its teeming race of 'glorious villains'. In them the superhuman is equated with the devilish; and thus the spirit of Renaissance humanism generated its own particular and peculiar replacement of the Devil in the earlier drama. In it glorification of the will represents an *inversion* of medieval values (in terms of which Lucifer fell through pride alone), while the 'Machiavel' side—a thing very different from the political thought of Machiavelli—combines in perfect fusion with the essences of Senecan tyranny. Machiavelli had written of the prudential uses of bad faith and broken promises, but the fusion with the Senecan villain made it almost *de rigueur* for the man-of-power to be a deliberate and delighted equivocator. The possibilities are seen at once in Atreus's very 'Machiavel' lines:

'Sanctitas, pietas, fides,
Privata bona sunt, qua iuvat reges eant.'[39]

Similarly, the 'Machiavellian' commonplace about its being better for a ruler to be feared than loved becomes an ideal aim: that of being hateful, and somehow enjoying this as a kingly title. It is equally Senecan. Two speeches of Tirell (the murderer of the princes) in Legge's Richard III play (1579) give the formula:

(*a*) Ars prima sceptri posse te invidia pati.
(*b*) Regnare non vult esse qui invisus timet.[40]

The second (*b*) is word for word from Eteocles in the *Phoenissae* (654); but (*a*) is only a slightly misquoted form of *Hercules Furens* 353; and both give what any intelligent reader could *deduce* about the prince in Machiavelli, though that sensible adviser is far indeed from holding up odium as an ideal. Indeed, the brag 'feared am I more than loved' is much more characteristic of the Senecan bogey-man than of the true Machiavellian, who would find it a political inconvenience to have 'Death' too conspicuously written in the furrows of his face. But it seems plain that the Elizabethans took this sort of thing for the genuine Florentine stuff: a heady spirit of 'Senecchiavellian' villainy which sang to them in the tones of the Demon Lover in the ballad:

> 'I'll show you where the wild lilies grow
> On the banks of Italee!'

All this fell opportunely into the expanded mould of the equivocating Vice, who was at once a double-crossing trickster, a tempter, a malicious humorist, and a clown. But for this condensation it would be impossible to explain why such villains as Barabas, Aaron, Richard III, Volpone, and Iago should enjoy such a remarkable sense of humour. If Seneca's villains laugh, it is with the cackle of the maniac; nor did any sane man ever take *The Prince* for a jest-book or the *Discorsi* for a collection of 'merry tales'. But already in *The Jew of Malta* the goblin humour is there. If Mr. T. S. Eliot had been more explicit, and, above all, more *historical*—more concerned with the *tradition*—in his attempt to diagnose the comedy of the terrifying-grotesque in that play, no one need ever have been outraged by his description of it as 'a farce'. It is so, but only in the way that a medieval gargoyle was farcical: as a grotesque distortion of the recognizably next-to-human, which shadows and gives 'a local habitation and a name' to the diabolic. It is serious, in a different way from what Greene meant when he wrote of 'daring God out of Heaven with that atheist Tamburlaine', but to a similar end. The qualities of humanistically observed or imagined humanity are developed and pressed to a limit. Marlowe presses *all* the qualities which interest him to such limits: indeed, *à l'outrance*—and so to the *outré*. With his own Guise he seems to say: 'That like I best that flies beyond my reach'; and in the queer shifts of aspect by which some of his *personæ* abruptly appear as 'prodigious caricatures' he almost recalls St. Augustine, when he looks into the incredible realm of his own consciousness with bewildered wonder and a nameless horror. In Marlowe the wonder predominates: in the later generators of 'Senecchiavellian villainy' it is mainly the horror. His explorations of the ideal will-to-power lead logically to the later men's terrifying investigations of evil. But the goblin jester is still present: in Marston and Tourneur as in Webster. In Jonson alone do we find the would-be superman adroitly twisted about in such a way that his very Renaissance *virtu* suddenly makes him a figure of fun. In short, 'the old Vice'—no longer with 'his dagger of lath'—was to take on a new vitality in the social-moralist comedies of the seventeenth century—e.g. in the best of Middleton's—as well as in the villain-intriguer of tragedy and tragi-comedy. In the more serious plays, comic or tragic, such figures represent the fear of man's potentialities which became predominant as the strictly 'Elizabethan' period drew to its close. With the growing scepticism of the 1600's, the Senecchiavellian rapidly turns into a terrified (but still fascinated and courageous) contemplation of the Frankenstein-monster of will, intellect, perfidy, and outrageous gusto which man might become, given freedom from all the Christian and medieval restraints.

If we seek for a sharp break between medieval and Renaissance ways with drama, it is to be found much rather with Kyd than with Marlowe. Kyd is small enough when set beside the man who in real life so alarmed him, but his innovations in the revenge-play appear great enough if we consider what they led up to. Like Marlowe, he studies evil and deals in the terrifying. He is, however, a true dramatist in his plotting; Marlowe, except in *Edward II*, is a dramatist only in his dramatic poetry—in great vistas of *mind*, rather than of the slip-knot of fate or events pulling tight on human lives. The theme of retribution is in the Moralities; but the sinner hunted by Bale's Vindicta Dei or the Nemesis of *Respublica* is never as exciting a theme as the revenges of *The Spanish Tragedy*, *Andronicus*, or *Hamlet*. The theme of retribution on prince and people in *Gorboduc* cannot compare with the emotional stimulation of its originals in Seneca, with their expositions of the psychologies of savage passion, frenzy, or sheer madness. Crude as those garish colours seem to us, they came to our ancestors with a shock of brilliant discovery. One has only to turn from a sufficiency of morality-play reading to Seneca's Latin to catch a glimpse of what this meant. To the Elizabethans his plays were full of a startling life-likeness such as they met—and shuddered at, snake-fascinated—in the Italian *novella*. Italy was at once to them a foothill to Parnassus and the Chicago *de ces jours*. Kyd's work shows both trends. On one side he is influenced by Garnier—a French Senecanizer, whom he translated in *Cornelia*—and *The Spanish Tragedy* attempts the academic, chorus-divided, five-act shapeliness. On the other, he is the first parent of the horror-mongerings of all the Jacobean specialists in the macabre and sensational. He established the ghost, both as stage-thrill and as messenger from an underworld variously compounded of Virgil and Seneca, if still with much of the smoky airs of Bosch and Bruegel in the background. If, as many believe, he was not only responsible for the *Ur-Hamlet* (?1586–7) but for *Arden of Feversham*, then the domestic tragedy was as much of his devising as the high-flown exotic revenge-plot.

By following the medieval traditions, we see that the domestic tragedy is a particular branch of 'moral history', in which impressive middle-class murder-stories were dramatized, with the usual suggestion that 'blood will have blood', as *The Mirror for Magistrates* had phrased it. Not many have survived; but it is notable that both *Arden* and the *Warning for Fair Women* take their material from books of history, not from criminal cases which had recently occurred. They are therefore further exemplifications of the 'moral' trend in the staging of 'history', and not entirely comparable with the later *Yorkshire Tragedy* (1607), which *is* concerned with a highly sensational contemporary crime. By degrees the writers in this genre seem to have recognized it as something less than 'tragic': as can be seen by Kyd's apology for the 'naked tragedy' at the end of *Arden*, which is echoed in Heywood's *Woman Killed with Kindness* (1603), and from the sentiments put into Tragedy's own mouth at the conclusion of *A Warning for Fair Women*. Possibly it was this sort of play which Dekker had partly in mind in making 'moral' a class distinct from the rest. Possibly it was a vaguer group which would include such 'social' plays—some overtly 'moral'—as his *Honest Whore* and Marston's 'reply' to it, *The Dutch Courtezan* (1604). The time was scarcely ripe for Bürgertragödie; but it is interesting to note that Lillo knew and adapted *Arden*, and it was his *London Merchant* (1731) which started a vogue which was to become of European importance in the eighteenth century. The morality tradition urged the Elizabethans towards considerations of ordinary ethical and social problems—from murder to remarriage, and mistressing to monopolies—and it is only when we look down the course of time in search of any penetrating investigation of such themes that we realize how completely the current of imaginative inquiry was shut off by the Puritan interregnum and the reaction to an empty frivolity at the Restoration. In a sense, the truest product of the English Renaissance, as a thing entirely separate from the Middle Ages, was the self-sufficiency of the Puritan: the man *outside* the theatre, whose only dramatic aim was its extinction. More authoritarian than any Tudor, more sure of his own inner light of conscience, the Puritan alone permitted no place for the inquiringness which was above all the spirit of the great age of the English drama.

We conclude that one great secret of the Elizabethan synthesis lay in the thoroughness of the co-action between the medieval layers and the new: predominantly, the Senecan and Italian. One special catalyst was that irrepressible taste for comedy on which most Elizabethan critics commented—rarely with favour. Above all, the characteristic English mode was the *mixed* one; for which only George Whetstone had his hurried good word to say, before packing together his papers and sailing off with Humphrey Gilbert, on a voyage from which he was prepared not to return. The dramatists, however, went their own way. Even in Lyly's sophisticated playlets this is as true as of Greene's *James IV:* of *Midsummer Night's Dream* as of *The Winter's Tale:* of *Hamlet* as of *Coriolanus.* Critics condemned it by foreign, neo-classical standards, just as they had done the 'barbarous' practice of rhyming in verse. But the Elizabethans found that though continental strictnesses might have their vogue among the temporary élite, for the rest nature had its own 'meer English' rules. Being *English* rules, they were case-law: some going back to vastly ancient rights and liberties. With that let this epilogue conclude.

Yet when I stand at that imaginary point of time and think of any dramatist of a later age looking over that seething world of creation and mind-adventure, I can only think of him as finding in his heart the echo of the sentiments of the poet in the prologue to Goethe's *Faust:*

> So gib mir auch die Zeiten wieder,
> Da ich noch selbst im Werden war,
> Da sich ein Quell gedrängter Lieder
> Ununterbrochen neu gebar. . . .
> Ich hatte nichts und doch genug,
> Den Drang nach Wahrheit und die Lust am Trug.
> Gib ungebändigt jene Triebe,
> Das tiefe schmerzenvolle Glück,
> Des Hasses Kraft, die Macht der Liebe,
> Gib meine Jugend mir zurück!

Just so might any but another Shakespeare cry:

> Give back to me those days for which I long
> When I was still *becoming*, still to grow,
> Teeming with birth on birth of crowding song
> Uninterrupted as a fountain's flow. . . .

Nothing was mine, yet all enough to prize
The urge for Truth, the lust for schemes and lies.
Give me those surging passions unconfined,
That deep delight as full of joy as pain,
Harsh strength of hate, love's mightiness of mind,
Give back my youth, let me be young again!

But time and evolution, like oblivion, are not to be bought. The words of Mercury, as Armado said in *his* epilogue, are harsh after the songs of Apollo. And in the oldest fertility-rite where spring contended with winter there were the same implications; a shadow of the same voice which divides all the worlds of time at their unseen turning-points: 'You that way—we this way.'

# NOTES

*A 'select bibliography' in a book of this kind and size would be merely ostentatious and intimidating. I therefore relegate 'suggestions on further reading' to these notes, with hints on where to find texts of plays, and some translations of quotations for those who cannot read other tongues. Where no translation is given, I have usually attempted to insinuate the meaning in the immediate context.*—A. P. R.

Note 1. Plate in Pickard-Cambridge: *Dithyramb, Tragedy and Comedy* (O.U.P., 1927), p. 152. Dubech's *Histoire Illustrée du Théatre* gives a version perhaps accommodated to the subtler sensibilities of Frenchmen, but otherwise rather pointless. Haigh's *Attic Theatre*, p. 257, is coy on the same subject, and Professor Cornford (p. 183 in book in the next note) very reasonably protests. Cf. Yeats' poem *The Scholars*?

Note 2. See refs. in Jane Harrison's *Epilegomena* (C.U.P., 1921), p. 23, or F. M. Cornford's *Origin of Attic Comedy* (C.U.P., 1934), p. 62.

Note 3. G. Murray: *Five Stages of Greek Religion* (Watts & Co., 1935), p. 33.

Note 4. See Chambers: *Medieval Stage*, i. 10, Note 4, and the stories of players converted to saints. The Reformation period provides a parallel use (or misuse) of theatricals for damning and defaming theological adversaries. See Chapter VIII, below.

Note 5. From Philostorgius. See Milman's note in Gibbon xxi.

Note 6. C. J. Sisson: *Lost Plays of Shakespeare's Age* (C.U.P., 1936), Chap. IV, on the May Game.

Note 7. From the *Concordia Regularis*, mentioned later. The main part is given, with English rendering, in a book I refer to for texts of plays throughout this work, viz. *Chief Pre-Shakespearean Dramas*, ed. J. Q. Adams (Harrap). The Latin quoted here means: '. . . the usage of certain of the religious (which as) worthy of imitation for the strengthening of faith in the untaught common-people and the newly converted . . . we have ordered thus . . .'

Note 8. Karl Young: *Drama of the Medieval Church*, i, 81. This, with Chambers' *Mediæval Stage*, is the standard work.

Note 9. Like Bottom the Weaver, these and the foregoing lines are but roughly translated. My intention is to give some idea of the *form* of the developed liturgical play for those who can only find their way to read the Latin through my doggerel.

Note 10. G. K. Chesterton quoted. He does not mean, as I do, that the donkey is also vulgarly famed for what Iago insinuated in 'foul disproportion'. It seems likely that the beast 'stood for' some original or equivalent of the *Cervulus* (a hobby-horse prototype, only the animal 'represented' was a buck), which the earlier Christian reformers repeatedly mention. See Chambers' Appendix N on 'Winter Prohibitions'.

Note 11. I use Gerhoh's words. See Chambers ii, 98 Note 5 (Latin). For detail here and on Herrad, consult Young, ii, 412–13

Note 12. The meaning is largely in the deft music, but in rough outline it runs:

> 'Worldly delectation, sweet and gratifying,
> All its conversation richly satisfying.'

Complete text in Young ii.

Note 13. 'Prefiguration' is a particular by-product of the medieval world-picture, with its emphasis on allegory and a principle of universal inter-relation. But this simple kind is derivable from the emphasis on fulfilled prophecies in St. Matthew. I am sorry to be unable to spare space for the late twelfth-century play on Isaac and his sons, in which everything is given an allegoric turn—expounded in parenthesis. See Young ii, 259 ff. and his remarks on 'figurative' and 'typological' interpretations, pp. 264 f.

Note 14. I give Stanzas 1, 2, 4 and 6 from the Sen version, with my own rough rendering, which will not always fit the tune: a harmonized form of which is still used for 'Soldiers who are Christ's below' in *Hymns A. & M.*, and for another hymn in *Songs of Praise* (which mentions *Orientis partibus*). Chambers gives all variants in Appendix L, and Young the Sens version (i. 551).

Note 15. 'Now a new offspring is sent from high heaven, the Virgin shall return, and Saturn's reign come back.' (*Bucolics IV*, 7).

Note 16. See the picture by Jordaens (1593-1678) called 'The Beanfeast' or 'The King drinks'. The bean was the precursor of the 'lucky threepennybit' in the Christmas pudding, and the finder became 'king'. But Jordaens includes the 'morality' tradition in the background inscription *Nil similius insano quam ebrius* (Nothing liker a lunatic than a drunk).

Note 17. They are exceptional in having no connection with craft-guilds, though they are of a comparable length (i.e. would imply a similar large-scale corporate interest), and also in the methods of production. The N-town cycle is so called because this phrase is used in the Banns announcing the show. It is taken to be like the 'N or M' for 'name or names' still used in the Prayer Book. The cycle has no connection whatever with the true Coventry cycle, from which two plays only have survived.

Note 18. A list of the York guilds, and of the episodes in all four cycles, is given in the useful *Everyman*, No. 381, with eight plays from four cycles, including the Cornish, but nothing from York or N-town. Adams gives the N-town banns, and a selection of eighteen plays, making a synthetic cycle. For York plays one must go to the edition by L. Toulmin Smith (1885); for the rest to the E.E.T.S. publications. I have seen no selection which does not fight shy of the characteristic brutalities of the Scourging and Buffeting, and also of what Chambers calls 'Joseph's trouble'.

Note 19. Since writing this book I have taken this matter further, in an article on *Bruegel's Ambivalences* in *The Cambridge Journal* (Vol. ii No. 3, December 1948) published by Bowes & Bowes, Cambridge. To illustrate the spirit of these scenes in Gothic Drama I have chosen Matthias Grünewald's *Christ Mocked*, exhibited with the Munich pictures at the National Gallery in 1949: because the Bosch *Crowning with Thorns* is not only in London, but obtainable as a National Gallery postcard (No. 361). The Grünewald combines the dramatic and the grotesque, the pathos of the Victim and the gusto of the tormentors, whose savage delight is infectiously rendered. Brutal callousness, with a kind of sadistic pleasure, is emphasized in the big oaf on the right, subtly contrasted with the troubled, hurt expression of the face behind him. There is a similar doubleness in the clown with tabor and pipe on the other side. The whole spirit of the Gothic art may be contrasted with Tintoretto's *Scourging of Christ* (exhibited with the Vienna pictures, 1949, and reproduced in Tietze's Phaidon Press volume).

Note 20. Rendering the Latin: 'Shut up . . . for I am lord of lords. I will take away the light from their eyes (who speak against me) . . . beware lest I stretch out the strength of my arm. . . . I call the laws of heaven to witness: Beware! I command the law in greatest majesty (?), and town and country shall go in terror of me.' I print 'jury' for *iure*, but it is probably meant for Latin, and, like the next line, mainly an impressive ritual-sounding noise.

Note 21. The source is the apocryphal *Protevangelion Jacobi*, X and XI, but there Joseph is accused of a secret marriage, and there is of course no Summoner. Summoners called people up for loose living, and as the play shows, the opportunities of blackmail were great. Huizinga remarks—not referring to drama or England—that 'the union of Joseph and Mary always remained the object of a deplorable curiosity, in which profane speculation mingled with sincere piety'. (*Waning of the Middle Ages*, p. 153.) Further evidence can be found in the bizarre gynæcological curiosity of the unbelieving midwife taken from *Protevangelion* XVI, and actually staged in the N-town cycle. For sources I have used *The Apocryphal New Testament*, printed for William Hone, London, 1820.

Note 22. *Narrenshiff:* the Ship of Fools. Title of a long satiric poem by Sebastian Brandt, published in 1494 in German, with very admirable woodcuts. It achieved a European reputation and was 'conveyed' (rather than 'translated') into English by Barclay in 1509. The basic idea is to label all classes of fools 'For export only', and to describe the kinds. Bosch painted one such allegorical ship (in the Louvre). See Jacques Combe's book (1946) on Bosch. (Now, 1948, translated.)

Note 23. The Isaac play mentioned in Note 14 is exceptional. The detailed expositions of the allegory of the not-very-moral story of Esau (the Jews) and Jacob (Christianity) are in Young, ii. 264–6.

NOTE 24. From Chambers' *English Literature at the Close of the Middle Ages* (p. 52), with the text modernized somewhat, e.g. I put 'from domain' for 'ut of the reyne' (*regnum, royaume*), and 'clay' for 'cleo', which apparently means *cliff* (or hillside?).

Note 25. General accounts will be found in Huizinga's chapter on 'The Vision of Death' in *The Waning of the Middle Ages*, Theodore Spencer's *Death in Elizabethan Tragedy* (1936) and Willard Farnham's *Medieval Heritage*. Emile Mâles *L'Art religieux de la fin du Moyen Age* has invaluable pictures, even if you cannot read French. The whole subject has recently been reviewed by Wolfgang Stammler in *Der Totentanz* (Carl Hanser Verlag, München, 1948): a monograph I was unable to consult in writing this chapter. It gives a photograph of Baldung's picture of a female corpse holding the hour-glass over the Three Ages of Woman (infancy, maturity and age), which some will have seen among the Vienna pictures.

Note 26. Above everything else, have plenty of action. They come for a *show*, what they want is something to see.' (From the *Prologue in the Theatre* in *Faust.*)

Note 27. *Tantum religio potuit suadere malorum* (such iniquities could religion persuade). Commenting on the sacrifice of Iphigenia before the Greeks sailed for Troy.

Note 28. Text in E.E.T.S., with *Castle of Perseverance* and *Mankynd*, as 'Macro Moralities'—from the name of an owner of the MSS. The contemporary evils here pageanted can be looked up in Trevelyan's *History of England*, pp. 259 ff.

Note 29. 'I have lived; nor can a worse fortune ever take away what better (earlier) hours have given.' The *memento vivere* sentiment is still more evident in the *Satyricon* (34) when an articulated silver skeleton is exhibited at Trimalchio's feast. Stammler notes that the myth of the Three Living and the Three Dead came from the East, and that the origin of Trimalchio's toy may be found in Herodotus' account of the customs of the Egyptians. I have seen this in B. R.'s Elizabethan translation (1584).

Note 30. The conclusion suggests a dependence on the *débats* which give contentions such as *Mens et Caro, Anima et Corpus.* See F. J. E. Raby: *Secular Latin Poetry* (1934) ii. 299 f. and compare his *Christian Latin Poetry*, p. 434, on Jacopone da Todi's dialogues of the Soul and its Body, and the inquisition of the dying corpse. Stammler notes the popularity of the *Dialogus mortis cum homine* ascribed to St. Bernard. But *Pride of Life* is quite certainly a *play*, not a *Contentio*: it is outdoors and has the King's *tentorium* as a property. Text in Brandl: *Quellen und Forschungen*, 1898, with German translation which eases the problem of missing words and the hideous spelling. This volume is a supplement to Hazlitt-Dodsley *Old Plays*, and contains *Nature* (Medwall's), *Respublica, King Darius, Horestes, Common Conditions*, and other elusive pieces.

Note 31. Chambers (ii. 220) gives the date as 1537. But he dates the play 1538! Cf. *C.H.E.L.*, VI, 296 and refs., which I accept.

Note 32. Lyndsay's main model is the *Jeu du Prince des Sotz* of Pierre Gringoire, acted in Paris in 1511. There La Commune, representing 'the People' also appears. See J. M. Smith's *French Background of Middle Scots Literature* (1934), Chap. VI and refs. Lyndsay's dramatic sense is shown in his making the 'cry' (or banns announcing the play) into a heterogeneous farce, astonishingly like the modern cinema 'trailer' used for advertisement. But neither the braggart-warrior theme nor that of the girdle of chastity (or 'Love laughs at locksmiths', taken quite literally) reappears in the play. The latter is quite the 'broadest' bit of farce in 'English' drama.

Note 33. Jonson's rude jest at Deuteronomy xxii, 5 in *Bartholomew Fair* (1614), where the puppet answers the Puritan, was by no means the end in this ancient game. The text was invoked in 1942 by a female conscientious objector from Brackley, who feared that she might be compelled to wear trousers in His Majesty's service. (Reported in *News Chronicle* of 16th or 17th July, 1942.)

Note 34. *Durham University Journal*, March 1945, in an article on *Woodstock*, which deals more widely with the Histories than I have been able to do here, and without the laboured detail of my Preface to that play. (Chatto and Windus 1946.)

Note 35. Horace in *Ars Poetica* advises the aspirant to play-writing. 'Do not let Medea kill her children in front of the audience.' Cambises does this—with someone else's child, admittedly; but has the heart produced *coram populo* to demonstrate that he scored a bull with his arrow. The moral use of such horrors as Preston stages can be seen from Gerard David's painting of the flaying of Sisamnes (at Bruges: colour-print in L. van Puyvelde's *Flemish Primitives*). The two pictures of the Judgement of Cambyses were made for the town-hall, as a warning to the burghers after a monetary scandal. See also Huizinga, p. 224.

Note 36. Malone Society Reprint, I. 330. The play is before 1600, and, I should say, well before.

Note 37. Cf. G. Wilson Knight in *The Wheel of Fire* and elsewhere. The value of my principle of ambivalence could be demonstrated merely by showing how its absence distorts Professor Knight's view of *Troilus and Cressida:* where despite all the evidence of 'fools on both sides' he has to make the Trojans somehow right in his own romantic-Christian scale of values.

Note 38. Horace, *Odes*, i. 3, 37-8. 'No ascent is too steep for man. We assail heaven itself (in our folly).' See also lines 25–6 of the same ode, and the following reference to Prometheus. In his own way, Marlowe too 'brought fire to the tribes of men'.

Note 39. 'Honour, virtue, faith, are goods to private men;
Let kings walk where they will.' (*Thyestes*, 217 f.)

These sentiments are behind the evil counsellor Hermon's advice to Ferrex in *Gorboduc* ii, l. 140–52. Miss S. R. Watson in *Modern Language Notes*, XXXIV, p. 361 calls them 'somewhat Machiavellian'. But the lines:

'Think you such princes do suppose themselves
Subject to laws of kind and fear of gods?'

plainly come from Seneca. And 'private men' are mentioned in the next line. Exactly the same passage in *Thyestes* is pillaged in *Selimus*, where Acomat says:

'Bare faith, pure virtue, poor integrity,
Are ornaments fit for a private man;
Beseems a prince for to do all he can.'

in the middle, however, Acomat goes over the Eteocles' speech in the *Phoenissae* (654 ff.) which follows on from the line quoted as (*b*) in the note following this, and then returns to *Thyestes* again. *Selimus* is ascribed to Greene—not very convincingly. Text in Temple Dramatists (lines 1385–1402).

Note 40. *Richardus Tertius*, Pt. III, Act. I (Shakespeare's Library, Vol. V, p. 188 in the 1875 ed.). A passage which looks exactly like a summary of Machiavelli on being loved and feared appears later, (p. 211):

'est imperandi principi duplex via,
Amor et metus: utrumque regibus utile.'

Richard himself is speaking. "There is a double way for princes' rule, the way of love and that of striking fear; each has its uses to the lords of men." The idea that security lies in fear is also in *Oedipus*, 703 ff. I cite these passages only to justify my invention of the term 'Senecchiavellian', the acceptance of which might divert attention from merely *literary* influences and set wits to work on what this synthesis *stood for* in European culture. What exactly comes from Seneca need bother none but aspirant PH.D.S; but what restates the notions of Thrasymachus in *The Republic* bears on what still splits the world.

# INDEX


A

*Abraham and Isaac*, 51, 66, 72
academic or neoclassic drama, 129f.
*Accidie, Ludus—see Sloth.*
actors, 29, 39, 63, 104, 149–50
——numbers of—*see length of plays.*
——names of: *histrio, mimus, planipes, scaenicus* (which see).
Adam of St. Victor, 43
Adam play (*Ordo . . . Adae*), 49.
Adams, J. Q., passim and 164, Note 7
Admiral's Men, 149, 150
Adso of Toul, 81
Aelred of Rievaulx, 49
Aeschylus, 24, 26
ages of man pattern, 95, 103
*agon*, 24, 26
Alabaster, Wm., *see Roxana.*
allegory, 87–90
Alleyn, Edward, 64, 148, 150
*Altercatio Ecclesiae et Synagogae*, 81
Ambidexter, a vice, 142–3
ambivalence, 53, 69–70, 72, 94, 110, 126–7, 128, 147, 155
*Amphitruo, see* Plautus.
amphoteric symbols, 92, 94
*anagnorisis*, 24, 26
Anne, St., pagan underlay of, 39, 61
*Antichristus* (of Tegernsee), 49, 81; (Chester), 71
antiphones, 42
*Antonio's Revenge* (Marston's), 156
*Apius and Virginia*, 73, 139, 141–2
'application', 81, 86, 116
*Arden of Feversham*, 161
Ariosto, 130
Aristophanes, 26, 30
Aristotle, 19, 26, 115, 116, 126
Arius, heresiarch, 32, 113
Ascension trope, 45
Ass, Balaam's, 47
Asses, Feast of, 57–61
Atellane 30
*Atheist's Tragedy*, 73
audience, Elizabethan, 9–12, 127
Augustine, St., 32, 36, 46, 159

B

Bacon, Francis, 61, 107
*Baculus*, Festival of, 56–7
bad language, 21, 59, 110
Balaam, 47, 65
*Balaam and Balaack* (Chester), 47
Baldung, Hans, 48, 167, Note 25
Bale, John, 115, 119–22, 123, 125, 126, 127
banns (prologues to plays), 97
Beddoes, T. L. 157
Bede, 36
Bernard of Clairvaux, 81
'Bessy' (fool in sword-dance), 109
Bethell, S. L., 79
Beverley, 52, 66, 68, 80
Black Death, *see* Plague.
Blackfriars Theatre, 149
blank verse, 131, 148
Boas, F. S., 109, 110, 113. 144
Bosch, Hieronymus, 64, 69, 70, 75, 98, 161 167
Botticelli, 73
boy-actors, 16, *see* Children.
Boy Bishop, 56, 61
Bowra, H. M., 26
Brandt, Sebastian, *see Narrenschiff.*
Bromyard, John, 32, 83
Bruegel, Pieter, 48, 64, 70, 72, 74, 89, 161 166, Note 19
Brute, King of Britain, 132
Burbage family, 149
Bürgertragödie, 161
burlesque ritual, 55f.
*Bussy d'Ambois*, 73
Byron, Lord, 67, 95
*Byron's Tragedy*, 73

C

*Cain and Abel*, 49, 70, 73
*Calisto and Meliboea*, 138
*Cambyses*, 73, 139, 142–4
Carmina Burana, 50
Carolingian Renaissance, 42
*Castle of Perseverance*, 80, 88, 95, 96–8, 99, 105, 113, 125
Chambers, Sir E. K., 34, 37, 38, 48, 49, 55, 57, 64, 80, 85, 115, 144
Chapman, Geo., 150, 151, 152, 155
character in medieval drama, 72
——in XIXth C. criticism, 79–80
Chaucer, 40, 42, 53, 54, 62, 74, 75, 83, 84, 90, 109, 110, 111, 118, 138
Chester plays, 47, 63, 65, 66, 73
Children's plays, 105–8, 129, 139, 149
Christian missionaries, 36–7
——opposition to plays, 29, 30–1, 33, 49–50, 55
Christmas, 22, 34, 45, 56
cinema, 16, 152
Cinthio, Giraldi, 145
Classical drama, 24, 131–2
——*see* academic, Seneca.
Clown, 20, 61, 90–1, 136, 137f., 151
*Coliphizacio* (buffeting play), 68, 69
Collier, J. P., 104
Collingwood, R. G., 11
Comedy, Greek, 19, 24, 26: Roman, 29: Medieval idea of, 138–9: general, 69, 71, 90–1, 102, 109, 130, 137–8
Commedia dell'Arte, 30
*Concordia Regularis*, 44
contemporaneity, 71, 73, 85–7, 102
*contentio, see débat.*
*Contention of Liberality and Prodigality*, 101
Cornford, F. M., 26
Cornish plays, 62–3, 64, 68

Cornish saints, 37
Corpus Christi festival, 62
Coventry plays, 65, 68
*Cradle of Security*, 153
craft guilds, 63, 66
Cranmer, Thos., 119, 120
*Creation*, 49, 51
Creeping to the Cross, 43
Creizenach, Whm., 88
Cromwell, Thos., 113, 114, 119–21
Crossing the Line ritual, 59
*Crucifixion*, 69–70
*Curtain* Theatre, 149
Cycles (mystery), 48–54, (development) and 62–74

D

*Damon and Pithias*, 139–40, 156
dance, 15, 16, 19
Dance of Death (danse macabre, Totentanz), 82, 84–6, 89, 93–4, 96
Daughters of God, *see Debate.*
David, Gerard, 168, Note 35
Death as character, 95, 96, 98, 153–4
*débat* or *éstrif*, a contention in arguments, 82, 109
*Debate of the Heavenly Virtues*, 81, 95, 98
*Decameron*, 135
*De casibus* stories, 118, 126–7, 134
dedication ritual, 43
Dekker, Thos., 84, 152, 161
*Depositio crucis*, 43
*Deposuit* sung at Feast of Fools, 57
*Deutronomy* damns disguise, 35, 50, 129
devils (dramatic), 49, 64, 68, 90, 91
diathetics, 114, 121, 133–4
Digby *Magdalene*, 95, 97
Dionysus, 20
divine right, *see Non-resistance.*
Dolce's *Giocasta*, 135
domestic tragedy, 161
donkeys, pagan symbols? 47
Donne, John, dramatic lineage of, 103
——refs., 66, 106
Dragon (St. George's), 22
dressing-up, wickedness of, 35, 50, 59, 129
*dromenon*, 21
Dryden, John, 100, 121
dumb-shows, 134–5
Dunbar's *Lament for the Makers*, 83
*Dutch Courtezan*, 161
*Dux Moraud*, 73, 96

E

Easter Candle, 37; eggs, 37
*Edmond Ironside*, 143
educational moralities, 105–6, 108
Edwardes, Richard, 139
*Elevatio crucis*, 42
Eliot, T. S., 89, 125, 134, 137, 156, 159
Elizabethan-Gothic continuities, 72–3
——tragic experience, 127–8
Epiphany plays, *see Magi*, *Stella* and Feast of Fools.
equivocators, 103, 116, 122, 124–5, 126–7, 130, 158
éstrif, *see débat.*
Ethenwold, St., 42, 44
Euripides *Bacchae*, 24
*Everyman*, 95, 98, 107, 117

F

*Fall* (*Adam* play), 51
Farnham, Willard, 117
*Fastnachtspiele*, 109, 153
Fate, 25
*Faustbuch*, 143
*Faustus, Dr.*, 52, 64, 143
Feast of Fools, 45–6, 47, 55–61, 109, 112
fertility-rituals, 15, 16, 19–24, 26–7, *see* also Spring-Winter.
Fescennine songs, 29
*Festum Stultorum*, 55–61
*Finding of Truth*, 104
fire-festivals, 37, 39
fireworks, 97, 109
*Floralia*, 30
flyting (slanging-match), 110
Ford, John, 155
Forman, Simon, 86–7
*Four Elements* (interlude), 106
*Four PP.*, 110–11, 112
*Friar Bacon and Friar Bungay*, 92
*Fulgens and Lucrece*, 102, 138
Fulwell, Ulpian, 145, and *Cradle.*

G

Gager, Wm., 129
gallimaufrey, 149
*Gammer Gurton's Needle*, 112, 130
Garnier, Robt., 160
Gascoigne, Geo., 130, 135
Gayley, C. M., 91
George, St., 22
Gerhoh von Reichersberg, 49
Ghost, 160
*Gismond of Salerne*, 135
gleeman or gleomon, 35
*Globe* Theatre, 148, 149
Goethe, 52, 53, 86, 147, 162
*Goodly Queen Hester*, 126
*Gorboduc*, 131, 132–4, 137, 139, 145, 149, 156, 160
Gothic drama, 48–54, 62f.
Grafton's Chronicle, 132
grammar schools, 105
Greece, Early drama in, 19
Greek Tragedy, 24–6
Greene, Robt., 84, 148, 159
Greg., W. W., 67
Gregory the Great, 36
Gringoire, Pierre, 168, Note 32
Grossteste, Robt., 40

grotesque in medieval drama, 70–72, 73
groundlings, 150
Grünewald, Matthias, 70, 166, Note 19
guilds, 63, 66
Guise, Duke of, in *Massacre at Paris*, 157, 159
*Gull's Hornbook* (Dekker), 152
gunpowder for devils, 97
Guy Fawkes's Day, 39

H

Hall, Joseph, 149, 154
Halle, Edw., 117, 118
Hamlet as interlude-writer, 117
hangings on stage, neck, 73, 123, 140
Haphazard, a vice, 141
Hardware, Hy., Mayor, 65
Hardy, Thos., 22
Hardy-dardy, a vice, 126
Harlequin, 30
*Harrowing of Hell*, 49, 51, 66
Harsenet, Samuel, 92
Hasenberg (anti-Lutheran), 118
Haywood, Jasper, 136
Hell-mouth, 64
Henry VIII, 104, 113–15, 118
Henslowe, Philip, 149
*Herod*, 45, 62, 64, 70, 73, 95
Herrad von Landsberg, Abbess, 50
Heywood, John, 103, 105, 108-12
Heywood, Thos., 161
*Hickscorner*, 95, 97, 99, 100
hieratic gestures, 42
Hilarius, author of a St. Nicholas play, 48, 138
Hilton, Walter, 79, 88
Hippolytus, 24
History and drama, 121, 122, 127–8
History books, Tudors encourage, 118
History plays, evolution, 113–28, 137f.
*histrio*, 31
Holbein, the younger, 82, 85, 93
Holy Innocents, Paris, 84, 93–4
Homer, 25, 33
*Homilies* (C. of E.), 121, 133
*Honest Whore* (Dekker's), 161
Horace (quoted), 60, 93, 142, 157
*Horestes*, 73, 140–1, 143, 156, 168, Note 30
Hroswitha or Hrotswith, 41
Hubris, 25
Hugo of St. Victor, 81
Huizinga, J., 68, 85, 94

I

Iniquity, a vice, 125, 126
Inns of Court plays, 129–31
Interlude, 102, 104
*Interlude of Youth*, 97
*Interludium de Clerico et Puella*, 82
Introit, tropes to, 43

J

Jack the Giant-killer, 21
*Jack Jugeler*, 125–6
*James IV*, 131, 154
*Jew of Malta*, 143, 153, 159
Jig (Elizabethan), 27, 112
*Jocasta*, 135
Joculator(es), 39, 73, *see* Minstrels.
*Johan Johan*, 69, 109, 112
John, King, 120–2, *see* also *Troublesome.*
Johnson, Sam, 12
Jonson, 65, 66, 75, 86, 102, 120, 130, 132 148, 155, 159
Jordaens, 165, Note 16
Jougleurs (Minstrels), 39–41
Judas as scapegoat, 37
Judgement Day, scenic reward, 32
*Juditium* (Last Judgement), 49, 51
Juvenal quoted, 29

K

Kabuki, 16
Kagura, 16
Kalends, 34, 59
*King Darius*, 126
King of Beans, 61 and note.
King of Fools, 34, 46, 57f.
Kinwelmershe, Francis, 135
Kirchmayer, Thomas, 119
*Knack to Know a Knave*, 154
Knight, G. Wilson, 169
Kyd, Thomas, 134, 148, 160
*Kynge Johan*, 79, 93, 119, 120–1

L

Langland, Wm., 40, 54, 75, 90
Laon *Prophetae*, 46–7
laughter a pagan veneration, 18, 38
laughter deprecated, 137
Lawrence, T. E., 114
*Lazarus*, 68, 69, 74
*Leir*, 136
length of plays, 95, 104, 112
Lenten veil, 43
Lewis, C. S., 87–9
*Like wil to like*, 145
liturgical drama, 42–54, 64
*Locrine*, 136, 137
Lodge, Thos., 139, 148, 154
*London Merchant* (*George Barnwell*), 161
Lord Chamberlain's Men, 149
Lord's Prayer (*Paternoster*) play, 80
love as comedy-theme, 138
*Love*, play of, 109, 112
*Love's Labours Lost*, primitive survivals in, 109, 153–4
Lucretius, 87
Ludus Coventriae (so-called), 63, 95
*Lusty Inventus*, 95, 104, 123
Luther, 114, 118–19
Lydgate, 41, 84, 86, 92
Lyly, John, 138, 148, 149, 152
Lyndsay, Sir David, 122, 125

M

Machiavelli, 157–8
Macro moralities, 167, Note 28

*Magi*, 45, 56, 66
magic and histrionic playing, 15f.
*Magnyfycence*, 103, 115–16, 117, 122, 124, 125
Mâle, Emile, 85
*Mankynd*, 92, 97, 99, 100
Manly, J. M., 144
Manning, Robt. of Brunne, 55
Marionettes, 16
Marlowe, 79, 99, 105, 106, 136, 148, 154–9, 160
*Marriage of Wit and Science*, 108
*Marriage of Wit and Wisdom*, 104, 106
Marston, John, 150, 155, 159
Mary Magdalene, 44, 50 and 95, 97
Masks, 15, 24, 34, 38, 56, 59
Mass, 42, 50
Maunday Thursday ritual, 42
May Queen, 27, 30
Medwall, Henry, 102–4, 106
Mercator (spice merchant), 44
Mercutio, 111
Messenger (*Nuntius*), 24
Middleton, Thos., 102, 155, 160
Midwives in religious plays, 45, 67
mime (Roman), *mimus* (actor) and *mima* (actress), 30
*Mind, Will and Understanding*, 91, 99
minstrels, 39–40, 56, 62, 69, 74, 111, 112
Miracle plays, *see* Cycles, Gothic drama.
*Mirror for Magistrates*, 118, 134, 161
*Misfortunes of Arthur*, 135, 149
*Misogonus*, 138
*Missel des fous*, 60
*Monachopornomachia*, 118
Money, moralities of, 101
monkey-song (*Sarugaku*), 24
Morality plays, 65, 79f., 95–101
Moralities, and allegory, 79–94: classified, 95: transitional or Tudor, 102f., 113f.
Moral History, 134, 161: development of, 113f.: Elizn., gallimaufries dependent on, 137f.
morals of State, 115, 133, 140f.
More, Sir Thomas, 102
*More*, play of *Sir Thomas*, 73, 104
*Mount Tabor* by R. Willis, 153
mummers, 22, 107
*Mundus et Infans*, 95
Murray, Gilbert, 24
Mystery-cycles (Miracle plays), *see* above.

N

N-town plays, 63, 95, 165, Note 17
Naogeorgos (Kirchmayer).
*Narrenschiff* (Ship of Fools), 75, 100, 167
Nashe, Thos., 83, 131, 148, 156
Nativity plays, 45, *see Pastores.*
*Nature* (Medwall's), 95, 102–4, 108, 112, 168, Note 30
*Nature of the Four Elements*, 104, 106
neums (*neumae*), 43
Newcastle plays, 68
*Newe Enterlude of Vice, see Horestes.*
New Learning values (in drama), 106–7, 116
Nicholas, saint's play, 48
*Nicodemus, Gospel of*, 51
Nō plays, 16, 18
*Noah*, 51, 55, 63, 69
Non-resistance doctrine, 121, 132
Norton, Thos., 132, 133–4
Norwich plays, 68, 95
Notker Balbulus, 43
Notre-Dame de Chartres, 54
*Nut-brown Maid*, 82, 138

O

Oberammergau, 140
*Octavia* (pseudo-Seneca), 155–6
Oedipus, 25, 135
*ordo* (a liturgic play), 46, 47
Orosius, 32
overdetermined symbols, *see* amphoteric.
Owst, G. R., 55, 67, 81, 83, 88, 89
Oxford Group technique anticipated, 124

P

pageants (pagond, etc.), or wheeled stages, 62
*Palamon and Arcite*, 139
Palmesel, 47
Palm Sunday procession, 42
*Pammachius*, 119
pantomime (Roman), 31
Pardon Churchyard, 84, 86
*Pardoner and the Frere*, 109, 110
Passion plays, 50
*Pastores, Pastorum* (Shepherd's plays), 45; and 63, 67, 69, 71–2
*Paternoster* plays, 80, 95
*pathos* (Greek: scene of suffering), 24, 26
patriotic motive (so-called) in Histories, 114, 134
Paul, St., 22
Paul's Boys, 118, 149
*Peregrini* (pilgrims to Emmaus), 44
*peripeteia*, 26
Petronius, 94
Phales, 20, 24
phallic rituals, 19, 20, 22–3, 26
*pharmakos*, 21
Pilate, 70, 72
Pikeryng, John 140
Plague, bubonic, 83–4, 98
*planctus* (lamentation), 44
*planipes* (actor in farce), 31
Plato, 26
Plautus, 29, 126, 130, 151
*Play of the Sacrament*, 73
plot (in moralities), 99
polemic plays (interludes or moralities), 113–128
political innuendo, dramatic, 115
Pollard, A. W., 48, 67
Porter, Henry, 130

*praesepe* (crib), 45
prayers ending interludes, 108, 144
preaching and drama, 55, 81–2
prefiguration, 51, 165
Preston, Thos., 139, 144
*Pride of Life*, 96
primitive survivals, 11, 109–10
princecraft, literature of, 118
'private' theatres, 150
*Processio asinorum* used of *Prophetae*, 47
*Processus Talentorum* (dicing play).
producers, illustrious, 31
*Promos and Cassandra*, 145
propaganda, 114f.
properties in medieval plays, 64–5
*Prophetae* (*Ordo Prophetarum*, etc.), 46, 51, 52, 66–7
prose comedy, 131
proses (*Prosa ad sequentias*), 43
Prose of the Ass, 57–8
*Protevangelion Jacobi*, 166, Note 21
Prudentius, 88, 89, 124
*Psychomachia*, 88, 96
Publius Syrus, 30
puppets, *see* marionettes.
*Pyrricha* or *pyrrhica*, 30

Q

'Q' on *Henry IV*, 144
*Quem quaeritis*, 43, 45

R

R.B. (Bower?), *see Apius.*
Racine, 24, 132, 151
*Ralph Roister Doister*, 112, 130, 138
Ramsay, R. L., 116
Rastell, John, 103, 105, 106, 108
——Wm., 103
Redford, John, 105, 107–8
Reformation, dramatic effects of, 113f.
*repraesentatio* (religious play), 42f.
*Respublica*, 103, 123, 124–5, 160, 168, Note 30
revenge plays, 156, 160
*Rex*, *see* King.
*Rex saturnalitius* (saturnal king), 34
*Richardus Tertius* (by Legge), 158
Riga, *comedia* at, 52
ritual, 15, 17, 21, 23, 29, 33, 42, 52
Ritwise, John, 119
Roman theatre, 29f.
Roo, John, 117, 121
*Rose* theatre, 136, 149
Rouen *Prophetae*, 46, 47
*Roxana* (Latin play), 136, 156

S

Sachs, Hans, 109
Sackville, Lord Buckhurst, 132–4
*Sacrament*, Croxton play of the, 73
Salvian, 32
Saturnalia, 33, 60
Satyr play, 19, 21, 27, 30
*Satyre of the Thrie Estaitis*, 122–3
scapegoats, 21, 37
scenic effects in liturgic drama, 64
Schelling, F., 132
school plays, 105–8, 129
scôp (bard), 35, 40
scurrility, 110
Seami (Nō play writer), 18
secularization of medieval drama, 48, 50, 55
*Secunda Pastorum* (2nd Shepherds' Play), 63, 69, 71–2, 109
*Selimus*, 169, Note 39
Seneca, 19, 88, 129, 130, 132, 134, 135, 136, 143, 150, 155–8, 159, 160
*sepulchrum*, 43
sequences (*sequentiae cum prosa*), 43
sermon, 46, 55, 81
*sermon joyeux*, 109
Shakespeare (general references), 65, 66, 74, 93, 101, 131, 132, 134, 137, 148–9, 150–5
Plays:
*Antony and Cleopatra*, 23
*As You Like It*, 35
*Comedy of Errors*, 130, 151
*Cymbeline*, 151
*Hamlet*, 118, 129, 134, 135, 151
*Henry IV*, 11, 93, 143, 144, 151, 154
*Henry V*, 36, 128
*King John*, 121, 154
*King Lear*, 72, 126
*Love's Labours Lost*, 93, 138, 153
*Macbeth*, 72, 137
*Measure for Measure*, 145–7
*Merchant of Venice*, 127
*Midsummer Night's Dream*, 9, 130, 155
*Much Ado*, 131
*Othello*, 30, 143, 153
*Richard II*, 36, 85
*Richard III*, 125, 153
*Taming of the Shrew*, 131, 153
*Titus Andronicus*, 136, 151, 153, 156
*Troilus and Cressida*, 151, 155
*Twelfth Night*, 10
*Two Gentlemen*, 10, 131
*Winter's Tale*, 35, 73, 86, 95, 151
Shepherds' plays, *see Pastores*
Sherrington, Sir Charles, 25, 53
shortening of Moralities, 95, 104–5, 112
Sibyl as prophet, 46
Sidney, Sir Philip, 118, 127, 131, 132, 136, 137, 143, 145
*Sir Clyomon and Sir Clamydes*, 145
Sisson, C. J., 38, 112
Skelton, John, 115–7, 121
skull symbol, 92–3
*Sloth*, play of, 80
Sophocles, 25
*sortes virgilianae*, 60
*sottie* (fool play), 60, 109
*Spanish Tragedy*, 9, 148
*spectacula*, 29
*Sponsus*, 49

Spring-Winter combats, 21, 27, 109, 154
*Stella* (star), Epiphany play, 42, 45
Stevenson, Wm., 130, 139
stooge, 30
*Streitgedicht* (éstrif), *see débat.*
*strenae*, 34
*Summer's Last Will and Testament*, 109
*Supposes*, 130–1, 138, 145
Supremacy, Act of, 114; royal, 121
*Swan* Theatre, 149
sword dance, 23, 109

T

Tacitus (quoted), 60
Taillefer, 35
*Tamburlaine the Great*, 84, 114, 143, 148, 154, 157, 159
*Tancre and Gismunda*, 135
Ten Brink, 68
Terence, 29, 41
*Terentius et Delusor*, 41
Tertullian, 32, 50, 88
Theatres, first English, 149
*Thersites*, 125
Thespis, 24
Thrace, mummers of, 22, 23
Three Dead and the Three Living, 84
*Three Laws, Comedy of* (Bale), 119, 126
*Thyestes*, 156, 169, Note 39
Tiberius, 31
*Tide tarieth no man, The*, 145
Titivillus, *see* Tutivillus.
*Tollite portas* (dedication rite), 43
*Totentanz*, a dance of the dead, 84–6, 89
Tourneur, Cyril, 99, 155
Towneley, *see* Wakefield.
Tragedy, 19, 24–6, 28, 99, 118, 127-8, 131, 132f., 136, 148f.
Tragical comedy, 126, 139
Tragy-comedy, 137f., 154
*Tres Reges* (Magi), 45, 66
Trevelyan, G. M., 114
*Trial of Joseph and Mary*, 71
*Tripudium* (a revel), 56
trope, 43
*Troublesome Raigne of* (*King*) *John*, 136, 154
Tudor politics and drama, 114f.
tug-of-war a fertility ritual, 27
Turkish Knight (mummer), 22
Tutilo, 43
Tutivillus (of Wakefield), 68, 70, 92; (of *Mankynd*), 100; (medieval demon, prototype of reporters), 130
*Two Angry Women of Abingdon*, 130

U

*Ubi sunt* poems, 82
Udall, Nicholas, 125, 130, 139
Underhill, Evelyn, 53
*Unguentarius* (merchant), 44
Unities, Gothic-Elizabethan contempt for, 72
Universities, playing in, *see* Academic.
University Half-wits, 139
University Wits, 139, 148, 154
*Ur-Hamlet*, 148

V

*Vado mori* verses, 85
Vaughan, C. E., 79
Vernacular languages, infiltration into Latin plays, 48, 49
Vice, The, and Vices, 10, 90–1, 97, 99, 102, 103, 109, 110, 125–6, 130, 139, 140, 141, 143, 153, 159
Vices' false names, 103, 116, 122, 124, 126, 139
Villain and Vice, 92, 125, 143, 159
Villain-hero, 127, 156f.
Villon, François, 83
Virgil as prophet, 46, 60
Virgins and fires, 37
Virgins, Wise and Foolish (*Sponsus*), 49
*Visitatio* ritual, 43–4

W

Wakefield Master, 68, 74–5
Wakefield plays, 62, 66, 67–70, 71, 72, 109, 138
Ward, A. W., 41
*Warning for Fair Women*, 152–3, 161
*Weather*, play of the, 110, 112
Webster, John, 151, 159
Wellerisms, 100
Westminster School play, 129
Wever, R. (*Lusty Iuventus*), 119, 123
Whetstone, Geo., 145 (quoted), 155, 162
Whitsuntide for plays, 62
William of Waddington, 55
William of Auxerre on Feast of Fools, 59
Willis, R., 42, 153
Wilmot, Robt., 135
Wind, age-old humours of, 30
*Wisdom*, *see Mind, Will*, etc.
*Wit and Folly* (*Witty and Witless*), 109, 112
*Wit and Science*, 106, 107–8
Wolsey, 116, 119
*Woodstock*, 137
*Women Killed with Kindness*, 161
*World and the Child* (*Mundus et Infans*), 95
Wylley, Thos., 119
*Wyt*, *see Wit.*

X

Xanthos *v.* Melanthos, 21
Xenophanes, 25
Xmas presents, 34
Xmas pudding, 165, Note 16

Y

Year-drama as tragic pattern, 25
*Yorkshire Tragedy*, 161
York plays, 63, 65, 66, 67
Young, Karl, passim and, 164, Note 8

Z

Zuccaro's portrait of Leicester, 93